Reading *Rocky* *Horror*

Previous Publications

Approaches to Teaching Poe's Prose and Poetry (with Anthony Magistrale)

Nothing That Is: Millennial Cinema and the Blair Witch *Controversies* (with Sarah Higley)

The Pedagogical Wallpaper: Teaching Charlotte Perkins Gilman's "The Yellow Wall-paper"

The Rocky Horror Picture Show

Scare Tactics: Supernatural Fiction by American Women

Spectral America: Phantoms and the National Imagination

Taking South Park *Seriously*

Reading *Rocky Horror*

The Rocky Horror Picture Show and **Popular Culture**

Edited by Jeffrey Andrew Weinstock

palgrave
macmillan

READING ROCKY HORROR
Copyright © Jeffrey Andrew Weinstock, 2008.

First published in hardcover in 2008 by PALGRAVE MACMILLAN® in the United States - a division of St. Martin's Press LLC, 175 Fifth Avenue, New York, NY 10010.

Where this book is distributed in the UK, Europe and the rest of the world, this is by Palgrave Macmillan, a division of Macmillan Publishers Limited, registered in England, company number 785998, of Houndmills, Basingstoke, Hampshire RG21 6XS.

Palgrave Macmillan is the global academic imprint of the above companies and has companies and representatives throughout the world.

Palgrave® and Macmillan® are registered trademarks in the United States, the United Kingdom, Europe and other countries.

ISBN: 978-1-137-52503-1

Reading Rocky Horror : The Rocky Horror Picture Show and popular culture / edited by Jeffrey Andrew Weinstock.
    p. cm.
   ISBN 978-0-230-61232-7 (alk.paper)
   1. Rocky Horror picture show (Motion picture)   I. Weinstock, Jeffrey Andrew.
   PN1997.R57543R43 2009
   791.43'72—dc22   2008019902

A catalogue record of the book is available from the British Library.

Design by Scribe Inc.

First PALGRAVE MACMILLAN paperback edition: June 2015

10 9 8 7 6 5 4 3 2 1

Contents

Acknowledgments

Academic publications like this one are labors of love, and this book is an homage to *Rocky Horror* from a group of wacky academics who like to think deeply and speculate about the cultural significance of sweet transvestites, audiovibratoryphysiomolecular transport devices, and cinema spectators who shoot squirt guns, wave lighters, and shout profanities at the screen. So first, I think I can speak safely for all the contributors to the volume when I say thank you to Jim Sharman, Lou Adler, Michael White, and all those responsible for creating and producing *Rocky Horror*, as well as Tim Curry, Susan Sarandon, Barry Bostwick, Patricia Quinn, Little Nell, Meatloaf, Peter Hinwood, Jonathan Adams, and the rest of the cast for giving us all so many hours of enjoyment. A special thanks goes to Richard O'Brien and Druidcrest Music Ltd for allowing me to quote from the song lyrics. Obviously, without the show and the movie, this book would not exist, and along those lines, I owe a huge debt of gratitude to the contributors, who stuck with this project longer than I had any right to expect. They waited and revised and waited and revised and, in general, made my life as editor as easy as possible. Thanks also to Gary Lane and Tim Gramza for their technical expertise and to Air'leth Aodhfin for providing the wonderful cover image.

Then there are all those lovely people who in one way or another made the book move from being a dream to a reality (yes, don't dream it. Be it!). My thanks to Farideh Koohi-Kamali, Brigitte Shull, Erin Ivy, Rosemi Mederos, and all the nice folks at Palgrave.

Finally, there are those people in my life who supported me and continue to uplift me in ways both obvious and subtle. The English department at Central Michigan University, especially Ari Berk, Kris McDermott, Mark Freed, Brooke Harrison, Matt Roberson, Gretchen Papazian, Marcy Taylor, and Stephenie Young, has been a consistent source of encouragement and assistance. Madeline and Alan Weinstock never blink when their son writes books on transsexual Transylvanians, and Astrid and Sophie and the kitty cat brigade make coming home as much a joy as working on volumes like this one. Thanks to you all.

Introduction

It's Just a Jump to the Left

The Rocky Horror Picture Show and Popular Culture

Jeffrey Andrew Weinstock

It's Astounding

Seldom are genres—cinematic, literary, musical, or otherwise—defined by a *single* text. When discussing science fiction, for example, one is hard-pressed to point to a single film and say, "*That's* the one! *That's* the essence of science fiction." One could debate the question, of course—something both film scholars and cinema fans enjoy doing. Sticking with science fiction for a moment, is the definitive film something heady like *2001*? An immense commercial success like *Star Wars* or *Alien*? Perhaps a throwback to times gone by such as (to take just two titles referenced by *Rocky Horror* itself): *The Day the Earth Stood Still* or *Forbidden Planet*? Each film—and certainly many others—likely would find its proponents, and if one put their fans in a room together and let them hash it out, per-haps a consensus would emerge as to which film *is* science fiction in its essence—but I wouldn't bet on it!

Cult film, however, is a different animal. In broaching the topic of "cult," one hastens to acknowledge at the outset that not all critics and theoreti-cians agree on what exactly makes a cult film a cult film. In attempting to grapple with this question, film critics have lingered reverently over *Casablanca* and *Citizen Kane*, wandered through the landscape of *El Topo*, shuddered at *Night of the Living Dead*, and self-referentially scrutinized their own guilty pleasures at enjoying John Waters' decided decadence. However, although not all critics agree on what constitutes the nature of the cult film, like Justice Potter Stewart defining pornography, they seem to know it when they see it because there is general agreement that, whatever a cult film is, *The Rocky Horror Picture Show* is it. *Rocky Horror* is almost universally hailed, as Danny Peary puts it in his book *Cult Movies*, as "The undisputed king . . . no . . . *queen* of the Midnight Movie circuit," and as "the very definition of the term 'cult picture'" (302).[1] Among the most astounding features, then, of *Rocky Horror* is the astonishing fact that a diverse group of scholars and critics *agree* as to its unrivaled status as preeminent cult film—and when was the last time a group of academics and critics agreed on anything?

However, beyond the fact of critical agreement concerning the generic affinities of the movie and its iconic status as cult film, one must also reckon with its unrivaled longevity and commercial popularity. In these respects, *Rocky Horror* is also unique. Completed for approximately $1.5 million and released in September 1975 (where it did well in Los Angeles, but bombed throughout most of the rest of the United States), the film today—over 30 years later—remains a fixture of the Midnight Movie circuit and still draws crowds on a regular basis that come to participate in the *Rocky Horror* experience. In addition to playing weekly in many large cities, college campuses routinely screen the film, and in 2000, Broadway mounted a revival of the stage version of *Rocky Horror* that starred Dick Cavett, Tom Hewitt, Alice Ripley, and rocker Joan Jett and that ran for fifteen months.

Rocky Horror, it must be acknowledged, is the oddest of things: a relatively low-budget gender-bending mish-mash of genres that somehow manages to provoke a response—famously from its audience, which dances, talks back to the film, and acts out the action along with the characters—but also from the critics and from American culture in general. *Rocky Horror* has wormed its way into America's collective unconscious. It's a movie virtually everyone has heard of and from which many can quote or sing songs, even if they haven't seen it. It's a movie that inspired its own newsletter—*The Transylvanian*—and one that is referenced by *other* movies, notably *Fame* (1980), in which the main characters take in a showing. It's an infamous addition to the resumes of Tim Curry, Susan Sarandon, and Barry Bostwick—one that Curry at least has tried his hardest to omit, but that no one will let him forget.[2] Finally, it remains the only movie that inspires its fans to pack an eclectic suitcase full of props (including toilet paper, rice, newspaper, squirt guns, and lighters or flashlights) to take along to each presentation.

For these reasons—the film's iconic cult status and continued prominence in American popular culture—as well as for its general importance to the history of cinema, its subversive position in relation to dominant culture mores, and its generic transgressions, the film that Tim Curry hates to acknowledge demands discussion—indeed, almost begs for analysis—and this collection of essays aims to redress *Rocky Horror*'s neglect by film and cultural critics. Surprisingly, *Rocky Horror* has received only a limited amount of scrutiny from scholars and film critics, who in a handful of isolated articles (and one doctoral dissertation) have focused mainly on the film's status as a cult movie, on its audience, and on its gender politics. These are all important topics that will concern this volume as well, and the authors included here are indebted to the astute observations of J. Hoberman, Jonathan Rosenbaum, Robert Wood, Barry Keith Grant, James Twitchell, Timothy Corrigan, J. P. Telotte, and others. However, given *Rocky Horror*'s unique status in American and British culture, it's time now, over thirty years after the initial release of the film, to consider it more closely and to expand the parameters of the investigation.

Let's Go See the Man Who Began It

Before turning to specific analyses of *Rocky Horror*, some background into the history of the film may be helpful.[3] The brainchild behind *Rocky Horror* was English performer Richard O'Brien (who plays Riff Raff in the movie). Hoberman and Rosenbaum report that O'Brien had already appeared in British productions of *Hair* with future *Rocky Horror* performer Tim Curry and been dismissed from a production of *Jesus Christ Superstar* directed by Jim Sharman (who would direct the *Rocky Horror* movie) when he decided in 1972 to create a rock musical originally entitled *They Came from Denton High* (4). *Denton High* subsequently became *The Rock Horroar Show* and then *The Rocky Horror Show*. O'Brien was able to attract the attention of British producer Michael White, whose extensive list of stage credits included *Oh! Calcutta* and *Sleuth* (Henkins 19), and director Jim Sharman and a stage production of *Rocky Horror* premiered in June 1973 at the Royal Court's experimental Theatre Upstairs—a sixty-three-seat venue in London's Chelsea, where O'Brien had previously played an extraterrestrial in Sam Shepherd's *The Unseen Hand* (Hoberman 6).

The original stage version of *The Rocky Horror Show*, which featured Tim Curry as Dr. Frank-N-Furter, as well as Richard O'Brien himself (Riff Raff), Patricia Quinn (Magenta), and Little Nell (Columbia), proved to be such a hit that it was relocated in London twice in quick succession, first to a converted movie house seating 270 on King's Road, and then to the five-hundred-seat King's Road Theatre—where it would play for seven years. In 1973, the production was named "best musical" by the *London Evening Standard*, and Curry was singled out for his "Jagger-like performance" (Samuels 128).[4] By 1974, the show was "a genuine London phenomenon" (Hoberman 8) that attracted popular culture luminaries including Mick Jagger himself, as well as David Bowie, Lou Reed, and Tennessee Williams (Samuels 128). Samuels reports that there were even *Rocky Horror* weekend travel packages from Paris to London (129).

Actress Britt Ekland, who saw the London production multiple times, apparently enjoyed the production so much that she convinced her beau, American film and music producer Lou Adler, to accompany her to a performance and he reached an agreement with Michael White to produce an American production at his Los Angeles rock club, The Roxy, less than two days after taking in the performance in October 1973 (Hoberman 6). Adler brought over part of the London cast, including O'Brien, Curry, and Meatloaf (Meatloaf played both Eddie and Dr. Scott in the stage production) and premiered *Rocky Horror* in America at The Roxy on March 21, 1974, where it sold out for nine straight months (Samuels 130). Encouraged by the success of the American stage production, Adler invited Twentieth Century Fox executive Gordon Stulbert—and his children—to see the show, and Stulbert was impressed enough to agree to invest one million dollars on a film version. After a ten-month run at The Roxy, Adler closed the show in early 1975 to allow Curry to return to London to work on the film production. Filming was completed in eight weeks, primarily at Bray Studies—the one-time home of the Hammer horror films—and to a lesser extent at a nineteenth-century château used as a hideout by Charles de Gaulle during World War II (Hoberman 9; Samuels 131). For the film version, Meatloaf retained the role of Eddie, and Jonathan Adams, who had played the role of the Narrator in the original London cast, assumed the role of Dr. Scott. Charles Gray, famous for playing the evil Blofeld in the James Bond film *Diamonds Are Forever*, was added as the Narrator and, most notably, two Americans—Barry Bostwick, who had played the part of Danny Zuko in *Grease* on Broadway for two years, and actress Susan Sarandon—were added as Brad and Janet. Adler's plan was to bring the stage show to Broadway before the release of the film version. It was anticipated that the Broadway production would be as big a hit as *Grease* and *Jesus Christ Superstar* and therefore would serve as a major publicity vehicle for the film (Samuels 131). As soon as Curry and O'Brien had completed filming in London, they were brought to New York to work on the stage production, which was mounted at the Belasco Theater. For the Broadway production, the theater's usual orchestra seating was removed, and the space was reconfigured with 120 café tables.

The Rocky Horror Show opened on Broadway on March 10, 1975, and was an unmitigated critical and popular disaster. Reviews were savage (Rex Reed called it "trash" [Samuels 132]), the play was hissed and booed, and it lost four thousand dollars. The play ran for fifty performances before closing, and Twentieth Century Fox executives became nervous about the impending film release (Samuels 132).[5] Anxious executives were not soothed when the film version of *Rocky Horror*, entitled *The Rocky Horror Picture Show*, previewed to poor response in Santa Barbara, California, in July 1975. The film was released on September 26, 1975, in Los Angeles and seven other American cities. In Los Angeles, it drew capacity crowds to the United Artists Westwood Theater; however, its performance elsewhere was dismal. The film grossed less than $400,000 in its first three weeks (Samuels 133) and was withdrawn by Fox before its planned New York City Halloween opening. In considering the Los Angeles success of the film and its dreadful performance elsewhere, Lou Adler and Tim Deegan, the publicist assigned by Fox to the film, discovered that many of the Los Angeles fans of the film were seeing it *repeatedly*. In consultation with Bill Quigley, a young publicist who worked for the New York–based Walter Reade theater chain, Deegan considered new ways to promote the film and was persuaded by Quigley to open *Rocky Horror* as a Midnight Movie at New York's Waverly Theater in Greenwich Village. *Rocky Horror* premiered at the Waverly at midnight on April Fool's Day (although technically, because it was midnight, it was April 2) in 1976, where it ran for a record-setting ninety-five weeks.[6] During this time, it opened as a Midnight Movie elsewhere, including Austin, Philadelphia, Toronto, Boston, and Tulsa. By the middle of 1978, *Rocky Horror* was playing at midnight on Fridays and Saturdays at over fifty locations around the United States (Samuels 134), and by end of the 1970s, Fox had two hundred prints of the film in constant circulation. The film reportedly grossed over $5 million a year (Hoberman 13). According to Samuels, "RHPS became the first motion picture to become a twice-weekly national institution. It spawned fan clubs, paraphernalia, posters, bumper stickers, record albums, videocassettes, pins, magazines, conventions, birthday parties, look-alike contests. A fan club for the film! The record album sold over one million copies. The RHPS phenomenon was born" (137).

Madness Takes Control

What makes *Rocky Horror* unique is the participatory nature of the audience response. As opposed to conventional viewing practices in which audience members sit quietly and absorb the presentation, attendees at

Rocky Horror shout remarks at the screen, dance along with the characters in the film, and vicariously participate in the onscreen action through the use of props—for instance (as all *Rocky* aficionados know), when it rains in the film, audience members shoot squirt guns in the air. Famously, many showings of *Rocky Horror* feature a simultaneous live performance referred to as the floor show or shadow cast, in which actors dressed as the film's characters lip sync the lines and mimic the motions of the onscreen characters. The film is, in Danny Peary's assessment, "the ultimate audience participation film" (302), and Wood has gone so far as to assert that the behavior of the *Rocky Horror* audience has "arguably altered the norms of behavior of a whole generation of filmgoers" (157). The origins of these practices are difficult to pin down and, among *Rocky Horror* devotees, are the stuff of legend. Although Henkin contends that "No one knows for certain how talking to the screen developed" and suggests that the practice may have started in several different places independently (102), Hoberman and Rosenbaum trace the convention of talking back to the screen back to Labor Day weekend in 1976, when five months into the *Rocky Horror* run at the Waverly in Greenwich Village, New York, schoolteacher Louis Farese, Jr., "felt compelled to talk back to the movie," and his quips were picked up by other *Rocky Horror* aficionados (176).[7]

Hoberman and Rosenbaum also locate the phenomenon of audience members dressing up as film characters as originating at the Waverly in 1976. They write that, independent of Farese's retorts, masqueraders taking great pains to duplicate the appearances of the film's characters began to show up a few weeks after the talking-back phenomenon began. This practice lead to a special Halloween costume party showing of the film at which fans got out of their seats, mimicked the on-screen action, and lip-synched the lines (177). This form of audience participation developed into the *Rocky Horror* floor show. These initial violations of conventional viewing practices seem to have liberated *Rocky Horror* fans, stimulating them to dream up "ingenious stunts involving diverse props that they would unexpectedly spring on fellow cult members during the movie" (Hoberman 179). Hoberman and Rosenbaum write, "The lineage was almost biblical, the way that rice begat candles begat water pistols begat newspapers, cards, and hot dogs aplenty" (181).[8] What this suggests is that part of the initial cult phenomenon of the film was the unusual—if not unique—opportunity it allowed for creative expression on the part of the audience, as well as the sense of community that developed out of not just the shared viewing experiences of audience members but their participation in the development of what film theorists J. P. Telotte and Barry Keith Grant have discussed as "supertext"—the combination of a film's text and reception and the "industrial practices" surrounding the film.[9] Audience members had the opportunity not just to absorb or even participate with the on-screen action but actually to originate new conventions of spectatorship.

Shivering with Antici ... pation

Given *Rocky Horror*'s unique place in cinematic history, a volume such as this one is long overdue. Essays included here have been organized into three sections that attend to what have emerged as the three most important topics for consideration of *Rocky Horror*: the film's appropriation and manipulation of various generic conventions, the "cultic" nature of the film and the viewership practices of its fans, and the film's representations of gender and sexuality. The first section of *Reading Rocky Horror* on genre groups together essays that situate *Rocky Horror* within the broader contexts of musical, theatrical, and cinematic genres, thus highlighting the ways in which *Rocky Horror* was a product of its historical moment that developed out of and manipulated the conventions of established forms and traditions. Sue Matheson, in "'Drinking Those Moments When': The Use (and Abuse) of Late-Night Double Feature Science Fiction and Hollywood Icons in *The Rocky Horror Picture Show*," carefully scrutinizes the ways in which *Rocky Horror* incorporates, appropriates, and cannibalizes elements of the cinematic science fiction tradition. *Rocky Horror*, in Matheson's assessment, is an invasion film indebted to 1950s science fiction. However, instead of expelling the alien threat at the end and reestablishing the social order, Matheson proposes that what *Rocky Horror* reveals is that "we are what we fear most."

Julian Cornell, in "*Rocky Horror* Glam Rock," rather than exploring *Rocky Horror*'s cinematic appropriations, attends to the film's musical indebtedness. Cornell situates the influence of glam rock on *Rocky Horror* within the broader context of the 1970s camp and pop aesthetics to which this musical style owes a significant debt, with the intention of demonstrating how the film is more than just a parody, a pastiche, or an instance of cult spectatorship—instead being a "polysemic text that reflexively addresses the issue of desire in mass culture."

In the same way that Matheson examines *Rocky Horror* in light of how it draws on and manipulates the cinematic science fiction tradition, and Cornell situates *Rocky Horror* within the context of 1970s glam rock and camp, Sarah Artt, in "Reflections on the Self-Reflexive Musical: *The Rocky Horror Picture Show* and the Classic Hollywood Musical," explores the ways in which the film both borrows and self-consciously departs from the conventions of the standard Hollywood musical. In Artt's assessment, *Rocky Horror* uses a conventional format to tell an unconventional story and thereby paved the way for more recent unconventional cinematic musicals, including *Chicago* and *Moulin Rouge.*

In section two, which focuses on the *Rocky* cult, the attention of contributors shifts from looking at the film in its historical context to focusing on what makes the *Rocky Horror* experience unique—the reactions of the film's audience. These observations are important not just for understanding *Rocky Horror* but for film studies more generally.[10] Jeffrey Andrew Weinstock, in "Heavy, Black, and Pendulous: Unsuturing *Rocky Horror,*" explores how *Rocky Horror* viewership practices are antithetical to conventional psychological film criticism predicated on spectatorial identification. For Weinstock, what *Rocky Horror* audience response demonstrates is a fetishization of interruption, rather than "suture." In the quest for mastery of the filmic text, *Rocky Horror* fans quite consciously break the diegetic flow, foregrounding both its rigidity and the failure of dialogue. Weinstock argues that evident in the playful, loving mockery of the film exhibited by fans is a more general but inevitably frustrated desire to *be* the movie. This failure to be the movie in turn stimulates a sadistic desire to master or control the film.

Heather C. Levy and Matthew A. Levy, in their "Mocking the Mirror: Film Spectatorship as Hyperreal Simulation," similarly assert that audience behavior during *Rocky Horror* calls into question psychoanalytic theories of viewership predicated on spectatorial "(mis)recognition." In place of this, Levy and Levy propose a new theory of viewership developed out of French postmodernist Jean Baudrillard's theory of simulation and description of the "postmodern hyperreal." The Levys conclude that what audience reaction to *Rocky Horror* demonstrates is the need for a psychosocial model that emphasizes the active nature of spectatorship—a model that they feel Baudrillard's theory of hyperreal simulation provides.

In "Wild and Untamed Thing: The Exotic, Erotic, and Neurotic *Rocky Horror* Performance Cult," Michael M. Chemers approaches the *Rocky Horror* cult by exploring the ways in which the film's eroticism generates audience response. Chemers here is attending to that most difficult of questions: Why *Rocky Horror*? What is it about *this* film that impels the audience to violate conventional viewing practices and provokes such allegiance? Chemers's answer is both simple and elegant: the "sincerity of its lust." However, in keeping with Kevin Bozelka's meditations in the sexuality section on the ease with which capitalism can absorb queer energies, this sincerity of erotic transgression is always on the verge of going out of existence, of being compromised by market forces. For Chemers, it is the "fragility" of the film's sincerity that galvanizes its adherents to rally around the film and preserve it for themselves.

Also preparing us for the analyses of *Rocky Horror*'s representations of queer sexuality introduced in the third section, Nicole Seymour in her contribution "'What We Are Watching' Does Not Present 'Us with a Struggle': *Rocky Horror*, Queer Viewers, and the Alternative Cinematic Spectacle," situates the *Rocky Horror* viewing event as a queer experience that allows for and encourages what she characterizes as "radical viewing." According to Seymour, viewing practices developed by *Rocky Horror* fans "suggest productive ways for queer and marginalized viewers to approach and read the average, mainstream film text" and "indicate that film-going need not always be a passive, rote experience, nor a solely analytical one devoid of personal enjoyment." Adopting an anthropological approach to fan response, Liz Locke, in her "'Don't Dream It, Be It': Cultural Performance and Communitas at *The Rocky Horror Picture Show*," turns to the work of anthropologists Arnold van Gennep and Victor Turner on liminality, communitas, and "interperformance" to explain the unique group dynamic that characterizes the *Rocky Horror* audience reaction. What *Rocky Horror* allows, according to Locke, is for a collectively experienced "sense of liminality" during which conventional subject positions can be briefly shed, producing a sense of liberatory exuberance. Rounding out the viewership practices section, in "The Cult and Its Virgin Sacrifice: Rites of Defloration in and at *The Rocky Horror Picture Show*," Kristina Watkins-Mormino situates the *Rocky* cult and its behavior within the broader social context of contemporary understandings of virginity. With interesting connections to Locke's analysis of liminality and *Rocky Horror* viewership, Watkins-Mormino makes the fascinating observation that perhaps the only widespread communal observance of the loss of virginity in America takes place at midnight screenings of *The Rocky Horror Picture Show* at which first-time viewers—"virgins"—are identified and subjected to certain rituals of initiation. Using this observation as the basis for her analysis, she scrutinizes the social understandings and implications of virginity that the film and its audience construct.

The third section of *Reading Rocky Horror* introduces essays that attend to *Rocky Horror*'s sexual politics. Leading off this section, Ben Hixon emphasizes the subversive potential of *Rocky Horror* in his "In Search of the Authentic Queer Epiphany: Normativity and Representations of the Queer Disabled Body in *Rocky Horror*." Here Hixon explores the film in terms of the ways in which its representations of disabled bodies subverts both heteronormative expectations and conventional attitudes toward corporal difference. Hixon maintains that although the film does manifest a tendency toward solidifying social norms, this conservative inclination is unable to offset the radical potential offered by its subversion of conventional mores and therefore offers a potentially liberating message and transformative experience for the viewer. Taking as his starting point Judith Butler's meditations on gender performativity and Michel Foucault's analysis of the production of sexed bodies, Zachery Lamm complicates Hixon's analysis with "The Queer Pedagogy of Dr. Frank-N-Furter." In his contribution, Lamm considers the radical implications of *Rocky Horror*'s subversive approach to gender and sexual preference. Important for Lamm, *Rocky Horror* is in fact a film concerned with pedagogy—with teaching—and Curry's Dr. Frank-N-Furter occupies the privileged role in this respect as instructor offering courses in both queer science and queer sexuality. At the end of the movie, not only Brad and Janet but also the audience graduate from Frank's queer classroom and emerge with an understanding of alternative sexual possibilities.

Reading Rocky Horror contributors Thomas G. Endres and Kevin John Bozelka are both far less sanguine concerning the radical potential of *Rocky Horror*'s representations of gender expectations and sexual orientation. In "'Be Just and Fear Not': Warring Visions of Righteous Decadence and Pragmatic Justice in *Rocky Horror*," Endres introduces symbolic convergence theory as a methodological tool to analyze the competing progressive and conservative messages communicated by *Rocky Horror*. As Endres explains, symbolic convergence theory provides a coherent and useful theoretical model for thematic analysis—one that leads him to conclude that the film ultimately forecloses the radical possibilities for social reorganization it seems to offer and instead reifies the status quo. In "'Your Lifestyle's Too Extreme': *Rocky Horror, Shock Treatment*, and Late Capitalism," Bozelka counters the critical emphasis on the film's "Dionysian" excesses and its celebration of counterhegemonic sexual practices by asserting that the film offers a critique of the "polymorphously perverse sexual politics of the counterculture," a critique that Bozelka reads as articulating a historically situated brand of 1970s cynicism. In opposition to those who focus on *Rocky Horror*'s subversive potential, Bozelka asserts that what *Rocky Horror*—and its less successful sequel, *Shock Treatment*—dramatize is the ease with which capitalism can absorb and co-opt the radical potential of counterhegemonic identity formations.

Taken together, the essays collected here offer the long overdue concerted attention to and analysis of *The Rocky Horror Picture Show* that the film, as one of the most important phenomena of twentieth-century cinema, deserves. Although they focus on what have emerged as the main issues in relation to the film, clearly other approaches are possible, and it is my hope that this volume will lay the groundwork for future such analyses. With that said, I would like, if I may, to take you on a strange journey . . .

Works Cited

Austin, Bruce A. "Portrait of a Cult Film Audience: *The Rocky Horror Picture Show*." *Journal of Communications* 31 (1981): 43–54.

Corrigan, Timothy. "Film and the Culture of Cult." *The Cult Film Experience: Beyond All Reason*. Ed. J. P. Telotte. Austin: U of Texas P, 1991. 26–37.

Day, Richard R. "*Rocky Horror Picture Show*: A Speech Event in Three Acts." *Sociolinguistics and Language Acquisition*. Ed. Nessa Wolfson and Elliot Judd. Rowley, MA: Newbury House, 1983. 214–21.

Eco, Umberto. "*Casablanca*: Cult Movies and Intertextual Collage." *SubStance* 14.2 (1985): 3–12.

Grant, Barry Keith. "Science Fiction Double Feature: Ideology in the Cult Film." *The Cult Film Experience: Beyond All Reason*. Ed. J. P. Telotte. Austin: U of Texas P, 1991. 122–37.

———. "Second Thoughts on Double Features: Revisiting the Cult Film." *Unruly Pleasures: The Cult Film and Its Critics*. Ed. Xavier Mendik and Graeme Harper. Guildford, UK: FAB Press, 2000. 13–28.

Henkin, Bill. *The Rocky Horror Picture Show Book*. New York: Plume, 1979.

Hoberman, J., and Jonathan Rosenbaum. *Midnight Movies*. 1983. New York: Da Capo, 1991.

Kawin, Bruce. "After Midnight." *The Cult Film Experience: Beyond All Reason*. Ed. J. P. Telotte. Austin: U of Texas P, 1991. 18–25.

Kilgore, John. "Sexuality and Identity in *The Rocky Horror Picture Show*." *Eros in the Mind's Eye: Sexuality and the Fantastic in Art and Film*. Ed. Donald Palumbo. New York: Greenwood, 1986. 151–59.

Kinkade, Patrick T., and Michael A. Katovich. "Toward a Sociology of Cult Films: Reading *Rocky Horror*." *The Sociological Quarterly* 33.2 (1992): 191–209.

Michaels, Scott, and David Evans. *Rocky Horror: From Concept to Cult*. London: Sanctuary Publishing, 2002.

Minor, Mary Eden. "The Folklore of Mass-Mediated Celebration: Audience Participation at *The Rocky Horror Picture Show*." Diss. University of Southwest Louisiana, 1995.

Peary, Danny. *Cult Movies: The Classics, the Sleepers, the Weird, and the Wonderful*. New York: Dell Publishing, 1981.

Piro, Sal. *Creatures of the Night: The Rocky Horror Experience*. Redford, MI: Stabur, 1990.

Prouty, Howard H. "The Rocky Horror Picture Show." *Magills American Film Guide*. 4th Ed. Frank N. Magill. Englewood Cliffs, NJ: Salem Press, 1983.

Robbins, Betty, and Roger Myrick. "The Function of the Fetish in *The Rocky Horror Picture Show* and *Priscilla, Queen of the Desert*." *Journal of Gender Studies* 9.3 (2000): 269–80.

Samuels, Stuart. *Midnight Movies*. New York: Collier Books, 1983.

Siegel, Mark. "*The Rocky Horror Picture Show*: More Than a Lip Service." *Science-Fiction Studies* 7.3 (1980): 305–12.

Telotte, J. P. "Beyond All Reason: The Nature of the Cult." *The Cult Film Experience: Beyond All Reason.* Ed. J. P. Telotte. Austin: U of Texas P, 1991. 5–17.

Twitchell, James B. "*Frankenstein* and the Anatomy of Horror." *The Georgia Review* 37.1 (1983): 41–84.

Wood, Robert E. "Don't Dream It: Performance and *The Rocky Horror Picture Show*." *The Cult Film Experience: Beyond All Reason.* Ed. J. P. Telotte. Austin: U of Texas P, 1991. 156–66.

Notes

1. This assessment is echoed by Wood, who characterizes *Rocky Horror* as "a paradigmatic cult film" (156); Kilgore, who asserts that the film has "risen to a position of preeminence among America's 'cult films'" (151); Samuels, who writes that *Rocky Horror* is "the king of the midnight cult films" (126); and Kinkade and Katovich, who contend that "Perhaps among all 'cult films,' *The Rocky Horror Picture Show* is the definitive exemplar" (198).

2. For example, in advertising a 2005 interview with Curry that aired on National Public Radio's *Fresh Air* program, the *Rocky Horror* song "Sweet Transvestite" was played and Curry was identified as "the star of *Rocky Horror* and other films."

3. A very thorough overview of *Rocky Horror*'s history is offered in Hoberman and Rosenbaum's excellent *Midnight Movies.* Helpful background is also provided in both Samuels and Henkin, and a rather muddled but at times entertaining discussion of the history of *Rocky Horror* is available in Michaels and Evans.

4. One of the most interesting features of the critical literature on *Rocky Horror* is the heights of rhetorical exuberance to which critics soar in attempting to characterize Curry's performance. For example, according to Michaels and Evans, Curry is a "*cross* between a megalomaniac boarding-school matron and a deranged circus ringmaster" (167); Prouty describes him as "half Auntie Mame, half Bela Lugosi, a hybrid Sophie Tucker and Mick Jagger, a cross between Greer Garson and Steve Reeves, and part David Bowie, part Joan Crawford, part Basil Rathbone" (qtd. in Minor 86); for Robbins and Myrick, he is "the spectacle of Dracula and Mae West" (5); for Kilgore, Frank is Pygmalion, Narcissus, and Percy Shelley "rolled into one" (156); Hoberman and Rosenbaum characterize Curry's Frank as an amalgam of Elvis Presley, Mick Jagger, and David Bowie (177–78).

5. In his history of *Rocky Horror*, Samuels considers reasons for the complete failure of the New York City stage production. In his estimation, the cabaret-style seating arrangement was primarily at fault because it prevented audience members from sharing the "make-believe world of RHS." In addition, the cabaret arrangement was at odds with the "flashy, expensive, ... overstaged" musical parody (132). Lou Adler reflects succinctly that New York "thought it was too L.A." (Hoberman 12).

6. Hoberman and Rosenbaum report that the promotional budget for the film's opening at the Waverly was four hundred dollars—"somewhere between one five-thousandth and one fifty-thousandth the amount customarily spent on a New York opening" (13).

7. Hoberman and Rosenbaum provide the detail that Farese's first *bon mot* was in response to Janet's shielding herself to the rain with a newspaper on the way to the Frank-N-Furter castle: "Buy an umbrella, you cheap bitch!" (176) and state that "Whenever the repartee went over well, it would be repeated the following Friday or Saturday [and] become absorbed within the general text" (176).

8. Hoberman and Rosenbaum provide an excellent overview of the development of the *Rocky Horror* cult, as well as its regional variations (see especially 176–88).

9. See Grant, "Second Thoughts," and Telotte.

10. The bulk of the surprisingly minimal academic attention paid to *Rocky Horror* has focused on the "cultic" nature of the film and its audience, as film theorists and critics alike have sought to analyze audience reactions and to isolate just what it is in the film that elicits such fervent audience response. For analyses of *Rocky Horror* as cult film, see Austin, Corrigan, Day, Grant, Hoberman and Rosenbaum, Kawin, Kinkade, Minor, Siegel, and Wood.

Part I

Rocky Horror and Genre

I

"Drinking Those Moments When"

The Use (and Abuse) of Late-Night Double Feature Science Fiction and Hollywood Icons in *The Rocky Horror Picture Show*

Sue Matheson

As Phillip Strick in *Science Fiction Movies* notes, science fiction invasion films found at the late-night double feature in the 1950s and '60s showcased things noticeably absent in the everyday lives of suburban teenage boys. The formula of these movies is simple: As any teenage boy would have known, "the aliens (or you could call them foreigners) are after our women and control of the world, whichever comes first. It would be unpatriotic to imagine otherwise" (Strick 9). Not only emblematic of problems faced by Americans during World War II, these aliens also functioned as metaphors of the "social ills" that American servicemen faced on returning home: among the lumbering, tentacled monsters signifying the calamities of fascism and communism, one also finds manifestations of the American family man's concerns with gender hierarchy and social status resulting from women reluctant to leave the workplace, as well as the rock and roll youth culture. In part, these movies—among them *Red Planet Mars* (1952), *She Devil* (1957), *The Attack of the 50 Foot Woman* (1958), *The Wild Women of*

Wongo (1959), *Teenage Monster* (1958), *Teenage Zombies* (1960), *Forbidden Planet* (1956), *Gigantis the Fire Monster* (1959), *The Leech Woman* (1960), and *Attack of the Crab Monsters* (1957)—showcased the state of anxiety in which average Americans were functioning throughout this period.[1] Underlying the political fear mongering, xenophobia, and gynophobia found in such movies, one finds the recurring nightmare of natural forces running amok as a result of scientific tinkering. Since the detonation of the A-bomb, the old problem of scientific megalomania, strongly voiced in the nineteenth century by Mary Shelley's *Frankenstein*, was understandably an overriding preoccupation for Americans in the 1950s. As Americans, and the rest of the world, grappled with the implications of Hiroshima and Nagasaki, movies like *Invasion of the Hell Creatures* (1957), in which "little green Martians with needle-like nails" inject alcohol into their victims, and *Invasion of the Star Creatures* (1962), during which the Earth is attacked by "strapping wenches armed with monster vegetables," offered their audiences reassurance that in the end, Middle American norms and forms—in particular, patriarchy and reason—could be restored to a world temporarily gone insane (Strick 10).

Accordingly, visitors from other planets in late night science fiction movies were diametrically opposed to the crewcut heroism of the Atomic Age: Exotic, flamboyant, and often leaking unpleasant bodily fluids, examples of these extraterrestrials include a fifty-foot woman squeezing her cheating husband to death and a poison-dripping, tentacle-lashing triffid chasing Janette Scott. In 1975, however, visitors from outer space even more outrageous than their predecessors appeared in *The Rocky Horror Picture Show*. These aliens challenged not only the prowess of the patriotic American male but also the puritanical social codes of Middle America: Richard O'Brien's Transylvanians wanted our men as well as our women.

An updated version of the midnight double feature, *Rocky Horror* parodies the science fiction genre established in the 1930s by movies like *Dr. X* (1932), *The Invisible Man* (1933), *King Kong* (1933), and *Flash Gordon* (1936). At the beginning of this movie, a pair of disembodied lips (known as Lips or the Usherette), floating in the vacuum of outer space, carefully prepares its viewers' expectations by reminding the audience that *Rocky Horror* follows directly in the footsteps of the following late night classics: *The Day the Earth Stood Still* (1951), *It Came From Outer Space* (1953), *Forbidden Planet* (1956), *Tarantula* (1955), *The Day of the Triffids* (1963), *Curse of the Demon* (1957), and *When Worlds Collide* (1951). For members of the audience who are not familiar with this genre—at times an uneasy blend of Gothic sensibility and hard science—Lips outlines its standard elements. Designed for the teenage imagination, the message from outer space contained in such pictures runs accordingly: A mad scientist—a

Dr. X—will "build a creature," and there will be "androids fighting." The viewer should expect to "get hot" when the alien monster is finally killed, and "some terrible thrills" will happen throughout the movie. True to this rather rudimentary formula, *Rocky Horror*'s Dr. Frank-N-Furter does build a creature, and Brad and Janet, who become like androids after experiencing the medusa ray, engage in a series of lovers' spats. By the time Riff Raff kills Frank-N-Furter, the latter draped across Rocky, who is climbing an unmistakably phallic RKO radio tower, the audience should be "hot," having witnessed two seductions and an orgy. In addition, there certainly are some terrible thrills—among them, Eddie the ex–delivery boy's untimely and bloody demise as he is ice picked to death, Riff Raff's dripping candelabra torture of the hapless Rocky, and Eddie's return as a mutilated corpse beneath Frank-N-Furter's dinner table.

To date, *Rocky Horror* has elicited a number of thoughtful examinations regarding its treatment of gender—its excessiveness, its celebration of transgressive sexuality, its playful treatment of Freudian dynamics, and its Gothic preoccupations.[2] Little critical attention, however, has been given to this film as a science fiction movie parody. It is the purpose of this chapter to do so, but oddly enough, to begin such an inquiry, it is necessary first to consider the significance of the past rather than the future—that is, Richard Nixon's resignation speech, which marks the beginning of Brad and Janet's farewell to American norms and forms.

Nixon's speech, which actually aired on the evening of August 8, 1974, has two functions at the beginning of *Rocky Horror*. First, because the "normal" young couple's adventure takes place not in August but during a dark November evening, Nixon's resignation suggests to viewers that Brad and Janet are in a time warp. Second, and arguably more important, Tricky Dick's assertion while quitting that he has "never been a quitter" points the viewer toward the movie's unrelenting deconstruction of Americana via elements of the science fiction movie. The significance of this Cold War Republican president's resignation lies in Nixon's strong identification with conservative, middle-class Americans. Many moviegoers in 1975 would have been initiated into their culture by way of the conservative, often paranoid, and generally politically reactionary medium of 1950s matinees and drive-in double features—arguably, the late-night double feature drive-in was the place where many of Nixon's middle-class voters, who later supported their government's policies in Vietnam, found their parents' social and religious attitudes reinforced.

In *Rocky Horror*, one finds Brad and Janet, leftovers from the '50s, beginning their night out in a mid-1970s version of a Woody Wagon listening to Nixon resign. Embodiments of Middle America, Brad and Janet are modern versions of the American Gothics found on Denton's Episcopalian

Church's steps after Ralph and Betty's wedding: Hopelessly out of date, their clothing and lifestyle denote a highly conservative approach to life in the sexually liberated and politically progressive '70s. Modeled after the 1950s emotionless, heterosexual, hypermasculine hero found in late night science fiction, Brad Majors embodies clean-living and God-fearing American values. Unfortunately for Brad, what was attractive in the '50s is not seen as such in the '70s. In his rectangular, dark-framed, Coke-bottle lenses, Brad is a caricature—that familiar type popularized in early science fiction movies and television serials as the nerd.

The nerd, whose social awkwardness conceals his true nature, has been an important mainstay in science fiction since Superman shed his socially inept Clark Kent exterior and began leaping tall buildings in a single bound. At first, Brad appears to have the heroic potential of Superman's Clark Kent and Captain Marvel's Billy Batson. Similar to Clark Kent, he has the deep voice and the lines of a late night hero: "It's alright, Janet," or "I'm here. There's nothing to worry about." Like Kent, Brad hints that he too can reveal his true nature by "pulling out the aces . . . when the time is right." However, unlike Kent (and Batson), Brad is unable to act heroically when the opportunity arises. Fixed to the laboratory floor, for example, he cannot save Janet from the medusa ray. The worst he can do is call Frank-N-Furter a hot dog. An ordinary human being, he lacks the finely tuned sense that superheroes have that danger or an alien menace is afoot. Clearly, there is a great deal for a late night science fiction hero to be concerned about at the Frankenstein Place, not the least of which is the odd appearance of the Transylvanians, the cobweb-covered mummy in the front hall, and Eddie's scarred and dripping forehead. Brad, however, notices none of these things. Thus, when Magenta pulls off Brad's pants, it is not surprising that his underwear is not made of silver, like Flash Gordon's, but ordinary cotton.

If heroic underwear is an indicator of super-masculinity in late night movies, one need look no further than Rocky's golden bikini for it. (It is no coincidence that Rocky wears the superhero's traditional golden boots to match his gleaming shorts.) Throughout, Rocky, played by Peter Hinwood, a professional model and bodybuilder, acts as a foil, emphasizing Brad's nerdhood. Compared with Hinwood, Bostwick appears to be the epitome of the ninety-eight-pound weakling—the bookworm who gets sand kicked in his face by a bully in the Charles Atlas ads found on the back of Marvel comic books in the 1950s and 1960s. In America, as elsewhere, it seems that muscles are an important measure of one's manliness and masculinity. Even Janet, who loyally tells Frank-N-Furter that she dates Brad because she doesn't like a man with "too many muscles," later confesses that she too is "a muscle fan."

As with all nerds, Brad is not only deficient in the area of deltoids but also lacks even the minimum amount of social delicacy that one would expect of a romantic late night lead. For example, when Janet urges him to leave the castle after "The Time Warp," he rudely grits his teeth and tells her "to get a grip on herself" because "it's just a party." The Transylvanians are "probably foreigners with ways different than our own," he reassures her patronizingly, and wanting to appear well-educated and broad-minded, he points out that "they may do some more . . . folk dancing." At this point, even Janet recognizes that Brad, playing anthropologist, is alienating the aliens in his attempts to be friendly. When he asks the Transylvanians after they do "The Time Warp" if anyone knows how to do "The Madison," she rolls her eyes, takes his arm, and heads for the door, saying, "Brad, please, let's get out of here." When he resists her suggestion, she resorts to terms that he can understand: "This isn't the Junior Chamber of Commerce, Brad," she tells him.

Unlike the Transylvanians, Brad is the epitome of the Junior Chamber of Commerce. Tastelessly dressed in white socks, flood pants, and a plaid cummerbund and bowtie at Ralph and Betty's wedding, he is the picture of a middle-class teenager attempting to ape Old Money. However, should the viewer miss the jarring ideological overtones of Brad's conservative suit, resplendent with a white carnation, and his embarrassing attempts to "swing" at the Frankenstein Place, the noisy and enthusiastic shouts of "asshole!" at Brad's appearance on screen at any public showing of *Rocky Horror* would at once rectify any false impression. Transcripts of this movie's cult following's responses to Brad's appearance demonstrate beyond a shadow of a doubt that they immediately recognize him as a reactionary representative of the conservative middle class—the butt of Sharman and O'Brien's jokes.

As Richard R. Day points out in *"Rocky Horror Picture Show*: A Speech Event In Three Acts,"* during this movie, meaning—especially irony—generally presents few problems for first-time viewers, because the verbal interjections by the audience anticipate the action on the screen, allowing the significance to become clear in short order. Moreover, should the viewer be confused by the audience's behavior, Brad's conduct quickly makes their interjections meaningful (217). Brad indeed proves through his chauvinism at Ralph and Betty's wedding to be as conservative as his attire: As the newly married couple leaves, he explains to Janet that Ralph and Betty's marriage will be a success because "Everyone knows that Betty's a wonderful little cook," and "Ralph himself will be in line for a promotion in a year or two." In the 1950s, Brad's rather Victorian analysis of the situation may have been deemed acceptable. In 1975 and later, however, his attitudes toward gender and marriage grow increasingly out of date.

Apparently having missed out on both the sexual revolution and women's liberation, he indeed is living in the past.

In short, Brad is the epitome of the Nice Boy Next Door. Respectful and sexually inhibited, he transmits that prepubescent sexual innocence found in episodes of *Leave It To Beaver* and *Mayberry RFD*. Poking fun at his reactionary opinions and "good" manners, the audience response mocks his character at every possible opportunity. For example, when a motorcyclist passes Brad's station wagon in the rain several scenes later, viewers shout, "Say something stupid, Brad (asshole)!" Dripping with bigotry, Brad's comment, "Yes, life's pretty cheap to *that* type," is greeted with shouts of "asshole!" and "yea that type!"[3]

The chorus' use of the word "asshole" simultaneously establishes and undercuts the notion of the science fiction late night hero's hypermasculinity and ironically foreshadows Brad's sexual experience with Frank-N-Furter later in the movie. A nerd, a bigot, and as the audience disapprovingly points out, an asshole, Brad is identified early in the movie as a burlesque character. Involved in a series of slapstick jokes, he literally falls at Janet's feet on the steps of the church when he proposes to her, finds himself caught with his pants down at the Frankenstein Place, and spends most of the movie parading about in his "charming underclothes." Only a fool would ask a party of gender-bending transsexuals if "any of you *guys* know how to *Madison*," or introduce his sexually repressed fiancé as Janet Vice to Frank-N-Furter. Arguably, one of the best examples of Brad's foolishness occurs during his marriage proposal to Janet. Parodying the lyrics of marriage proposals often found in Hollywood musicals, Brad's offer of matrimony, which marks the end of his freedom as a bachelor, begins in a graveyard and concludes in front of a coffin. His musical proposition is constructed as a series of clichés that have occurred and reoccurred in popular love songs *ad nauseam*: Brad's entirely predictable, interminable, and overused metaphors include "The river was deep but I swam it. The future is ours so let's plan it. The road is long but I ran it. There's a fire in my heart and you fan it." He ends his declaration of undying love in a medley with Janet that reduces his beloved to a handful of letters in a doowop duet reminiscent of songs sung by The Chords, The Platters, and The Shirelles: "J-A-N-E-T. I love you."

Similar to Brad, Janet too is a send up of the '50s suburban Puritan. Her bifurcated nature also reflects the cultural contradictions of her period. Embodying the sexual double standard for women during the 1950s, in the movie's opening scenes, Janet is dressed in a conservative white hat that covers her head in church and a modest mauve suit buttoned to her neck that shows off her legs above the knees. Later, as the Criminologist points out, in her pink Peter Pan collar and white cardigan, she is, in the vernacular of the Eisenhower Era, just a "healthy, ordinary kid."

In Janet's case, the 1950s American terms "healthy" and "ordinary" translate into the nice girl next door, who supports the power of patriarchy and its values. It is not surprising, then, that she upholds the ideals of the patriarchal family system, perfected almost a century before in the Victorian home. In this system, marriage and the sex life it licensed provided men with a status of which polite society approved. Indeed, marriage was "deemed almost a necessity for the pursuit of a conventionally acceptable career, or occupation, or simply existence" (Calder 9). As a result, acquiring a homemaker, who preserved the standards and values of Victorian family life well into the twentieth century, was generally considered by men (and women) to be an indication of social and economic success. Thus, after Ralph and Betty leave for their honeymoon, Janet wistfully gushes to Brad, "I can't believe it. Just an hour ago she was just plain old Betty Munro. And now she is Mrs. Ralph Happshatt," before heaving a deep sigh of regret that she is still single. When Brad presents her with an engagement ring, therefore, Janet's first reaction is not to ponder her forthcoming spiritual transformation and elevation but to leave Brad lying with his face on the doorstep and run into the church to show off her prize, triumphantly shouting, "It's nicer than Betty Munro has." A suburban girl, she is interested solely in her social and material elevation, keeping up with the Joneses next door.

The product of the American marriage market, Janet's possessiveness of Brad is a matter of personal property. By proposing marriage, he becomes Janet's. With apologies to *Frankie and Johnny*, he is *her* man, and it is Janet's responsibility to make sure that he does her no wrong. After all, in a monogamous, heterosexual, Episcopalian marriage, not only does the man take the woman but the woman also takes the man. Thus, when Brad gallantly offers to walk to the Frankenstein place in the rain to find a phone, Janet insists on accompanying him, because "the owner of that phone might be a beautiful woman, and you might never come back again." Ironically, the sexual predator awaiting Janet at the Frankenstein Place reveals itself not to be another competing angel of the house but something Other.

Accompanying Brad proves to be Janet's undoing. As Jenni Calder points out in *The Victorian Home*, modern women, if they were to become the middle-class male's refuge from the pressures of the world outside the home, could only be good wives "if they were unsullied by the horrors that lay without" (10). At first, J-A-N-E-T appears to be perfect for her essential function as Brad's future wife, because she seems to be innocent and puritanical. That is, her morals, like her hymen, appear to be intact. It soon becomes apparent, however, that by venturing outside the walls of her own domestic sphere into a competitive arena, the nice-girl-next-door becomes no longer so N-I-C-E after all. After her first sexual encounter, Janet discovers a voracious sexual appetite that she proceeds to satisfy. She tells Rocky she needs "action." She has "tasted blood," and she wants more. As the Criminologist points out in his dictionary, Janet's state of mind is not what one would expect of the pure, demure, passive virgin she was before intercourse. According to the dictates of polite American society, she has become "abnormal," possessed by that state of "agitation or disturbance of the mind," which is "an irrational and powerful master." As the Criminologist explains, enslaved by emotion, she is no longer the passive, forgiving lover found in popular American love ballads. Instead, her appetites have become aberrant. Wanting blood, she has become something alien, socially abhorrent, immoral, and un-American—a vampire.

Amittai F. Aviram points out in his excellent article "Postmodern Gay Dionysus: Dr. Frank N. Furter" that blood-sucking vampires have long been associated not only with extramarital seduction but almost subliminally with homosexuality in the European popular imagination (188). A horrifying expression of reproductive aberrance in the Gothic, the vampire, originally found in European folklore is always a sexually experienced predator operating outside generally accepted social and religious boundaries. In the Gothic, the sexually experienced villain's triumph, of course, is the inexperienced victim's social, moral, and spiritual ruin. Once "bitten," she becomes a fallen woman—a Lilith who joins her seducer in seeking and destroying others' sexual innocence.

Similar to Magenta and Columbia, who voyeuristically hiss and slaver like Dracula's brides in a late night feature while watching Janet seduce Rocky, Janet proves that she wants to be not only a competitor but also a predator and a hedonist—a "creature of the night." During this scene, her allusion to Bram Stoker's *Dracula* reminds the viewer about and reinforces the Gothic treatment of sexuality that begins at the Frankenstein Place with the appearance of Frank-N-Furter, wrapped from head to toe in the sort of vampire cape seen in late night horror movies. As a sexual predator, however, Janet is comical. In fact, she is so clumsy while seducing Rocky that Magenta and Columbia roll about together and howl with laughter while they view and parody her betrayal of Brad. In spite her transformation from victim to vamp, Janet is still very much a novice in pleasurable matters. As she tells Rocky, who is even more inexperienced than she, all she wants to know is "how to go" when she should be teaching him "how to come." Ironically, Rocky is the person most unsuited to become Janet's tutor at the Frankenstein Place, because he has never experienced intercourse with a member of the opposite sex. Therefore, it is she who must initiate him, not he who initiates her.

Similar to Janet's unlikely vampirization, almost every Gothic convention from the late night science fiction genre appears in *Rocky Horror* and is remorselessly lampooned: to name but a few, the serendipitous dark and stormy night on which the adventure takes place; the tree branches that clutch like hands at Janet as she walks on the castle grounds toward one light showing in the entire Gothic complex, when she could have taken the road; the "Enter At Your Risk" notice repeatedly illuminated by lightening bolts and tacked to a ridiculously high iron fence; the bolts of lightening striking within and without the castle; the outrageously large, Igor-like hump that mysteriously shifts about on Riff Raff's back and changes its size in each scene; the wolf howling on cue as Frank-N-Furter enters Janet's and Brad's boudoirs; and "the dogs," rather than the traditional hounds guarding the grounds, that Magenta releases (see Figure 1.1). These parodies, especially those associated with the movie's hero and heroine, offer, as Aviram notes, a critique of "such apparently reasonable institutions as home and family, dad and mom and apple pie" (185). Moreover, as generic and social conventions collapse on the screen, the result is complete carnival. All that is marginalized and excluded in American culture—the mad, the scandalous, the aleatory—takes over the center in what Robert Stam would identify as "a liberating explosion of otherness" (86).

As Stam points out in *Subversive Pleasures: Film, Literature, and the Carnivalesque*, carnival involves a constellation of interrelated tropes and ideas engaged in the overturning of social norms and forms. Among these

Figure 1.1

subversive tropes are the notion of bisexuality and the practice of transvestitism as a release from the burden of socially imposed sex roles that rigidly
prescribe procreative norms of sexual activity (93). A prime example of
the freedom that carnival produces occurs at the movie's end, when Janet,
dressed in black fishnet stockings, high heels, and a Merry Widow corset,
experiences her liberation. Freed from the procreative sexual norms borrowed from the Victorians by the 1950s, she sings, "I feel released . . . my
mind has been expanded." Moving into the '70s, she finally gives herself
"over to absolute pleasure" and "swim[s] the warm waters of sins of the
flesh." Perhaps a comment on the plight of the Middle American male in
the '70s, poor Brad, although similarly dressed, finds his transsexual freedom frightening: Instead of celebrating his bisexuality and "feeling sexy,"
he is a reluctant carnival-goer, whimpering, "It's beyond me; help me
Mommy! I'll be good; you'll see. Take this dream away."

During the orgiastic carnival in the swimming pool that follows, the five
celebrants' bisexual natures are emphasized (see Figure 1.2). With wet flat-
tened hair and wearing similar costumes, Rocky, Frank-N-Furter, Columbia, Brad, and Janet are virtually indistinguishable from one another.
As Aviram notes, the movie effectively removes gender differences and
subverts the institution of heterosexual reproduction via heavy makeup,
burlesque brassieres, corsets, and fishnet stockings with garters and high
heels (190). More important, during the orgy, distinctions between Self
and Other break down, as swimming men look like women and swimming
women look like men. In the water, it seems sexual behavior cannot be

Figure 1.2

gender specific. As a result, heterosexual norms are overturned: There is no top or bottom in the water, no pairing, and no aggressive or passive partners. As Frank-N-Furter, the master of the carnival, promises, this exercise is about pure pleasure, not the act of procreation.

The swimming pool scene in *Rocky Horror*, however, is not only about promoting the pursuit of pleasure—be it homo- or heterosexual. At its campy core, *Rocky Horror*, similar to other works of science fiction, is seriously concerned with the problems created by man's desire to create life. In addition, as in Mary Shelley's *Frankenstein*, patriarchal ideology based on biology is also at stake in *Rocky Horror*'s blurring of gender and genre.

Oddly enough, science fiction, which is often considered a lowbrow form of entertainment by critics, is a perfect medium for such a serious discussion. From spectacularly bad B movies such as *Teenage Zombies* (1960) and *The Leech Woman* (1960), to such a classic work of literature as Shelley's *Frankenstein*, mad scientists suffer from what has come to be known as the Frankenstein complex and simply cannot resist the desire to appropriate the power to create life and hubristically play God, thereby inviting suitably tragic ends. *Rocky Horror* signals its central concern regarding the question of creation when Lips dissolves after the opening credits to become part of a cross mounted on a steeple. Indeed, given the tongue-in-cheek nature of this movie, one cannot help noting here that both Frank-N-Furter and Jehovah, who are not of this world, must have come from outer space. As *Rocky Horror* begins, it is tempting to think that that Sharman and O'Brien may have borrowed material from the gospel of Michael Valentine Smith concerning the nature of free love in Robert Heinlein's classic science fiction satire *Stranger in a Strange Land* for their movie, but it soon becomes evident that Frank-N-Furter is not a god—or even godlike—but merely suffering from a god complex. Before the orgy in the swimming pool begins, Frank-N-Furter leaps feet first into what appears to be a cloud. When the mists dissolve, he is found floating in a swimming pool on a life preserver from the *Titanic*. Although this life preserver foreshadows that he is inevitably and irrevocably doomed, the bottom of the pool, a sepia-toned mural of Michelangelo's *The Creation of Adam*, points to the cause of his downfall. Ironically, the master of carnival is floating in the blank space in which the creative current occurs between Adam and God at the moment Adam is given life. Paddling in circles in the area between Adam and God's forefingers, Frank-N-Furter delivers a Promethean message, which could not be more withering. The ideal he invokes is that of Hollywood's America by singing, "Don't dream it. Be it." Frank-N-Furter's creative current is not the electricity found in the lab, as in Frankenstein's case, but the flashing lightening bolts of the RKO Radio Picture's tower that serve as his backdrop. Mistaking the illusion of life (or art) for life itself, Frank-N-Furter asks, "Whatever happened to Fay Wray?" and then becomes her, reenacting her performance in *King Kong* (1933), as Rocky, in an attempt to revitalize his master, climbs the RKO tower like Kong climbing the Empire State Building.

As a Romantic attempt to realize the American Dream promoted by Hollywood, Frank-N-Furter's social and sexual experiment is a failure. Indeed, he himself points out that being a creator is anything but a bed of roses. While turning "tiny fools" who should "quake with fear," into stone, he observes, "It's not easy having a good time. Even smiling makes my face ache." When Frank-N-Furter promises earlier that "in just seven days" he can make Rocky, his creation, a man, he is, of course, plagiarizing Genesis. What Frank-N-Furter has forgotten—or has arguably never known—while paddling above *The Creation* in the swimming pool is that man's place in the universe is not that of the creator, but of the creation.

Conventionally, then, it is entirely appropriate that Frank-N-Furter is finally punished for his intellectual and biological hubris. At first, Dr. Everett V. Scott seems, logically and generically, to be the agent of society's retribution. As Rolf Eichler suggests in "In the Romantic Tradition: *Frankenstein* and *The Rocky Horror Picture Show*," it is possible to view Scott as "a guardian of morality from the real, everyday world" (112). In late-night double features, wheelchair-bound scientists, with the paralyzed bottoms of their bodies draped in plaid car rugs, typically represent the social norms of order, reason, and patriarchy divorced from the distractions of the flesh.[4] A representative of these forces, Scott understands the criminal enormity of Frank-N-Furter's madness that leads him to tamper with the laws of nature. Scott warns Frank-N-Furter that he has finally gone too far when, Janet—feet fixed to the floor—really does appear to be endangered. He reminds Brad that Frank-N-Furter must be executed because of "what became of Eddie. Society must be protected." Even when the lower half of his body, dressed in fishnet stockings, garters, and high heels, appears to take on a life of its own, Scott realizes that "We've got to get out of this trap before this decadence saps our wills. I've got to be strong, and try to hang on, or else my mind may well snap, and my life will be lived . . . for the thrill!"

Here it seems that Sharman and O'Brien are calling for a Gothic reading of their film. If Scott, alive only from the waist up, embodies the principle of pure intellect in *Rocky Horror*, it should follow that Frank-N-Furter is his evil twin, in much the same manner that Eddie is "the wild and ugly source that was sacrificed in order to produce his double, the gentle, handsome Rocky" (Eichler 110). However, when one considers the possibility of a doppelgänger in this case, an interesting problem arises. By seducing his own child and engaging in what he terms "erotic nightmares beyond any measure," Frank-N-Furter clearly represents the dark side of the self in all its sexuality and aggression. But what does Scott represent? Regarding Scott as the purveyor of logocentric thinking is problematic, as the good doctor is simply not very bright. No match for the wily Frank-N-Furter, Scott is himself a parody of the late night science fiction movie's epistemological hero, whose superior brain allows him to rationalize and defeat the threat of the irrational and the Unknown. Armed with a pair of binoculars and a magnifying glass, Scott's slow-witted and low-tech attempts to save his nephew merely serve to bore Frank-N-Furter and most of the dinner party. In fact, his lines are so clichéd that when greeting his competitor for the first time, like Stanley meeting Livingstone, he says, "Frank-N-Furter. *We meet at last.*" His scientific credentials are based on the "fact" that he knows "a great deal about a lot of things." Even the device on which he and Brad have been working is a cliché: Like the transporter on *Star Trek*, it too is "capable of breaking down solid matter and then projecting it through space and who knows perhaps even time itself." Happily, Scott's performance is interrupted by the medusa ray. Notably, before being turned to stone, he is unable to come up with even one original thought—all he can do is parrot Brad's insult that Frank-N-Furter is a "hot dog."

Later, however, Scott begins to resemble his nemesis. When Frank-N-Furter bursts from the swimming pool as "a wild and an untamed thing," Scott, a "rival scientist," joins the chorus line, wheeling about and kicking his heels in the air from his wheelchair. Other carefully constructed parallels between Scott and Frank-N-Furter also serve to undermine Scott's trustworthy posture as the man of science. Similar to Frank-N-Furter, who incorporates elements of the maniacal eugenicist in science fiction B movies in the 1950s and 1960s inspired by Nazi science—Rocky is "the triumph of [his] will"—Scott also displays foreign intellectual tendencies, sporting an exaggerated German accent. He punctuates his discoveries in the Zen Room with loud "achs," which are later replaced by louder "unds." Like Frank-N-Furter, Scott too is interested in tinkering with the forces of nature. He has also been spending his time building gadgets—in particular, an "audio-vibratory-physio-molecular transport device."

Throughout *Rocky Horror*, Sharman and O'Brien's spoofs of late night movie elements are delightful and instructive, but their careful and calculating parodies of Hollywood icons supporting and strengthening their use (and abuse) of other Hollywood movie staples are what ultimately rescue this movie from becoming something that can be appreciated only by Trekkies and B movie fans. A number of Hollywood screen goddesses, arguably themselves parodies of human beings, make up Curry's presentation of Frank-N-Furter—in particular, the middle-aged Joan Crawford, whose androgynous appearance has prompted a good deal of attention from reviewers, and Mae West, whose throaty intonations and seductive pauses when inviting men upstairs to her boudoir made her a star in movies like *Goin' To Town* (1935).

As Gaylyn Studlar notes in "Midnight S/Excess: Cult Configurations of 'Femininity' and the Perverse," the Otherness of Frank-N-Furter's transvestitism and bisexuality are normalized by his very masculine qualities that confirm his active, phallic power (8). Curry's sideburns and the five-o'clock shadow under his makeup do reassure the audience that Frank-N-Furter's masculine aggression is testosterone-based. Curry's sideburns, however, are also an important part of his character's burlesque of womanhood because they undercut the powerful appeal of the diva that rests upon her hyperfeminine attributes. Here it is important to note that, during the Cold War, hyperfemininity became a bifurcated affair for women: The diva was popularly conceived of not only as a charming, ladylike hostess in the living room but also as a whore in the bedroom. Unlike the Victorian wife, who was taught to endure her husband's activities in the bedroom, in 1963, the modern woman looked, walked, and talked like an angel but, as Elvis Presley pointed out, was actually a devil "in disguise." With this in mind, on the one hand, throughout *Rocky Horror*, playful flaws in Frank-N-Furter's wardrobe deconstruct the divinity of the 1950s diva of the hearth. In what is arguably the most charming parody of Joan Crawford on the planet, the mad scientist appears in what seems to be a '50s Coco Chanel cocktail dress. Frank-N-Furter's tasteful lab coat, worn back to front, is actually an exact copy of Dr. Frankenstein's in James Whale's *The Bride of Frankenstein* (1935). Frank-N-Furter's exaggerated cherry-sized pearls and his gloves further undermine the seriousness of his announcement to the unconventional conventionalists gathered in the spectators' gallery. Made of pink rubber, Frank-N-Furter's household cleaning gloves burlesque the modest, ladylike ideal transmitted by the cotton, linen, and lace fashion accessories donned by '50s women for formal public occasions, such as a tea. To emphasize the inappropriate nature of his gloves, Frank-N-Furter snaps them on like a homemaker protecting her hands from the dishwater in an Ivory soap or Palmolive commercial.

When not parodying Crawford's matronly appearance, Curry overuses elements of Mae West's character to poke fun at the less puritanical aspects of American womanhood. Arrested for obscenity in the 1920s, West was known as "The Baby Vamp" at age fourteen and was Hollywood's first sex clown. As flamboyant and shocking as West, whose earliest Broadway plays were "Sex" and "Drag," Frank-N-Furter lacks her forty-three-inch bust but wears her trademark six-inch platform heels. Performing on a gymnast's horse, shaped like a red, beribboned dildo, he parodies not only her sexual innuendo and double entendres but also her stage presence, salaciously rolling his eyes and singing, "Honey, I can make you a man." Much more sexually explicit than West, Frank-N-Furter informs his Transylvanians that "a hot groin" makes him want "to take Charles Atlas by the ha-ha-hand." To ensure that no one in the audience can mistake the source of his parody, Curry even borrows from what are arguably West's most recognized lines from *Goin' To Town*: "Come up and see me some time." Pausing for effect like West, he invites Brad and Janet to "come up . . . to the lab and see . . . what's on . . . the slab."

Sharman and O'Brien's delightfully irreverent treatment of late night movie staples and Currie's send up of the Hollywood star system suggest that the Other in *Rocky Horror* should ultimately be recognized as that Cold War phenomenon, the enemy within. In the final analysis, Frank-N-Furter and his Transylvanians are precisely what the puritanical social norms and forms of America during the Cold War were designed to suppress. It seems that every character in *Rocky Horror* subverts the sexless 1950s suburban dream of a white picket fence and twin beds in the master bedroom. Wearing her Mouseketeer hat, even Columbia is a member of the Disney inner circle. In *Rocky Horror*, similar to those alien Others of the 1950s invasion films, characters with antisocial tendencies are suffering from a malaise generated by the United States itself.

As Lips says at the beginning of *Rocky Horror*, the 1950s late-night double features tell "us where we stand." Typically, human beings in these films, whatever their vices and follies throughout, fare well in the end. Late-night double features, whether they may be classified as As or Bs, conclude with order being restored (in America, on Earth, and throughout the galaxy). The alien Other is killed, returns—or is returned to—outer space, and the Earthlings, the hero, the heroine, and what is left of the supporting cast, gratefully resume their humdrum lives in the suburbs as the dominant species on Earth, a little older and much wiser. Toward the conclusion of *Rocky Horror*, however, human beings prove themselves to be no wiser than the aliens. It is disturbing that they are like the aliens and have nowhere else to go. In yet another carnivalesque overturning of genre, the insanity, aberrance, sex, and vulgarity of the late-night double feature is not flushed into outer space. It remains on Earth. Having fallen into a garden, rather than from it, Brad, Janet, and Scott stay dressed in their corsets—unable to get to their feet and writhing about like worms on the ground. As the Criminologist points out, human beings have been revealed to be that lowliest of Others, mere insects, and as he spins his illuminated globe before turning out the lights, it seems inevitable that the carnival will continue. Following in the tradition of *The Day The Earth Stood Still*, *Rocky Horror* reveals that we are also that which we most fear, Otherness, which we project on those whom we do not know.

Works Cited

Aviram, Amittai F. "Postmodern Gay Dionysus: Dr. Frank N. Furter." *Journal of Popular Culture* 26.3 (1992): 183–92.

Calder, Jenni. *The Victorian Home*. London: B. T. Batsford, 1977.

Day, Richard R. "*Rocky Horror Picture Show*: A Speech Event In Three Acts." *Sociolinguistics and Language Acquisition*. Ed. Nessa Wolfson and Elliot Judd. Rowley, MA: Newbury House, 1983. 214–21.

Eichler, Rolf. "In the Romantic Tradition: *Frankenstein* and *The Rocky Horror Picture Show*." *Beyond the Suburbs of the Mind: Exploring English Romanticism*. Ed. Michael Gassenmeier and Norbert H. Platz. Essen: Blaue Eule, 1987. 95–114.

Kilgore, John. "Sexuality and Identity in *The Rocky Horror Picture Show*." *Eros in the Mind's Eye*. Ed. Donald Palumbo. New York: Greenwood, 1986. 151–59.

Robbins, Betty, and Roger Myrick. "The Function of the Fetish in *The Rocky Horror Picture Show* and *Priscilla, Queen of the Desert*." *Journal of Gender Studies* 9.3 (2000): 269–80.

The Rocky Horror Picture Show. 20 July 2004. http://www.ccs.neu.edu/home/image/rocky-horror.html.

Ruble, Raymond. "Dr. Freud Meets Dr. Frank N. Furter." *Eros in the Mind's Eye*. Ed. Donald Palumbo. New York: Greenwood, 1986. 163–68.

Stam, Robert. *Subversive Pleasures: Bahktin, Cultural Criticism and Film*. Baltimore: John Hopkins P, 1992.

Strick, Philip. *Science Fiction Movies*. London: Octopus Books, 1976.

Studlar, Gaylyn. "Midnight S/Excess: Cult Configurations of 'Femininity' and the Perverse." *Journal of Popular Film and Television* 17.1 (1989): 2–14.

Warren, Bill. *Keep Watching The Skies!: American Science Fiction Movies of the Fifties*. Volume 2: 1950–1957. Jefferson, NC: McFarland, 1982.

———. *Keep Watching The Skies!: American Science Fiction Movies of the Fifties*. Volume 2: 1958–1962. Jefferson, NC: McFarland, 1986.

Notes

1. Bill Warren points out in volumes 1 and 2 of *Keep Watching The Skies!* that science fiction movies that played as late-night double features were preoccupied to a great extent with America's domestic problems that surfaced during the Cold War. These domestic problems, among them the communist threat, women in the workplace, and motorcycle-riding teenagers who listened to rock and roll, manifest themselves as the Other or as aliens from outer space. For example, *Red Planet Mars* (1952), a hysterically anticommunist religious science fiction picture, showcases a scientist and his family who are "Just Folks" and save the world from the "Red" Martians (vol. 1, 90). Similar to the forces of communism, women in science fiction movies often became part of the forces threatening the gender norms and social forms of Middle America. The original *She Devil* (1957), for example, features an aggressive Jekyll-and-Hyde woman,

who—having been injected with fruit fly serum—will stop at nothing to get what she wants. In *The Attack of the 50 Foot Woman* (1958), a radiated wife exacts revenge on her philandering husband and ends "the saga of Handsome Harry Archer, the most inept fortune hunter since Daffy Duck" (vol. 2, 10). *The Wild Women of Wongo* (1959) features a number of dissatisfied, beautiful, and savage wives who trade their ugly husbands in for more attractive models. Rebellious youth threatening the status quo is a major concern in *Teenage Monster* (1958), a science fiction Western in which a meteor strikes down a miner and his son in the Old West: The son recovers to become a teenager only a mother could love—"hairy, ugly and stupid, occasionally killing sheep and cattle" (vol. 2, 196). According to Warren, the ads for *Teenage Zombies* (1960) promised "Young Pawns Thrust Into Pulsating Cages of Horror in a Sadistic Experiment" (vol. 2, 446). In *Teenage Zombies*, youth is not entirely to blame for the threat posed to society: The mad scientist, Dr. Myra, who "resembles Vampira after a muscle-building course," is "working for an Unnamed Foreign Power which will transform people into obedient zombielike slaves" (vol. 2, 445). Likewise, *Forbidden Planet* (1956) also investigates the problems that the Frankenstein complex can cause for the average American—among them, the misuse of science and technology and incest. Scientific meddling is again an issue as the forces of nature, a tyrannosaur, and an anklyosaur revived by a Japanese-U.S. geological/paleontological team threaten life and limb in *Gigantis the Fire Monster* (vol. 2, 1959). In *The Leech Woman* (vol. 2, 1960), an interesting variant on the vampire theme, an unscrupulous endocrinologist who specializes in the rejuvenation of elderly women unleashes on an unsuspecting America a patient who drinks pineal fluid. *Attack of the Crab Monsters* (1957) merely features the perils of two huge radiated land crabs.

2. For example, see Gaylyn Studlar's illuminating examination of excess and transgressive sexuality in *Rocky Horror* in "Midnight S/Excess: Cult Configurations of 'Femininity' and the Perverse"; Amittai F. Aviram's provocative reading of the movie as a "pastiche of Great Books and other portions of Western culture" and a gay response to Euripides' *The Bacchae* in "Postmodern Gay Dionysus: Dr. Frank N. Furter"; John Kilgore's thorough investigation of sexual subtexts in the movie in "Sexuality and Identity in *The Rocky Horror Picture Show*"; Betty Robbins and Roger Myrick's discussion of gender ambiguity, the institution of marriage, the political uses of drag, and sadistic masculinity in *Rocky Horror* in "*The Function of the Fetish in* The Rocky Horror Picture Show *and* Priscilla, Queen of the Desert"; Raymond Ruble's discussion of O'Brien's playful incorporation of Freud's psychoanalytic theory in "Dr. Freud Meets Dr. Frank N. Furter"; Rolf Eichler's excellent examination of Gothic elements, especially the treatment of the doppelgänger, or the double, in *Rocky Horror* in "In the Romantic Tradition: *Frankenstein* and *The Rocky Horror Picture Show*"; and Richard R. Day's useful and illuminating discussion of audience participation during a screening of *Rocky Horror Picture Show* in "*Rocky Horror Picture Show*: A Speech Event In Three Acts."

3. For a popular set of audience responses, see the complete script of *Rocky Horror*, available from the Dartmouth College Computing Center at http://www.ccs.neu.edu/home/image/rocky-horror.html.

4. The wheelchair-bound scientist appears in *Dr. X* (1932), a movie that Lips mentions at the beginning of *Rocky Horror* in "Science Fiction/Double Feature." Dr. Scott closely resembles the wheelchair-bound Boris Karloff who sports what appears to be the same plaid car rug draped over his lap in *Monster of Terror* (1965). Perhaps the most recent memorable example of a wheelchair-bound scientist (with a German accent) in science fiction film is Dr. Strangelove in Stanley Kubrick's *Dr. Strangelove or: How I Stopped Worrying And Learned To Love The Bomb* (1964).

2

Rocky Horror Glam Rock

Julian Cornell

Hot Patootie
Bless my soul
I really love that Rock and Roll

—*"Hot Patootie Bless My Soul"*

The many and varied interpretations of *The Rocky Horror Picture Show* have provided keen insights, but few seem to have considered how the film specifically uses glam rock, a particular genre of rock and roll, which enjoyed a brief, though significant, commercially successful, and influential vogue in the early 1970s. Described by director and screenwriter Todd Haynes as "nothing short of a Camp attack on rock and roll," glam represented a "queering" of the masculine hegemony of popular music (Hoskyns x). Called glitter in the United States because of the propensity of the glam rockers to wear face paint and put sparkles in their hair and on their clothes, the musical genre was primarily a British phenomenon. As the term itself indicates, glam—short for glamour—placed star image and fashion on equal footing with the music itself. Glam emerged as a mass cultural form during a time when the American and British rock and Pop charts were ruled by '60s holdovers (the Who, the Rolling Stones, the Grateful Dead, Bob Dylan, the former members of the Beatles), introspective singer-songwriters (James Taylor; Joni Mitchell; Crosby, Stills, Nash, and occasionally Young; America; Cat Stevens; John Denver; the Carpenters), boogie-based southern rock (the Allman Brothers, the Marshall Tucker Band), portentous art school progressive rock (King Crimson; Jethro Tull;

Yes; Emerson, Lake, and Palmer; Pink Floyd; Genesis) and hard-rocking progenitors of heavy metal (Deep Purple, Grand Funk Railroad, Led Zeppelin, Aerosmith, Black Sabbath).[1] Although glam rockers shared the sonic landscape with artists of all kinds in the United States, they dominated the UK charts for the brief period from 1971 to 1975 until being superceded by punk and disco.

Despite its chart-topping popularity with music fans, glam rock proved troubling and controversial in many respects, especially in the rock press. Much of the denigration of glam came from the genre's winking, reflexive awareness of popular music as being an inauthentic image driven commodity. Because "authenticity" had long been—and continues to be—a central concern in rock music criticism, glam's acknowledgement of the constructed nature of the rock star persona represented a quandary. Where the confessional sincerity of the singer-songwriter, virtuosity of the progressive-rock instrumentalist, or blues-based musicianship of the southern rocker implied little separation between the performance and the authentic human being behind it, glam continually referenced the artificial, showbiz nature of rock and roll. In doing so, glam suggested not only that there might be a disparity between performer and performance but also that the musician was first and foremost a performer heavily invested in projecting a rock star persona. Glam demonstrated that rock and roll was an economic and cultural phenomenon and an industry, as opposed to an organic entity that was a natural expression of rebellious youth. Unlike other genres of pop music, glam celebrated the artificiality of rock music rather than attempting to deny it or cover it up. Glam not only contested the idea of authenticity but was also anticraft, antivirtuoso, and image based. The embrace of ideas seemingly antithetical to previous mainstream expressions of rock and roll may have reinvigorated popular music, but it might also account for the genre's relatively brief stint in the public consciousness.

At the same time, glam marked a return to structural and lyrical simplicity in reaction to the complexity, length, and compositional indulgence of art rock and hippie music. In place of concept albums and overblown rock operas, glam harkened back to the tighter, shorter song structure of the 1950s and early 1960s, emphasizing driving rhythms and anthemic, catchy choruses in lieu of extended jams, guitar workouts, and displays of technical virtuosity.[2] The nostalgia indicated by a return to a "classical" rock and roll song structure was inflected with self-consciousness rather than merely providing updates, rewrites, or cover versions of earlier forms of pop music. Glam songs were quite often *about* rock and roll classicism and songwriting, rather just being a straightforward repetition of previous songs and styles. Because reflexivity and irony were normally lacking in the music of the 1960s, glam's reinvigoration of the golden oldies presented a marked contrast to its predecessors in the pop world. More significantly, perhaps, glam's engagement with visual indulgence and decadence reveled in the very aspects of the entertainment industry that the hippies, folkies, and art-rockers had seemed to deny. Performers like Davie Bowie, Bryan Ferry, and Freddie Mercury presented themselves as showmen—not merely musicians—consciously embracing their role as entertainers as part of their stage personas. The reflexivity and ironic nostalgia of the music was absorbed into the rock star icon in glam performance.

The espousal of excess, showmanship, and ironic nostalgia embraced by glam rock made it, in many ways, the logical choice for the musical numbers of *Rocky Horror*. In contrast to the pensive sincerity of early 1970s singer-songwriters and former hippies or the lyrical obtuseness of art rock, glam dealt in transgression and was profoundly reflexive. For example, glam's biggest stateside hit was Lou Reed's "Walk on the Wild Side," a knowing tribute to Andy Warhol's Factory scene, which contains references to oral sex, cross-dressing, prostitution, and drug use. Iggy and the Stooges' "I Wanna Be Your Dog" is an ode to masochism, and Alice Cooper's songs often trafficked in sadism and images of wanton mayhem, as in the apocalyptic destruction of the hit single "School's Out." As in glam, the lyrical content of the musical numbers in *Rocky Horror* is nothing if not transgressive.

Decoding glam lyrics often requires familiarity with the history of pop music and culture. For example, in Mott the Hoople's "Honoloochie Boogie"—a song celebrating the discovery of rock music by a new fan—Ian Hunter sings "Wanna tell Chuck Berry my news," which refers not just to '50s rock pioneer Berry but to his song "Roll Over Beethoven," which is also about being introduced to rock music.[3] In *Rocky Horror*, to look ahead a bit to the following discussion, an analogous form of intertextuality is expressed through movie references (as opposed to musical ones), such as the long list of science fiction films and stars in the opening number "Science Fiction/Double Feature," but musical references exist as well. For instance, in the floor stomping number "What Ever Happened to Saturday Night? (Hot Patootie)," Meatloaf's Eddie notes that "a saxophone was blowing on a rock and roll show" and "Buddy Holly was playing his very last song" as the adolescent male in the song makes his move on his date in the backseat of his car. Glam's retrieval of the musical stylistics of the 1950s fits nicely with the film's intertextual celebration of that decade's science fiction and horror B movies and the iconographic drive-in theater, site of sexual activity for many teens.

Although it was the British glam artists who experienced the greatest commercial success, the genre had its roots in New York City's underground theater, the Warhol Factory scene, and American Pop art aesthetics.[4] Of particular influence were Warhol's notions of stardom and the constructed nature of fame. Warhol's "superstars" challenged the notion of how "stardom was attained by showing how easily it could be manufactured" and demonstrated how unstable the notion of celebrity was—themes also expressed in Warhol's Pop art paintings (Buckley 107). For artists such as Warhol, according to Andrew Ross in *No Respect: Intellectuals and Popular Culture*, Pop was a discursive practice whose commitment to the disposable, mass-produced artifact was a "direct affront to those who governed the boundaries of official taste" (149). Warhol's paintings of Coke bottles, Campbell's soup cans, star portraits, and car crashes are prominent examples of this tendency. In a sense, Pop symbolized the promise of liberal pluralism, as well as of democratic access to cultural production and reception—something that rock music, with its commitment to authenticity also suggested. Critically, Pop art acknowledged and celebrated the obsolescence of the mass-produced artifact and culture. In the British context, the specific milieu from which both glam and *Rocky Horror* emerged, Pop represented "American-ness" as an alternative to British cultural traditions. Pop embodied America in such things as science fiction, cars, comic strips, Detroit, rock and roll, Hollywood genre films, and advertisements—the very stuff that built both *Rocky Horror* and glam (Ross 148–49).

In addition to embracing elements of the Pop aesthetic, glam was influenced by camp and its treatment of star image. Camp's appropriation of classical Hollywood can be seen as a perversion of nostalgia itself—one that can be directed against the original representation, such as a movie star image, and thus facilitates oppositional readings of gender stereotypes. As Ross contends, camp signified differently to different classes, genders, and sexualities, and interpretation of camp performances varied widely. Before Stonewall, camp was a survival strategy, though not an oppositional one, in some homosexual communities. By using Hollywood star iconography in camp, disenfranchised gay subjects found "a way of imaginatively communicating its common conquest of everyday oppression" (157). Images of Hollywood straightness were "appropriated and used to express a different relation to the experience of alienation and exclusion in a world socially polarized by fixed sexual labels" to suggest an "imaginary control over circumstances" (157–58). This suggests the possibility of understanding *Rocky Horror* and glam rock in a similar manner as forms of camp performance. Glam's retrieval of 1950s rock and roll iconography and musical styles, wedded with an emphasis on gender fluidity, can be seen as an appropriation of camp's strategy of reinterpreting forgotten or obsolete cinematic iconography to challenge popular culture's rigid representational strategies. It is, therefore, possible to see *Rocky Horror*'s shifting signifiers of gender as coterminous with the glam rock project, perhaps accounting for the music's appropriateness for the film itself.

As a text, glam can be read as being principally about stardom and identity—two of the main preoccupations of camp. Appearing at the very end of this fertile period in rock and roll, *Rocky Horror* represents, in a certain sense, a culmination of glam rock's recurring thematic preoccupations with stardom, identity, gender fluidity, and desire. However, the glam star was not the macho, virile virtuoso of the blues or art rock scene. Instead, glam artists consciously blurred the line between straight and gay, male and female. David Bowie, for example, actively courted the gay press. Although it is easy to dismiss Bowie's pronouncements of bisexuality and homosexuality as cynical publicity stunts, they did, in fact, dovetail with the rocker's larger project of constructing the self.[5] Indeed, much of glam is about the multiplicity of identity, a central theme of much of Mott the Hoople, Iggy Pop, Lou Reed, and Roxy Music's *oeuvres*.[6]

In terms of glam's noted androgyny, a flattening out of the differences between male and female was enacted, but without losing the masculine power over the image and the self. It is possible to view glam's male rock stars in terms similar to the ones Richard Dyer uses to analyze the androgynous persona of Judy Garland. As Dyer observes, "to be glamorous is to be asymptotic to the feminine, to feminize the masculine self, to arrive at a de-sexed space but without relinquishing male privilege and aggression" (Dyer 167). The idea is to become a gender "in-between," existing in a space that allows for a more complex conception of gender than a male/female binary permits. At the same time, this is not quite as rebellious as it seems. Although many drag performances problematize the boundary between the female image and male privilege, glam performs androgyny and bisexuality in a manner that still retains masculinity at its core.

Glam's obsession with the plasticity of sexuality and its expression in stage personas results in an intense preoccupation with stardom—a construction that informs *Rocky Horror*. In *Rocky Horror*, androgyny and stardom are both displayed through the film's most transgressive character, Dr. Frank-N-Furter, but in a complex manner. Frank-N-Furter is introduced in the number "Sweet Transvestite" in visual fragments. He descends into the frame by means of an elevator and a close-up on his sequined, star patterned shoes—a shot that is repeated, and one in which Frank taps in time to the music. After Janet shrieks in horror, the film cuts to a long shot and a quick track-in to a close-up of the face of Frank. Contrary to critics Betty Robbins and Roger Myrick, I do not think that this is a simple recapitulation of the introduction of the female star common to many Hollywood narratives, which restates the objectification of women. Instead, cinephiles instantly will realize that it is a quotation or parody of that type of entrance; it requires familiarity with the conventions of female representation in classical cinema and has little meaning outside a particular, cinematic construction of "woman." Frank cautions Brad and Janet,

> Don't get strung out by the way I look
> Don't judge a book by its cover
> I'm not much of a man
> By the light of the day
> But at night I'm one hell of a lover
> I'm just a sweet transvestite from transsexual Transylvania.

The critical moment occurs when Frank discards his cloak, revealing his gender-bending attire. His black leather corset complements his excessively made-up face, torn fishnet stockings, garter belt, sequined shoes, and perfectly coiffed hair.

As Robbins and Myrick note, Frank's appearance is clearly meant to disrupt conventional notions of gender, as it is an amalgam of masculine and feminine. His dress and manner eroticize his gender fluidity and provide the source of his power, which Robbins and Myrick term sadomasochistic. Despite the shifting signifiers of gender, Robbins and Myrick contend that masculine power and authority constantly implicate him, thus undermining the oppositional potential of, his drag. Perhaps this might be the case if Frank is read as a conventional glam idol, rather than the complex one he portrays. For example, the authors conveniently ignore Frank's crotch bulge, which complicates his drag. As Chris Straayer observes, Frank is not just a man giving a drag performance, wearing the signifier of "woman," but is "bi-sexed" (81). Frank is powerful because he is able to contain multiple sexual identities on a single, eroticized body. As the song indicates, the signifiers of gender continually revise and reconfigure one another. If one is a transvestite from a transsexual planet in a Transylvanian galaxy, then one can be presumed to be constantly crossing back and forth between gender positions and boundaries. This type of continually shifting gender association is a direct corollary to the star personas of such noted glam figures as Freddie Mercury, David Bowie, and Roxy Music's Bryan Ferry and Brian Eno.[7] It is perhaps conceivable that the good doctor's character is a camp performance of a glam rock idol. Frank's persona can be understood as an allusion to the iconography of the male glam idol, which was dependent on a similar deployment of signifiers of excessive gender identity but with an additional layer of excess and self-consciousness that underscores glam's unwillingness to disengage completely from male privilege. Frank's glam performance, in contrast, camps both masculinity and femininity; moreover, his act denaturalizes the figure of the scientist—a paragon of masculine knowledge and power familiar to fans of horror and science fiction film. This denaturalization can be seen as analogous to the manner in which the glam performer denaturalizes the figure of the rock star.

Finally, the glam rock music allows for the articulation of Frank, not just as character in a narrative but also as a comment on the star persona. His dramatic arrival could also be seen as similar to that of a rock star making a grand entrance in the tradition of Bowie, Mercury, Alice Cooper, or the members of Kiss. To underscore this point, Frank ascends the podium (stage) to reveal his provocative attire. Frank is constructed as "star" by the film (both a Hollywood movie star and a musical rock star) but also as the focus of a non–gender specific "desire" on the part of the audience. Frank explodes the androgyny common to glam, replacing it with the previously noted shifting signifiers of gender. If glam desexes the star by flattening gender through androgyny, Frank resexualizes stardom and connects it to desire when he sings,

I could show you my favorite obsession
I've been making a man
With blond hair and a tan
And he's good for relieving my tension.

Thus, Frank signifies a desiring male body clothed in the feminine—asserting the power of both genders—whose desire is expressed not just for another man but for a man of his own creation, his own object of obsession. Here, the star is expressed in terms not just of glam's construction of the self but also of the ability to project that self outward, to construct the very object of one's desire. If, like camp, glam fetishizes stardom, then Frank takes it one step farther and models a stardom of the fetish.

In one sense, the main structuring narrative device in the film is desire itself. This is expressed in the opening song "Science Fiction/Double Feature" and becomes a framing device when the song returns in reprise at the conclusion. This number, with its dizzying array of cinematic allusions, foregrounds the act of desire *for* cinema and the space of the cinema as a place where sexual desire is enacted. The entire cinematic or cult film experience operates in the realm of desire; it need not be consigned to be a function of the narrative or its effects. The lyrics are a list of classic and B-movie stars and moments, and the song ends,

I wanna go
To the late night, double feature, picture show
By RKO
To the late night, double feature, picture show

In the back row
To the late night, double feature, picture show!

Thus, desire is framed in terms of cult knowledge (the compendium of obscure genre film references), the desire to experience the film in the plentitude of the theater (late night, double feature), and sexual possibility (in the back row, where adolescent sexual initiation often takes place). The song is camp in Andrew Ross' sense of retrieving history's detritus and re-energizing it; it engages glam at the musical level and cult cinephilia through the references to science fiction and horror films. In other words, the song is polysemic, engaging multiple levels of desire in multiple locations. In case that is not enough, we see only full, painted lips continually linking cinema and glam to desire in indeterminate space and time, where desire is expressed in an excessive way, detached from a desiring body. The song returns at the end to sum up the film and to posit the continuance of cinematic desire:

Science fiction double feature
Frank has built and lost his creature
Darkness has conquered Brad and Janet
The servants gone to
A distant planet
Wo, oh, oh, oh
At the late night, double feature
Picture show
I want to go
To the late night, double feature picture show.

The implication is that the movie has satisfied the very desire framed by the song and that the experience can, and even must, be repeated endlessly—in a sense, equating sexual activity and spectatorship.

That desire is fluid and is expressed in a number of the songs, but none so forcefully as in Janet's solo "Touch-A, Touch-A, Touch Me." Significantly, the song allows for the expression of female sexual desire—in this case for the idealized male body Rocky. She sings,

I'd only ever been kissed before
I thought there's no use getting
Into heavy petting
It leads into trouble and seat wetting
Now all I want to know
Is how to go
I've tasted blood and I want more

and

Touch-a, Touch-a, Touch-a, Touch Me
I want to be dirty
Thrill me, chill me, fulfill me
Creature of the Night.

As the song reaches its conclusion, Magenta and Columbia, inspired by the Rocky and Janet coupling, fool around with each other. For the coda, each of the major characters is intercut with Janet writhing in ecstasy, as if they are all pleasuring her. The camera setup and the editing extend her desire and orient the spectator in her spatial position; thus, while she and Rocky are having sex, the implication is that anyone could take her or Rocky's place, establishing both the fluidity and equivalence of desire. The point of view expressed in the shot and editing addresses the audience in terms of that same equivalence—in other words, the film literalizes multiple sexualized viewing positions. It should also be stated that Rocky, the constructed expression of the powerful bisexed Frank's desire, is conquered and possessed by Janet on one level and by the spectator on another. Rocky, by his very name, refers intertextually to the film itself (as his name comes from the movie's title) and to rock and roll (from which his sobriquet is ultimately derived). Finally, the line that is repeated by each character as they pleasure Janet and the audience is "Creature of the Night," which refers to deviance; to existence in a shadowy, nocturnal world; to horror films; and to cinema patrons, who, similar to club and concert goers, can be construed as creatures of the night. (In the play, Rocky counterpoints her song with "Bless my soul / I really love that rock and roll" from the previous number "What Ever Happened to Saturday Night?" linking desire with glam as well as cinema.)

One portion of the film that makes little sense outside of a glam context concerns the brief appearance of Eddie. Frank's number "I Can Make You a Man" is interrupted by the entrance of Eddie to great acclaim from the onlookers. Meatloaf's only number presents a vision of skewed heteronormativity, depicted as excessive masculinity. He enters on a Harley, clad in leather and blue jeans, with a phallic saxophone in tow, love and hate tattooed across the knuckles of his hands, and sings a "conventional" glam number, "What Ever Happened to Saturday Night?" about adolescent heterosexual love. This symbol of conventional masculinity also happens to have a big red scar on his forehead, indicating that half his brain has been removed. Although some commentators have noted that Meatloaf's hairstyle and leather jacket mark him as Elvis, a better comparison would be Gary Glitter, an extremely popular glam idol who is best known for the UK hit "Rock and Roll Part Two."[8] Glitter glammed up Elvis, so his persona and music referred back to that previous icon, though with a liberal coating of glam androgyny, parody, and irony. Meatloaf's song refers further to such glam hits as Bowie's "Drive In Saturday" and Mott's "Golden Age of Rock and Roll" and "Saturday Gigs," all British chart successes. All these songs, similar to Meatloaf's, highlight the connection of music and sexuality, but in a fashion that betrays an awareness of ironic nostalgia.

"What Ever Happened to Saturday Night?" does not just ask about that day of the week but also about masculine privilege and an adolescent conception of sexuality. Frank responds by murdering Eddie and labeling it a "mercy killing." The first line that Frank utters after dispatching Eddie is "one from the vaults," a disk jockey expression for an old record. The doctor then reprises "Charles Atlas," thus circumscribing Eddie's disruptive, conventional, brainless masculinity and suggesting the viability of constructing one's own fetish object rather than recapitulating traditional ones. The segment ends with the playing of the wedding march and the marriage of Rocky and Frank as the scientist jumps into his creation's arms in front of a "matrimonial" bed. Here the film privileges Frank's desire, depicts Eddie's conventional man as deviant and disruptive, and asserts that masculinity is a problem if it has become ossified, as represented by Eddie. The answer that the film poses to the song's question is perhaps that heteronormative nostalgia for adolescent groping is outmoded and unfulfilling. All male desires in the film are, in fact, problematic. Where Eddie is anachronistic and brain-dead, Brad is vacuous and normative, Riff Raff is incestuous and ultimately repressive, Rocky is pure libidinal energy, and Dr. Scott arguably is impotent. The sexual indeterminacy of Frank is more appealing than these other configurations of masculinity, which allows Frank-N-Furter to appropriate and overtake them with his free-floating desire. In a similar vein, the glam rock idol represented a more appealing and more fluid vision of the male pop star than previous incarnations.

The relation of this type of fluid desire to camp, cult, and glam is explored in the film's lengthy closing sequence,

> Rose Tint My World,
> Floor Show,
> Fan Fare,
> Don't Dream It Be It,
> Wild and Untamed Thing,
> I'm Going Home.[9]

In this rousing closer, Frank dresses up Columbia, Janet, Brad, and Rocky in his preferred clothing, equips them with feather boas, makes their faces up in close approximation to his, and puts them onstage. The action takes place in an empty theater, with rows of deck chairs constituting the audience. Each of the four players takes a verse of "Rose Tint My World," in which they individually express their differing identities and sexualities. For Columbia, named after both a film studio and record company, it is fandom and love; for Rocky, it is unadulterated lust; for Brad it is Oedipal confusion; for Janet it is sexual empowerment and liberation. All of their identities are figured in relation to Frank-N-Furter: Columbia is a fan of his, he has created Rocky, and he has deflowered Janet and Brad. In other words, the signifier of the slippage/fluidity of desire—Frank, the glam rock idol—defines the four characters. Rose tinting suggests an escape into this desire. The four characters perform an approximation of Frank and of his star qualities, and their performance configures desire as a refusal of psychological depth and unconscious processes; it is a conception of stardom consonant with the glam rock idol. In addition, the group's song is a literal warm up and opening act for the main event, the star of the film, Dr. Frank-N-Furter.

When they finish their song, the film cuts to a long shot of the empty theater with the principals onstage. Trumpets herald Frank's imminent arrival. The curtain pulls back to reveal not just the star but Frank standing in front of an exact replica of the RKO studios logo, with the looming radio tower behind the doctor. RKO, of course, was best known for Astaire-Rogers musicals, so it is possible to see the closing sequence as a camp performance of glam, musicals, and also horror films, given the reference to *King Kong*. In "Don't Dream It," Frank sings,

What ever happened to Fay Wray
That delicate, satin-draped frame
As it clung to her thigh
I started to cry
For I wanted to be dressed just the same.

He continues, "Give yourself over to absolute pleasure" and "Don't dream it—Be it," a line taken up by the chorus as they frolic in a pool in a parody of Esther Williams' nautical spectacles.[10] "Don't Dream It" refers back to the "Science Fiction/Double Feature" framing device, contextualizing Frank's desire to be Wray—not merely to assume her gender but also to perform her function in the supertext of genre film. When he sings, "give yourself over to absolute pleasure," he connects sexuality and cinema spectatorship. The pleasure to which he refers is the satisfaction of desire by cinematic or sexual means. If we configure his wish as expression of lack, then the film's dénouement, in which a lifeless Frank is carried by Rocky up the phallic tower, itself an overdetermined reference to excessive masculinity expressed as a parodic recapitulation of Kong's tragic finale, is an ironic, self-aware, reflexively artificial fulfillment of desire. Thus, the text is engaged in avowing the power of cinema to compensate for lack, to satiate desire. The film works to give Frank what he wants: He can be both Fay Wray and King Kong.

Some critics—Barry Keith Grant, Gaylyan Studlar, and Robbins and Myrick included—have interpreted the narrative's resolution to indicate the restoration of normative and recuperation of the deviant spectacle by patriarchy. If one considers the destruction of the monster at the end of the horror film to restore normativity, then perhaps Frank's death does reassert conventionality. The musical genre, for its part, is concerned with the construction of community and the consolidation of heteronormativity. The singing and dancing in the musical genre film is a metaphoric, paradigmatic circumscription of heterosexuality and gender roles; the narrative trajectory is toward the reconsolidation of the heterosexual couple who have been kept apart in the body of the text. In *Rocky Horror*, this is not the case. Heteronormativity is exploded by the film, and the escape of the romantic couple and their authority figure friend and government operative, Scott, at the end suggests that normative heterosexuality cannot be restored. The penultimate image of the film has them writhing on the ground still wearing their Frank-style clothing—hardly an image of normativity restored. Furthermore, the agents of "restoration" are brother and sister, Riff Raff and Magenta. No normal couple, they are instead presented as incestuous. The film also implies that Frank has slept with both of them. Their attire in the scene where Riff Raff asserts his control over Frank and then murders him and Rocky is a combination of drag and space suit—a camp performance of science fiction authority. Riff Raff's stated reason for killing Frank has nothing to do with restoring order; he does it because he thinks Frank does not like him. The entire castle is then beamed back to the planet of Transsexual in the galaxy of Transylvania, undoubtedly a transgressive place. Frank's death is, finally, framed by "Science Fiction/ Double Feature," indicating the fulfillment of cinematic desire, not necessarily patriarchal restoration.

The excessiveness of the closing sequence, and even the film as a whole, prevents the reaffirmation of heteronormativity; instead, perhaps, once exploded it can never be restored. Where the glam rock idol never relinquished his masculine privilege, here the film's playing with popular culture suggests that heteronormativity, not heterosexuality, is the repressed and repressive thing that returns. Certainly, it can be argued that by "queering" genre film, musicals, and glam, *Rocky Horror* either effaces gayness or relegates it to one form of deviance among many, but as the film performs the same operation on heterosexuality, it asserts the viability of the marginalized over the dominant. Heterosexuality is just one possibility for sexual identification. Sexuality, as such, comprises traces of all potentialities. By camping so many genre film elements at the same time, *Rocky Horror* does not just parody the musical, the horror film, the science fiction spectacle, or the glam rock performance; it reveals an absence of normative reception that was always implicit in the way the genre film mobilized desire and exposes the cinema's economy of desire by literalizing it. The film acknowledges, through the final sequence and the framing device, that Frank is a fantasy himself—a creation of the cinema, one derived from camp and glam, and an expression of the fluidity of desire that film is empowered to mobilize. The link between star and film—both commodities and circulated texts—creates a space for the articulation of desire coded in terms of a particular, shared knowledge. It is the cinema and knowledge of film, film history, and genre codes, of stars and stardom, and of rock and roll and glam that is the locus of power.

Works Cited

Buckley, David. *Strange Fascination: David Bowie: The Definitive Story*. London: Virgin, 1999.

Corrigan, Timothy. "Film and the Culture of the Cult." *The Cult Film Experience: Beyond All Reason*. Ed. J. P. Telotte. Austin: U of Texas P, 1991. 26–37.

Dyer, Richard. *Heavenly Bodies*. New York: St. Martin's, 1986.

Gill, John. *Queer Noises: Male and Female Homosexuality in Twentieth Century Music*. Minneapolis: U of Minnesota P, 1995.

Grant, Barry Keith. "Science Fiction Double Feature: Ideology in the Cult." *The Cult Film Experience: Beyond All Reason*. Ed. J. P. Telotte. Austin: U of Texas P, 1991. 128–36

Harper, Phillip Brian. *Private Affairs: Critical Ventures in the Culture of Social Relations*. New York: New York UP, 1999.

Hebdige, Dick. *Subculture: The Meaning of Style*. London: Routledge, 1979.

Hoskyns, Barney. *Glam! Bowie, Bolan and the Glitter Rock Revolution*. London: Faber and Faber, 1998.

Kawin, Bruce. "After Midnight." *The Cult Film Experience: Beyond All Reason*. Ed. J. P. Telotte. Austin: U of Texas P, 1991. 18–25.

O'Brien, Richard. *The Rocky Horror Show*. London: Samuel French, 1983.

Paytress, Mark. *The Rise and Fall of Ziggy Stardust and the Spiders From Mars*. New York: Schirmer, 1998.

Robbins, Betty, and Roger Myrick. "The Function of the Fetish in *The Rocky Horror Picture Show* and *Priscilla, Queen of the Desert*." *Journal of Gender Studies* 9.3 (2000): 269–80.

Ross, Andrew. *No Respect: Intellectuals and Popular Culture*. New York: Routledge, 1989.

Samuels, Stuart. *Midnight Movies*. New York: Collier Books, 1983.

Sontag, Susan. "Notes on 'Camp.'" *Camp: Queer Aesthetics and the Performing Subject: A Reader*. Ed. Fabio Cleto. Ann Arbor: U of Michigan P, 1999. 53–65.

Straayer, Chris. *Deviant Eyes, Deviant Bodies: Sexual Re-orientations in Film and Video*. New York: Columbia UP, 1996.

Studlar, Gaylyn. "Midnight S/Excess: Cult Configurations of Femininity and the Perverse." *Journal of Film and Television* 17.1 (1989): 2–14.

Taubin, Amy. "Todd Haynes: Fanning the Flames." *The Village Voice*. 43.44.3 (1998): 46–49.

Telotte, J. P. "Beyond All Reason: The Nature of the Cult." *The Cult Film Experience: Beyond All Reason*. Ed. J. P. Telotte. Austin: U of Texas P, 1991. 5–17.

Notes

1. A family tree of glam rock acts would include such UK artists as Marc Bolan and T. Rex, David Bowie, Roxy Music, Mott the Hoople, Slade, Gary Glitter, Sweet, David Essex, Queen, the Sensational Alex Harvey Band, Steve Harley and Cockney Rebel, as well as acts that incorporated some glam aspects into their stage personae and music such as 10cc, Elton John, Alvin Stardust, the Bay City Rollers, and Showaddywaddy. In the United States, the best known domestic acts were Iggy Pop and the Stooges, Lou Reed, the New York Dolls, Sparks, Alice Cooper, Kiss, and for a brief period, Todd Rundgren.

2. There were notable exceptions to the rejection of experimentation, such as the explorations of song craft and structure by Roxy Music or the vocal pyrotechnics of Queen, but in general, glam dispensed with the musical immoderation of progressive and art rock or the emotional intimacy of the singer-songwriters.

3. In the song, Hunter's recent convert to glam rock exclaims "Now my hair gets longer / as the beat gets stronger / Wanna tell Chuck Berry my news / I get my kicks from guitar licks / and I've sold my steel-toed shoes." In Berry's original, he sings "You know my temperature's risin' / And the jukebox blowin' a fuse / My heart's beatin' rhythm / And my soul keeps singin' the blues / Roll over Beethoven / And tell Tchaikovsky the news."

4. Connected to Warhol's Factory scene were underground theater groups that involved many of the same people. Prominent at the time were Charles Ludlum's Ridiculous Theater Company and John Vaccaro's Playhouse of the Ridiculous Theater, both of which used camp performance and drag in many productions. Much of the costumes, makeup, and transgender images of glam, as well as the deployment of androgyny, drag, and bi- and homosexual themes, was developed in the New York theater underground. In terms of music, David Johansen, founder of the New York Dolls, was also a member of the Ridiculous Theater, and Lou Reed was the main force behind the Velvet Underground—the legendary house band for the Factory. In addition, the

music club Max's Kansas City served as a hangout for both Factory and theater personnel (Hoskyns 24–27). Tony DeFries, prominent partner in arts management firm Main Man Productions, was pivotal in both the production of *Pork* and the career of David Bowie. Apparently, it was at DeFries' suggestion that Bowie familiarize himself with the New York theater scene and with the Factory (Paytress 58–59). Bowie's well-known fascination with Warhol manifested itself in a song on his 1971 album *Hunky Dory*, named after the Pop artist. Bowie would later portray Warhol in Julian Schnabel's 1996 film *Basquiat.*

5. As early as 1969, Bowie was interviewed in *Jeremy* (which, according to Richard Dyer, was geared to a bisexual audience) and in *Gay News* (a key British gay liberation journal) in July 1972. In the latter article, Peter Holmes stated, "David Bowie is probably the best musician in Britain now. One day he'll become as popular as he deserves to be. And that'll give gay rock a potent spokesman." He also appeared in drag on the cover of his 1970 album *The Man Who Sold the World*, spawning a series of articles about his propensity for wearing frocks (Paytress 53). In a famous January 1972 interview in *Melody Maker*, Bowie announced, "I'm gay and always have been." Taken together, these controlled images of Bowie helped create the myth of Queer David (Gill 107).

6. For instance, in "All the Way From Memphis," Hunter claims, "you look like a star but you're still on the dole" and "you look like a star but you're really out on parole." Mott also dedicated two albums, *Brain Capers* and *Mad Shadows*, both commercial failures, to the exploration of the multiple sides of Hunter's would-be rock star persona.

7. Roxy Music in particular is a musical touchstone for many of Richard O'Brien's compositions. Bryan Ferry's mixing of older rock and roll styles with Broadway show tunes can be seen in "Dammit Janet" and "Over At The Frankenstein Place." Perhaps more strikingly, "The Time Warp" is lyrically and compositionally quite similar to Roxy Music's early hit "Do the Strand."

8. Glitter's hit was common at American sporting events until recently. Glitter, whose real name is Paul Francis Gadd, made headlines when he was imprisoned in Vietnam on charges of sexual misconduct with a minor.

9. A common criticism leveled at the film is that it is incoherent. Stuart Samuels in *Midnight Movies* claims that the film falls apart in the last half hour. In the context of genre musicals, it should be noted, the ending makes perfect sense: How else would you attempt to resolve tensions in a narrative except by putting on a show? In addition, Frank's naming of the performance the Floor Show refers, perhaps, to David Bowie's 1973 television special *The 1984 Floor Show.*

10. It is virtually impossible to account for all of the intertextual references in the final sequence, let alone the entire film. Many have tried, as a visit to the official fan club Web site attests. A comprehensive list of all the cinematic allusions exists at http://www.rockyhorror.org/faq/.

3

Reflections on the Self-reflexive Musical

The Rocky Horror Picture Show and the Classic Hollywood Musical

Sarah Artt

> Whenever an art form is highly conventional, the opportunity for subtle irony or distanciation presents itself all the more readily.
>
> —*Jean-Loup Bourget, "Social Implications in the Hollywood Genres"*

Most critical and popular work on *The Rocky Horror Picture Show* acknowledges that the film demonstrates a variety of cultural references that open it up to many possible aesthetic and theoretical interpretations. In interviews conducted for the music video channel VH1 and now included in the special features of the twenty-fifth anniversary edition of the *Rocky Horror* DVD, writer Richard O'Brien has confirmed this view, citing influences as diverse as old lingerie ads and Sergei Eisenstein's *Ivan the Terrible* (1944). Much has already been said about *Rocky Horror*'s status as a cult film and its use of sexuality, but as yet no one has offered an in-depth analysis of *Rocky Horror* as a musical. The music and songs that make up much of *Rocky Horror*'s narrative have long been treated as an aspect of the film that feeds into other theoretical readings of *Rocky Horror* as an example of camp, cult, or queer cinema (or indeed, all of the above). Without wishing to diminish the richness of those other readings, I would like to propose that an examination of *Rocky Horror* as a musical is long overdue. *Rocky Horror*, with its theatrical origins and its annual presence as a Halloween screening for the better part of three decades, deserves to be included in a genre that ranges from classics like *42nd Street* (1933), *Top Hat* (1935), and *Easter Parade* (1948) to the surreal heights of *Cabaret* (1972), *Hairspray* (1988), and *Dancer in the Dark* (2000).

The musical has had a checkered academic history and did not really gain acceptance as a genre worthy of study until the 1970s, in part because of the recuperation and rediscovery of Vincente Minnelli (*The Band Wagon* [1953], *Gigi* [1958], *An American in Paris* [1951]) as an auteur of the musical genre, as well as feminist film theorists' academic championing of "women's genres," which often included the musical alongside melodrama and costume drama. The musical was initially reclaimed as a genre that appealed to a female audience by celebrating fantasy and pleasure, but it could also be interpreted as subversive. Molly Haskell claims the woman's film, which can include the musical among other previously denigrated genres, "ranged from films that adhered safely to the formulae of escapist fantasy, films that were subversive only 'between the lines' and in retrospect, and the rare few that used the conventions to undermine them" (21).

The classic Hollywood musical I have chosen to refer to in this chapter, *Summer Stock* (1950), falls into Haskell's "between the lines" category but maintains a traditional romantic ending. Jane Feuer in her book *The Hollywood Musical* comments that "*Summer Stock*, a fascinating and undervalued 1950 MGM musical ... is unique among musicals of its period in achieving a fifty/fifty blend of folk and backstage themes" (20). Although *Summer Stock* (in the United Kingdom the film was released with the title *If You Feel Like Singing*) is a lesser known example of a classic musical, it stars Judy Garland and Gene Kelly and contains Garland's first performance of her now well-known "Get Happy" number, which later came to be as closely associated with Garland's star persona as "Over the Rainbow" from *The Wizard of Oz* (1939). Although Feuer references *Summer Stock* throughout *The Hollywood Musical*, the film remains underseen and understudied. By using it as a comparison for my analysis of *Rocky Horror*, I hope that these two films may illuminate each other, shedding critical light on neglected aspects of both texts.

Jean-Loup Bourget states, "the musical, like a court jester, is allowed a saturnalian freedom because it is not a 'serious' genre" (472), and it is this freedom associated with musicals that allows *Rocky Horror* to be interpreted and enjoyed on so many different levels. It is, among other things, a cult film, a sex film, a horror film, a film about social misfits, and a film that articulates popular social movements of the 1970s. The blending of all these ideas is possible under the all-encompassing rubric of the musical, where nothing has to be particularly realistic, or even make sense. (If you've ever seen the Busby Berkeley number with Carmen Miranda singing "The Lady with the Tutti-Frutti Hat" with its giant banana set pieces in *The Gang's All Here* [1943], you'll know that the Hollywood musical entered the realm of the ridiculous long before *Rocky Horror*.) In terms of theories of the musical, I have chosen to make substantial use of Feuer's writing because I feel that her ideas provide the most comprehensive scope for a study of how *Rocky Horror* demonstrates many of the characteristics of the classic Hollywood musical and then takes them even further—into the realm of the subversive. Feuer also remains one of the few academics to undertake a sustained critique of the Hollywood film musical in book form.

In her landmark 1977 essay, *The Self-Reflexive Musical and the Myth of Entertainment*, Feuer claims that, within the classic Hollywood musical, "entertainment is shown as having greater value than it does" (487). What Feuer means here is that entertainment, in the form of the songs and dances, or the "show within the film," takes precedence over everything else. In the world of the classic Hollywood musical, singing and dancing become more important than the mundane realities of everyday life. This holds particularly true for what Feuer dubs the "backstage musical," in which the putting on of the show is the most important thing. In the backstage musical, songs and dances usually occur in the context of a rehearsal and serve to further backstage romance. *Summer Stock*, the 1950 musical starring Gene Kelly and Judy Garland, is a classic example of the backstage musical. The plot consists of a wayward troupe of performers headed by director Joe Ross (Kelly) attempting to convince skeptical farmer Jane Falbury (Garland) of the importance of putting on their show in her barn. When Jane eventually joins in the performers' fun, it is happily at the expense of running her farm and ruining her engagement with an upstanding local shopkeeper. In *Summer Stock*, entertainment in the form of the show, *Fall In Love*, conquers Jane and the rural community's suspicions about "show people," privileges the production of entertainment, and trivializes things that would, in reality, be serious responsibilities.

Rocky Horror, rather like Mervyn LeRoy's classic musical *Golddiggers of 1933* and its comical take on surviving the Depression, takes this idea of privileging fantasy over reality to its extreme. Entertainment in the form of sexual pleasure is upheld as the ultimate goal in the fictional world of *Rocky Horror*—even Dr. Frank-N-Furter's scientific achievement in creating Rocky is a triumph of entertainment, as Rocky's primary function is to serve as a sexual plaything. The climax of *Rocky Horror*'s equation of entertainment and pleasure is, of course, the pool orgy, during which Frank sings, "Give yourself over to absolute pleasure." However, even though it is implied that Frank, Magenta, and Riff Raff hail from a planet where hedonism is encouraged ("sweet Transsexual, land of night"), Frank has managed to give his desire for entertainment too much importance: "your lifestyle's too extreme" Riff Raff sings to him. Feuer comments, "perhaps the last step along the road away from the vision of the classical period is *All that Jazz* (1980) which terminates in the death of the artist and the negation of show business" (*Hollywood* 85). I would argue that *Rocky Horror*'s conclusion also represents a break with the vision of the classic musical. *All that Jazz* ends with the death of its protagonist, the hard-living choreographer Joe Gideon. Joe suffers complications after a heart attack brought on by his drug use and frenetic lifestyle, but his final moments are a montage of ironic performance to the song "Bye Bye Life" and a series of dreamlike appearances by his family and former lovers. *Rocky Horror* concludes with Frank's death, the spaceship's return to Transsexual, and the disheveled figures of Brad, Janet, and Dr. Scott amid the rubble. Both *Rocky Horror* and *All that Jazz* show a definitive curtailment of entertainment and pleasure with their conclusions that differs dramatically from the upbeat send-off typically employed by the classic Hollywood musical, as exemplified by *Summer Stock*, which ends with the engagements of Jane and her sister Abigail, followed by a reprise of the song "Howdy Neighbour," celebrating community spirit. Indeed, most classic Hollywood musicals conform to the expectations of the romantic comedy in terms of their conclusions: *Easter Parade* (1948), *Singin' in the Rain* (1952), *Funny Face* (1957), *Silk Stockings* (1957), and even *Les Girls* (1957), which uses the unusual narrative technique (unusual for the musical, anyway) of a court case over a tell-all book about a former musical act, all conclude with the romantic union of one or more couples.

When entertainment is relegated to a less prominent position in the musical, it is usually the result of an unsuccessful performance. As Feuer remarks, "Only unsuccessful performances are demystified. The musical desires an ultimate valorization of entertainment; to destroy the aura, reduce the illusion, would be to destroy the myth of entertainment as well" (488). *Singin' in the Rain* famously engages in a simultaneous demystification and valorization of entertainment in the form of "natural" talent in the sequence toward the end of the film when Lina Lamonte's (Jean Hagen) singing talent is exposed as fraudulent when the curtain of the theater in which she is performing drops away to reveal the "real" singer, Kathy Selden (Debbie Reynolds). This is the case with Frank's final song in the floor show sequence "I'm Going Home." Up until now, Frank's costuming has been as seamless as that of any '40s starlet: His costume changes happen off screen, and his makeup has been flawless. However, just before the floor show, we see Frank with messy hair, in his dressing gown, with cold cream on his face. The seamless image of Frank as an emblem of sexual entertainment is compromised, and when Riff Raff enters in his gold lamé uniform declaring his status as the new commander, Frank is finally exposed: His costume is wet and unraveling, his makeup is sloughing off, and he sings, with no apparent irony, "I'm Going Home" in torch song style. It is fitting that *Rocky Horror*, coming decades after the golden age of the Hollywood musical, takes the myth of entertainment to its fullest extent and then exposes it precisely as a myth.

Both *Summer Stock* and *Rocky Horror* can be considered "self-reflexive" musicals in that each thematizes the putting on of a show—they are both to varying extents musicals about mounting musicals. According to Feuer's model, the self-reflexive musical displays three main myths: spontaneity, integration, and audience. Feuer defines spontaneity both as "musical performance['s] . . . spontaneous emergence out of a joyous and responsive attitude towards life" and "spontaneous talent" (488). Within the genre of the classic Hollywood musical, there are countless examples of this first definition of the myth of spontaneity; virtually every musical employs the conceit that singing and dancing are natural, everyday ways of expressing emotion and, therefore, do not need to be integrated into the narrative as part of a show, as is often the case with the backstage musical. *Gentlemen Prefer Blondes* (1953) deploys the myth of spontaneity throughout its narrative, particularly in two solo numbers by Jane Russell as Dorothy Shaw: when she performs "Ain't there Anyone here for Love" surrounded by the Olympic swim team on the deck of the cruise ship, and when she gives her own performance of "Diamonds are a Girl's Best Friend" in the Paris courtroom. As viewers, we accept this myth as an aspect of the genre, just as we accept that in a conventional horror film, though it is always unwise for characters to enter dark basements alone, they do it anyway. It is also this spontaneous bursting into song that detractors of the musical cite as seeming particularly ridiculous to their sensibilities—they cannot accept the myth of spontaneity.

Summer Stock actually opens with just such a spontaneous moment: Jane sings a song about how pleasant it is to sing to yourself for no reason as she gets ready for her day. This is our first indication of Jane's spontaneous talent, and the lyrics are telling: "if you feel like singing, sing" is the refrain, showing the audience that any emotion or occasion can be expressed by a song within the narrative world of this film. A more contemporary example of a film that counts on the myth of spontaneity is Lars von Trier's *Dancer in the Dark* (2000). In *Dancer*, the musical performances do not occur in the context of a show, or even on stages; instead, they occur in real, but also highly unusual, places: a railway car, a factory floor, and most incongruously, an execution chamber. It is the myth of spontaneity that accounts for how actors in a musical burst into song and dance to signal their highly complex emotions, as if we all did this everyday.

Rocky Horror also uses singing and dancing as the preferred modes of emotional expression for both mainstream and underground society. Brad and Janet perform their duet "Dammit Janet" as they become engaged, signaling that rapturous joy can only be expressed through song in the filmic world of Rocky Horror. Of course, because Rocky Horror is a parody, Brad and Janet's wholesome style of singing would not be out of place in a classic musical—musically, it stacks up well against Joe and Jane's courtship song, "You Wonderful You," in Summer Stock. However, the humorous lyrics of "Dammit Janet" (e.g., "there's three ways that love can grow / that's good, bad or mediocre") and the monotone repetition of their names by the church staff send up the staid suburbanite façade of Brad and Janet. Singing and dancing are also the way in which we are famously introduced to the world of Dr. Frank-N-Furter through the musical numbers "Time Warp" and "Sweet Transvestite." These two numbers signal that the audience, along with Brad and Janet, have now entered a world where conventions are ridiculed and hedonism reigns. Frank sings,

> I'm not much of a man
> By the light of day
> But by night I'm one hell of a lover
> I'm just a sweet transvestite.

These lyrics, in tandem with the synchronized dancing and strangely erotic costumes, all contribute to Rocky Horror's own myth of spontaneity.

Feuer also defines the myth of spontaneity as the expression of spontaneous talent and cites the performances of the three stars of Singin' in the Rain (1952), who not only make singing and dancing seem like "an involuntary response, like breathing" (489) but also "[make] use of props at hand" (489). Kelly is the real master of making this technique look natural, epitomized by the dance he appears to improvise in Summer Stock with the sound of a squeaky floorboard and a sheet of newspaper. Feuer also cites this performance as an example of spontaneity in The Hollywood Musical: "Of all Kelly's environmental conceptions, the one which gives the greatest impression of spontaneity springs from a stage's squeaky floorboard and an old newspaper" (6). The squeak of the floorboard in combination with tap dancing becomes a whole routine as a crumpled and ripped newspaper is added to the melody and the dance. The scene culminates with Kelly noticing a story of interest in the newspaper and gradually stopping dancing, wanders off reading the paper. Kelly's dance here is a perfect example of the myth of spontaneity, "us[ing] the proscenium stage not as an arena for the dance but rather as material for the dance" (6). Kelly goes to great lengths to make a carefully rehearsed number seem effortless and part of everyday life through the use of ordinary objects as props. Kelly's work in *Summer Stock* contrasts dramatically with his performance in the fanciful, self-consciously elaborate Toulouse Lautrec–inspired sequence that ends *An American in Paris*, which was released only a year after *Summer Stock*.

It is hard to apply the myth of spontaneity to *Rocky Horror* because so much of the film relies on the unnaturalness of Frank's castle and the elaborate symbolism of its sets. Ordinary, everyday objects do not really exist in *Rocky Horror* as they do in the classic Hollywood musical. However, I argue that part of the film's enduring appeal for its hardcore fans is undeniably connected to the film's costumes, particularly the way underwear and high heels are given an iconic sexual status. Clothing that is typically hidden and characteristically feminine, including bikini underwear, corsets, garter belts, fishnet stockings, and high heels, is transformed by Frank into clothing that indicates an aggressive sexual attitude for any gender. Suddenly, these clothes are allowed to be on the outside—in fact, all the major characters are mostly underdressed throughout the film—which, in the filmic world of *Rocky Horror*, is made to appear normal and natural. Two examples of similar performances in classic Hollywood musicals come immediately to mind, where the revelation of undergarments and elements of burlesque enter into the classic musical. The first is Mame Carson's (Jane Russell) striptease performance "Lookin' for Trouble" in *The French Line* (1954). The second is Peggy Dayton's (Janice Paige) salacious number "Satin and Silk" in *Silk Stockings*, in which she performs in an elegant but brief negligee for the composer Boroff in the private showroom of an expensive dress shop. Brad and Janet are spontaneously undressed before their trip to Frank's lab under the premise of removing their wet clothes, but the real reason seems to be so that they can be more easily integrated into Frank's world. Given the assumed conservativeness of Brad and Janet, they are remarkably calm when their outer clothes are removed, signaling the normality of being underdressed in Frank's world. In *Rocky Horror*, the myth of spontaneity is perhaps best expressed as the myth of spontaneous and natural seminudity, whereas in the classic Hollywood musical, these sartorial displays are relegated to the proscribed areas of the performance space or the boudoir.

The myth of integration, according to Feuer, is evident when "successful performances are intimately bound up with success in love, with the integration of the individual into a community or a group, and even with the merger of high art with popular art" ("Self-Reflexive" 491). In *Summer Stock*, Jane's integration into the community of performers comes when a square dance is held in her barn. The performers—"the kids," as they are often called—are banished to the upper reaches of the barn, where they observe and gently mock the stiff and staid dancing of the farming community. Joe ends up dancing with Jane to distract her from two boys who are about to reveal that one of the performers has accidentally destroyed her new tractor. At the sight of Joe dancing, the kids leap down from the hayloft and take over the band: One of them takes over the drums and enlists the help of a sympathetic saxophonist. The square dancing music and dance moves evolve seamlessly into swing style as the performers jive and jitterbug. Jane tries to maintain the original stately pace but soon shrugs and gives herself over to Joe's more energetic style. As Joe sets up a series of steps, Jane effortlessly follows him, demonstrating the spontaneity of her talent and beginning her transition from the farming to the performing community. After she and Joe finish dancing, the kids crowd around to congratulate them.

This demonstration of Jane's "natural" talent proves crucial when the two stars of *Fall in Love*, Jane's sister Abigail and "the name" Harrison Keyes, abandon the show for more lucrative opportunities in New York. Although Joe quickly decides he can do the male lead himself, Jane has to be persuaded to take the female lead. By the time her stuffy fiancé Orville vents his disapproval at her performing in the show, Jane is already committed to its success and to her growing attraction to Joe. When rumor has it that Orville has convinced the other townspeople to boycott the show, Jane storms into a meeting of the town council and proclaims she is "fighting tooth and nail for this show," which must go on because "it means too much to Joe." On opening night, Jane's stage fright is soothed by Joe's promise of a romantic courtship after the show's success, and Jane goes on to give a flawless performance. In contrast to the success of Jane's performance and its link to the increasing success of the romance between her and Joe, Abigail's performance during rehearsal before her abandonment of the show begins to suffer the more she opposes Joe's direction and the more they quarrel. Once it is clear that Abigail sees herself, despite her inexperience as a performer (this is her first real acting, dancing, and singing experience), as being on a higher level than the rest of the cast, she becomes segregated from the performing community, which culminates in her escape with Harrison. As one leading lady becomes segregated, the new one is in the process of embracing the performing community, ensuring a seamless musical performance and upholding the myth of integration.

The myth of integration in *Summer Stock* also represents the mythical integration of two disparate communities—the rural and the urban, or as Feuer characterizes it, the relationship between mass art and folk art (*Hollywood* 20). The show people come from New York and make their living by entertaining others. The rural community of Windgate Falls traces its ancestors back to the earliest European settlements, and its members make their living by farming. The initial merger of these two communities is expressed by Joe and the kids in the musical number "Dig for your Dinner," performed in the Falbury Farm kitchen and filled with lyrics that can only be described as "Protestant work ethic goes Hollywood":

> You gotta dig dig dig
> Dig for a dollar
> T'aint as simple as you think
> You can't purloin a sirloin or the butcher'll put you in the clink
> You just can't be a lazy bird
> You gotta get off of your twig
> So you can afford
> Your room and your board
> And it's nice to have the price of a cig
> Hey you gotta pay the fiddler manif you wanna do a jig
> You gotta be as busy as a bee
> To be a Mr. B-I-G
> And if you want some dig dig dignity
> You gotta dig dig dig dig dig for your dinner
> dig, etc.

This number reinforces a shared work ethic, and it is this aspect that eventually unites both communities.

Rocky Horror also demonstrates the myth of integration through the merger of disparate aspects of society. Brad and Janet represent the conservative middle class: Their modest clothes, plans to marry after college, and shared virginity all signify this. These two are thrown into the madcap world of Frank's laboratory: bisexual aliens, scientific experimentation, and spontaneous undressing. After some initial resistance, Brad and Janet are completely absorbed into this hedonistic community—especially once Frank seduces them both. After their separate deflorations, they both go on to mimic Frank's image in the floor show sequence while ruminating on their respective sexual awakenings: "My mind has been expanded" sings Janet, for example.

Although Brad does not demonstrate a successful integration in the film despite his sexual encounter with Frank (even his portion of the floor show is awkward and helpless), Janet is another story. After her encounter with Frank, she appears to be suffering some remorse: "Oh Brad my darling, how could I have done this to you?" she cries as she returns to the laboratory. She finds the lab empty but observes Brad on one of the TV monitors having a postcoital cigarette as Frank reclines on his bed. This revelation causes Janet to weep even more until she hears whimpering and discovers the wounded Rocky hiding in his tank. Janet begins to dress his wounds until Rocky touches her hand and the Narrator intervenes with the following voiceover: "Emotion: agitation or disturbance of mind; vehement or excited mental state. It is also a powerful and irrational master. And from what Magenta and Columbia eagerly viewed on their television monitor, there seemed little doubt that Janet was indeed its slave." What follows is Janet's first successful performance, "Touch-A, Touch-A, Touch Me." Having realized that Brad too has slipped, and on the strength of her sexual success with Frank, Janet is now free to choose Rocky as a sexual partner, which coincides with her solo performance of this song:

> Touch-a, touch-a, touch-a, touch me
> I wanna be dirty
> thrill me, chill me, fulfill me
> creature of the night.

Just as successful performances in the classic Hollywood musical are linked with romantic success, *Rocky Horror* uses the same trope in relation to sexual success.

To seal the myth of integration, the classic Hollywood musical usually ends with a public consummation of romance. Feuer's example is *Singin' in the Rain*'s final "shot of the lovers embracing in front of a billboard." This shot, asserts Feuer, "emphasizes the unity-giving function of the musical for both the couples and the audiences *in* the film and for the audience *of* the film" ("Self-Reflexive" 491). Other musicals that culminate with the public validation of romance include *An American in Paris* (1951), *Easter Parade* (1948), and *Summer Stock*, the latter in which Jane and Joe finally kiss in public before performing a reprise of the number "Howdy Neighbour" (performed by Jane alone at the beginning of the film), which celebrates the virtues of farming and rural life.

However, the myth of integration, similar to the myth of spontaneity, is not maintained in *Rocky Horror*. At the end of the film, Brad and Janet are cast out of the castle/spaceship, and as they crawl on the ground in their disheveled corsets, they sing the melancholy "Super Heroes" number:

> I've done a lot
> God knows I've tried
> To find the truth
> I've even lied
> But all I know
> Is down inside
> I'm bleeding.

The dark tone of the final song dispels the myth of integration. Rather than ending on a note of communal high spirits and heady romance in the manner of the classic musical, *Rocky Horror* shows us that Brad and Janet are no longer enveloped in Frank's paradise of sexual freedom, and as the lyrics of "Super Heroes" imply, they will now have to deal with the deeper ramifications of their experiences.

Feuer maintains that the myth of integration can also be symbolized through the merger of high and popular art ("Self-Reflexive" 491 and *Hollywood* 20); I argue that both *Summer Stock* and *Rocky Horror* demonstrate this. In the case of *Summer Stock*, the merger of high and popular art is symbolized by the penultimate number in *Fall in Love* (the show within the film). The number is "Get Happy," a song Garland went on to perform throughout her career. Unlike the rest of the fairly conventional musical numbers, "Get Happy" stands out for a number of reasons: First, it is essentially a gospel song about death ("Sing Hallelujah / c'mon get happy / get ready for the judgment day"), which sets it apart lyrically and musically from the rest of the show and its conventional romantic or comic numbers. In addition, this song is performed solo by Garland in a striking ensemble of fedora, tuxedo jacket, fishnet tights, and high heels, surrounded by anonymous male dancers in black suits against a stark red backdrop. Most of the other numbers in *Fall in Love* are ensemble ones with several cast members singing and dancing. Garland does little dancing here, but the men around her dance in a way that appears almost modern and sculptural as they form walls of movement with their bodies around Garland. The style of this number contrasts sharply with the otherwise conventional performances that punctuate the film, and "Get Happy" seems to be a number in which an effort is being made to do something different with the musical within the context of the conventional Hollywood musical—perhaps to merge the spheres of popular and high art through the daring costuming of the normally wholesome Garland in something reminiscent of Marlene Dietrich, through the minimalist set, and through the modernist influenced dancing. Feuer points out that "Get Happy" was in fact Garland's last appearance in an MGM musical. The song marked both the end of Garland's wholesome image and her contract with MGM. The stark visual imagery and sexualized costuming of Garland in the "Get Happy" number hint at the "new singing style with its histrionic excess and awkward gestures" (*Hollywood* 119) and the tragic image she would assume in her next film, *A Star is Born* (1954).

The myth of integration can also be extended to the way *Rocky Horror*, similar to many classic musicals, attempts to fuse high and low artistic influences in both its music and its mise-en-scène. Analogous to Dick Hebdige's theories of subcultural style, *Rocky Horror* can be said to engage in "semiotic warfare" by incorporating into its camp aesthetic both images of classical Western art and its Oakley Court setting for numbers like "Time Warp." (The film was shot partly at Oakley Court, a former stately home that had long served as the set for the Hammer Horror films and is now a hotel.) Oakley's Court's history as a private home for the upper class, a set for popular films, and a middle-class hotel, reflects this intersection of high and low cultures. Frank's lab has replicas of Michelangelo's *David*, and Frank and Rocky's honeymoon suite contains a stained-glass depiction of Atlas holding the world. The image of the mythical Atlas is of course tied into the camp references to 1950s bodybuilder Charles Atlas when Frank sings "The Charles Atlas Song" to Rocky. Another Italian renaissance image appears in the floor show sequence: Michelangelo's fresco of God and Adam decorates the bottom of the pool. These are just a few examples of how *Rocky Horror* mixes its high and low cultural influences. In these various ways, *Rocky Horror* presents itself as a site that displays the myth of integration in terms of narrative, music, and visual imagery.

The final element that Feuer identifies as defining the self-reflexive musical is the myth of audience, which also relates to the idea of the successful performance: "successful performances will be those in which the performer is sensitive to the needs of the audience and which give the audience a sense of participation in the performance" ("Self-Reflexive" 493). This idea of the sensitive performer reacting to a responsive audience is also related to the idea of the star as articulated by John Ellis: "the star is at once ordinary and extraordinary, available for desire and unattainable" (614). This is certainly the case with the stars of *Summer Stock*, Judy Garland and Gene Kelly. *Summer Stock* plays off this contrast of ordinary and extraordinary by making Garland's character someone exceptionally ordinary—the owner of a rural farm—but with an extraordinary talent for singing and dancing that is discovered by accident. Kelly's character is made ordinary by his poverty—the fact that he has risked all his money and even sold his car to put on *Fall in Love*. Ellis remarks that "the star is present in the same social universe as the potential film viewer" (617), and this connection to the ordinary is evident in the theme of financial constraint that pervades *Summer Stock*, as well as the type of characters played by Kelly and Garland. The rest of the performers in *Fall in Love* are also ordinary. They are portrayed as amateurs, just "kids" as Joe calls them, with little experience of being in a large or successful show. Their inexperience is also the reason they are happy to put up with the unusual conditions: sleeping in the hayloft and doing farm chores in addition to rehearsing the show. At the same time, as with Ellis's star theory, the kids are elevated by the seamless perfection of their performances in the final sequences of the film. They too become simultaneously ordinary and extraordinary.

Although a classic Hollywood musical such as *Summer Stock* relies partly on the mythology of the extraordinary Hollywood star in contrast with the ordinary character to create that sense of connection with the audience, *Rocky Horror* also fulfills the myth of the audience despite the relative obscurity of most of its actors, few of which could be deemed stars at the time. Possibly, it is this combination of relatively unknown actors joyfully singing and dancing to catchy tunes about hedonism that is at the core of *Rocky Horror*'s appeal. The ordinary appearance of Brad and Janet contrasts sharply with their hedonistic experiences and desires, but we are also presented with a world in *Rocky Horror* in which "giving yourself over to absolute pleasure" is totally permissible.

Feuer's theory of the myth of the audience was originally formulated in relation to the musical's diegetic audience (i.e., the audiences we see witnessing performances within the musical's narrative), but I believe that in the case of *Rocky Horror*, it can also be applied to this film's extraordinary, participatory fan audience. Therefore, it is not only the diegetic and extradiegetic audiences' rapport with the film's performers that fulfills the myth of audience in *Rocky Horror* but also the direct address of this extradiegetic audience of cinema spectators through the Narrator and various characters' takes to the camera. The first instance in which the audience is really acknowledged by a character other than the Narrator occurs during "Sweet Transvestite," when Frank pauses midperformance for a drink of water, which he then tosses into the camera. This has since given birth to the audience response line "Hey Frank can I have some water?" or "Throw it!" The audience is also implicated in Janet's performance of "Touch-A, Touch-A, Touch Me" during the final refrain of the lyric "creature of the night." In this sequence, we hear Janet sing the lyric "creature of the night," which is then repeated by different characters. What is interesting about this sequence is that the shot is from Janet's perspective underneath Rocky as they make love, and she appears to be imagining other characters in Rocky's position: Brad, Frank, Magenta, Riff Raff, Columbia, and finally Rocky. Because this is one of the few shots in which where the audience shares the perspective of a particular character, we are invited to share in Janet's performance rather than remain merely spectators. These two specific instances in which the extradiegetic cinema audience is invited to respond to or share in a character's on-screen performance perfectly captures Ellis's theory of the star as both ordinary and extraordinary. The lesser-known actors of *Rocky Horror* are appealing to the audience because there is not a mythology of fame surrounding them, and yet by creating performances that are so "sensitive to the needs of the audience" that both the internal and external audiences want to respond *en masse* with actions and words, the film renders these performances extraordinary and fulfills the traditional function of the star. Feuer also acknowledges this theory when she states that "star iconography can be a means of manipulating audience response" ("Self-Reflexive" 495).

Feuer stresses that the classic Hollywood film musical lacks the "fluidity and immediacy" of a theater show: "the out-of-town try-out, the interpolation of new material after each performance, the instantaneous modulation of performer-to-audience response—none of these common theatrical practices is possible for film" (493). What Feuer stresses here is that a musical theater show has a capacity for change with each performance, whereas a filmed performance is the same each time it is viewed. *Summer Stock*, similar to many backstage musicals, attempts to incorporate something of this immediacy of the musical by including scenes of rehearsal and choreography. In these scenes, the cinema audience is given the illusion of change, of seeing a musical number as it is being created, even though we realize that these scenes are entirely scripted and not spontaneous at all. *Summer Stock* shows us a montage of an exhausted Jane making entrances and struggling to learn new steps during the intense rehearsal period before *Fall in Love* opens, which gives the audience the illusion that it is seeing a work in progress.

Rocky Horror is quite possibly the only exception to the lack of immediacy characteristic of the Hollywood film musical, in that it is a film in which a live element (the audience and the shadow cast) is present, giving it the fluidity and change attributed to live theater. This may partly be because the story began life as musical theater. The unpredictable combination of the film, the shadow cast, and what must be the rowdiest cinema audience anywhere—in costume, sometimes drunk, and armed with everything from spare tires to raw meat—stands alone and changes every time. *Rocky Horror* thus is unique when it comes to the theory of the myth of audience, mainly because it is the extradiegetic audience that makes the experience of viewing the film so unusual. This is a film in which audience members feel such an overwhelming "sense of participation in the performance" that they physically participate in their own version of the performance. All films are different with an audience, but there is no *Rocky Horror* experience without a live cinema audience that participates.

Feuer comments that, "The backstage musical . . . manages to incorporate the immediate performer-audience relationship into films, thus gaining all the advantages of both media. Musical numbers can be shot from the point of view of a front-row theatrical spectator and then move into filmic space—combining the immediate contact of the theater with the mobility of perspective of the camera" ("Self-Reflexive" 493). Structurally, *Rocky Horror* shares the traits of a backstage musical such as *Summer Stock*. Examples of this technique can be found throughout films similar to *Golddiggers of 1933*, in which each musical number begins with a shot of the proscenium arch stage, from the perspective of a theatergoer, before rapidly moving into film space, with close-ups, cut-away shots, and of course the Berkley top shot—Busby Berkley's overhead shot, which he invented to showcase his famous synchronous, geometric dance routines. Examples of this technique can be found in the final part of *Summer Stock*, when the show *Fall in Love* has its debut. The first shot of the opening number "All for You" takes in the stage from the perspective of a seated theatergoer and then moves around throughout the following numbers to give a privileged, filmic perspective on the performances. The film's final frame is also in keeping with the theater: a long shot of the entire cast of *Fall in Love* on stage singing "Howdy Neighbour."

In *Rocky Horror*, alongside unconventional techniques such as Frank's takes to the camera, with which the film seems to be actively acknowledging the extradiegetic cinema audience, there are also sequences that give the cinema spectator the best seat in the house for the musical performances in the style of the classic Hollywood musical. Throughout most of *Rocky Horror*, the spectator has this mobile, filmic perspective Feuer describes. The floor show sequence, with its overtly theatrical costumes, underwater swimming pool sequence reminiscent of a pornographic Esther Williams feature, and RKO Pictures logo backdrop, opens by showing us a proscenium arch stage and then moves, as Feuer describes, into filmic space.

Before this movement, the audience is treated to a backstage shot of Frank preparing the "medusaed" Columbia, Rocky, Brad, and Janet for their performance. Then there is a long shot taking in the entire proscenium arch stage and the four characters, followed by a close-up on Columbia as she begins to sing the first verse of "Rose Tint My World." Next is a low-angle shot that takes in the whole figure of Columbia but also the bottom edge of the stage, giving the perspective of a seated theatergoer. The entire floor show sequence alternates between techniques employed by the classic Hollywood musical to imply the perspective of a diegetic or traditional theatrical audience and filmic techniques—such as the rear shot of Brad performing—that also reveal the empty seats in the theater. The fact is, during this performance there is no diegetic audience. Just before Frank's entrance, there is a long shot, as if from the back of the theater, and then a second curtain rises and a spotlight picks out a perfectly made-up Frank in front of the RKO Pictures backdrop. As Frank moves downstage, a plank lowers as he sings:

> Give yourself over to absolute pleasure
> Swim in the warm waters of sins of the flesh
> Erotic nightmares beyond any measure

And sensual daydreams to treasure forever
Can't you just see it,

at which point he jumps into the mist. The mist parts to reveal Frank floating in an *S. S. Titanic* inner tube in the pool. Once the pool sequence begins, filmic perspective takes over, even moving underwater. A theatrical perspective resumes when Frank and the others emerge after their orgy-like interlude to sing, "we're wild and untamed things." As all six (Dr. Scott has also succumbed by this point, wheeling around in his chair and waving fishnet clad legs in the air) characters take the stage once more, the camera draws back to a long shot, revealing the lit archway of the stage and the empty seats until Riff Raff and Magenta burst in with "Frank-N-Furter it's all over."

One intriguing thing about the floor show sequence and the myth of audience is that, unlike most of the other musical numbers in *Rocky Horror*, there is no diegetic audience. "Dammit Janet" has the church staff to observe, and "The Time Warp," "Sweet Transvestite," "Sword of Damocles," "Whatever Happened to Saturday Night," and "The Charles Atlas Song" all have an audience of the "unconventional conventioners." "Touch-A, Touch-A, Touch Me" has Magenta and Columbia watching via a television monitor, and "Eddie's Teddy" is performed at the dinner table. Unlike these songs, the floor show song "Rose Tint My World" has no audience apart from the extradiegetic spectators in a cinema or a living room, and it is this song sequence that adheres most closely to Feuer's theory of the structure of the classic Hollywood musical, beginning with a shot of Frank, Janet, Brad, and Rocky on a proscenium arch stage and then moving gradually into filmic space when the characters enter the pool, while alternating between theatrical and filmic perspectives throughout. When Frank sings "I'm Going Home," he has to imagine an adoring diegetic audience of ghostly figures from a bygone era applauding and cheering him. Magenta shatters Frank's myth of his own audience when she comments acidly "how sentimental." The myth of audience in *Rocky Horror* is displayed through the camera techniques it shares with the classic Hollywood musical and its use of a diegetic audience. The experience of the cinema audience that accompanies screenings of *Rocky Horror*, and the audience rapport established by the stars' successful performances, constitute a unique extension of Feuer's theory of the myth of the audience.

With the myth of spontaneity, we are treated not only to the spontaneous musical performances of characters such as Frank-N-Furter, Eddie, and Columbia but also to spontaneous hedonism as well. The myth of integration is represented by Brad and Janet's absorption into Frank's world, but the film then acknowledges that this fantasy cannot be sustained and ejects them back into reality. The myth of audience is expressed through camera shots that imply the perspective of a theatrical audience, through the presence of diegetic audiences like the conventioners, and through the cinema audience that participates in the *Rocky Horror* experience. As I claimed at the beginning of this chapter, *Rocky Horror* fulfills the qualities that Feuer attributes to the classic Hollywood musical and takes them farther—into the realm of the subversive. When we look at a classic musical such as *Summer Stock*, its rare moments of unconventionality stand out against its otherwise conventional story, just as the "Get Happy" number stands apart from the rest of *Fall in Love*.

In her conclusion to "The Self-Reflexive Musical and the Myth of Entertainment," Feuer states, "self-reflexive musicals are conservative texts in every sense" (497). *Summer Stock* is no exception to this rule: Both Jane and Abigail are paired off at the end, the show is a success, and the two disparate communities resolve their differences. However, it is difficult to make the same assertion for *Rocky Horror*, and I would in fact argue that *Rocky Horror* is one of the first musicals to conform to the overall style of the genre while striving to tell a less conventional story. In *The Hollywood Musical*, Feuer mentions Bob Fosse's 1980 musical *All that Jazz* as one of the only examples of a musical that ends in tragedy. Fosse's 1972 version of *Cabaret* also has a less than upbeat ending, and *Rocky Horror*, released in 1975, slots comfortably in between these two examples. *Cabaret* is unusual as a musical in that it draws its inspiration from a dark historical period—decadent Weimar Berlin just before the Nazis came to power—which gives its performances a certain doomed, voluptuous quality. *Rocky Horror*, although largely camp, dips into both the realms of horror with Eddie's murder and the price of excess with its penultimate song, "Super Heroes." *All that Jazz* presents us with largely ironic, frequently surreal performances dwelling on the nature of paternity, drug addiction, and death. These three films, made over a period of eight years, can be seen to form a trend that shows an attempt to continue to make the film musical culturally relevant by attempting to explore the darker, more adult themes that characterized American cinema in the 1970s more generally.

Curiously, Feuer does not include *Rocky Horror* in the revised second edition of her book *The Hollywood Musical*, which appeared in 1993. The absence of *Rocky Horror* in Feuer's otherwise highly comprehensive analysis seems odd, particularly when discussing films such as *Hairspray* (1988), which share a similarly irreverent approach to song topics and mise-en-scène, and is reflective of the generally critical dismissal of *Rocky Horror* by academics and theoreticians. *Rocky Horror* demonstrates many of the classic traits of a Hollywood musical. However, alongside the later musicals of Bob Fosse, it also represents an important attempt to revitalize the musical as a contemporary film genre by tackling nontraditional subjects and allowing the possibility of a downbeat ending, paving the way for both the darkly experimental *Dancer in the Dark* and the spectacular pastiche of *Moulin Rouge!* (2001).

Works Cited

Bourget, Jean-Loup. "Social Implications in the Hollywood Genres." *Film Theory and Criticism*. Ed. Gerald Mast, Marshall Cohen, and Leo Braudy. 4th ed. Toronto: Oxford UP, 1992. 467–74.

Ellis, John. "Stars as a cinematic phenomenon." *Film Theory and Criticism*. Ed. Gerald Mast, Marshall Cohen, and Leo Braudy. 4th ed. Toronto: Oxford UP, 1992. 614–21.

Feuer, Jane. "The Self-Reflexive Musical and the Myth of Entertainment." *Film Theory and Criticism*. Ed. Gerald Mast, Marshall Cohen, and Leo Braudy. 4th ed. Toronto: Oxford UP, 1992. 486–97.

———. *The Hollywood Musical*. 2nd ed. London: Macmillan Publishing, 1993.

Gledhill, Christine, Ed. *Home is Where the Heart Is: Studies in Melodrama and the Woman's Film*. London: BFI Publishing, 1987

Haskell, Molly. "The Woman's Film." *Feminist Film Theory: A Reader*. Ed. Sue Thornham. Edinburgh: Edinburgh UP, 1999. 20–30.

Henkin, Bill. *The Rocky Horror Picture Show Book*. New York: Plume, 1990.

Kilgore, John. "Sexuality and Identity in *The Rocky Horror Picture Show*." *Eros in the Mind's Eye: Sexuality and the Fantastic in Art and Film*. Ed. Don Palumbo. New York: Greenwood, 1986. 151–59.

Robbins, Betty, and Roger Myrick. "The Function of the Fetish in *The Rocky Horror Picture Show* and *Priscilla Queen of the Desert*." *Journal of Gender Studies* 9.3 (2000), 269–80.

Ruble, Raymond. "Dr. Freud Meet Dr. Frank-N-Furter." *Eros in the Mind's Eye: Sexuality and the Fantastic in Art and Film*. Ed. Don Palumbo. New York: Greenwood, 1986. 161–68.

Wills, Nadine. "'110 per cent woman': the crotch shot in the Hollywood musical." *Screen* 42.2 (2001), 121–41.

Part II

Rocky Horror and Cinema Spectatorship

4

Heavy, Black, and Pendulous

Unsuturing *Rocky Horror*

Jeffrey Andrew Weinstock

The bulk of *Rocky Horror* participation is verbal. There is an almost constant dialogue between the audience and the film, similar to that between priest and congregation.

　　—Mark Siegel, *The Rocky Horror Picture Show: More Than a Lip Service*

AUDIENCE: Is it true you masturbate?
NARRATOR: It's true, there were dark storm clouds . . .
AUDIENCE: Describe your balls!
NARRATOR: . . . heavy—black and pendulous, toward which they were driving.
AUDIENCE: Is it also true you're constipated?
NARRATOR: It's true also, that the spare tire they were carrying was badly in need of some air.

Discussions of cult films in general, and of *Rocky Horror* in particular, frequently emphasize, as Mark Siegel does in the epigraph at the beginning of this chapter, the religious character of audience response. Along these lines, Richard Day asserts that cult movies are events similar to religious rites (215), Hoberman and Rosenbaum compare midnight movies to midnight mass (16), and Kinkade and Katovich claim that cult films "represent one of the many secular replacements for religious symbols in the postmodern age of electronic imagery" (191). Speaking of *Rocky*

Horror in particular, Bruce McDonald describes the film as a "different church" (219), Rosenbaum refers to audience response as "a mutant form of organized religion" (qtd. in Siegel 306), and Jonathan Adams, the originator of the characters of the Narrator and Dr. Scott in the theatrical version and the actor who plays Scott in the movie, commented in a 1998 interview concerning *Rocky Horror* aficionado Sal Piro, and *Rocky Horror* "cultists" in general, that they are "Obsessed a bit. It's like a holy church, and the script is the holy text" (Michaels and Evans 164).

Although there most certainly is a ritualistic quality to *Rocky Horror* spectator practices—and I do agree with Day, Grant, Kawin, Minor, and others who assert that cult movie viewership practices construct communities of admirers that connect people in intimate ways and provide "renewable source[s] of delight" (Minor 16)—this comparison between audience response to *Rocky Horror*, in which the audience talks back to the film, and religious rites seems problematic in at least three respects. First, although the bulk of the discussion of the *Rocky Horror* cult has focused, as Siegel previously does, on the audience's verbal responses to cinematic text, this emphasis overlooks the audience's use of props, the important role of the shadow cast during which live actors mime the onscreen action, and the dancing that the audience does during "Time Warp." With these features in mind, the claim that "the bulk of *Rocky Horror* participation is verbal" is questionable at best. Second, as opposed to Siegel's contention, no "dialogue" is in fact created between audience and film. "Dialogue" implies an interchange or discussion of ideas—that is, a conversation between (at least) two participants who respond to one another. *Rocky Horror* fans are not having a conversation with the film because the film does not respond to or specifically address audience comments—indeed, as I discuss later, what audience comments shouted at the screen reveal is precisely the failure of dialogue and the inability of the film to change or respond. Rather, what *Rocky Horror* fans do is to construct out of what I will refer to as the film's primary script a secondary script, which is then overlaid on the primary script for the benefit of other audience members. Third, as my juxtaposition of epigraphs here is intended to illustrate, the secondary script that *Rocky Horror* fans construct for one another is one that primarily *debases* the primary script. The vast majority of the witticisms hurled at the screen are humorous quips poking fun at the characters and their actions and highlighting production gaffs.[1] The comments produced by audience members hardly are the sorts of things one would say to a priest or about a holy text—at least not out loud. Paradoxically, although *Rocky Horror* fans may venerate the *Rocky Horror* script, the script itself is hardly sacrosanct. Indeed, it is travestied at every turn.

Rather than solely demonstrating reverence, I argue here that what *Rocky Horror* audience response, through both its love and its iconoclasm, makes evident is the attempt to realize two unspoken desires inherent in cinematic spectatorship in general—the desire, as Robin Wood puts it, to "be" the film—to be a part of the film, to enter into the filmic world—and the desire to control the film—to seize control of discourse and to speak, rather than to be spoken. The two forms of audience response—to which I will refer as empathetic and ironic—exhibited by the *Rocky Horror* audience demonstrate the simultaneous and contradictory pull of both of these desires during the viewing experience of the conventional plot-driven Hollywood film, as well as the impossibility of their realization. No matter how perfectly one mimics the screen action or attempts to reproduce in the theater the environment represented in the film, one will never be part of the film. Finally, despite the most inflammatory rhetoric, the film will never yield or change. What *Rocky Horror* audiences perform then, week after week, is precisely the failure not only of their desires but also of cinematic desire in general.

Empathetic Behavior

Audience responses to *Rocky Horror* during the film can be categorized in terms of their temporal relationship to the onscreen action and then divided into three categories that I refer to as predictive, reactive, and simultaneous. Predicative actions are audience actions—in the case of *Rocky Horror*, almost entirely verbal—that reveal foreknowledge of what is to come. My second epigraph provided earlier is one example of predictive action because the audience, having memorized part or all of the *Rocky Horror* script, can insert its own lines between the lines of onscreen dialogue in such a way that the intended meaning of subsequent lines of the filmic script is altered or subverted. For this secondary script produced by the audience to be coherent and produce humor, lines generated by the audience must appear to be answered by the film. The origination of such lines thus demands an awareness of what is to come and fosters the illusion of control.[2] Another example of a predictive action occurs during the song "Sweet Transvestite," when, following Frank-N-Furter's statement that he'll remove "the cause," the audience shouts "What about the symptom?" Frank then concludes the song by shouting "but not the symptom!" seemingly answering the audience's query.

Reactive responses are comments that respond to and evaluate onscreen action. Similar to predictive actions, reactive responses are verbal interjections generated by cues in the primary text. However, their humor is derived from their relationship to a preceding line or action in the primary text, rather than an ensuing one. For example, when interrupted while fellating Brad by a summons from Riff Raff, Frank-N-Furter responds, "Coming!" to which the audience adds, "So is Brad!" Another example of a reactive response occurs when Magenta greets Brad and Janet by sliding down the banister while shouting, "You're lucky, he's lucky, I'm lucky." The audience (refined as always) here adds, "The banister's lucky!"

Predictive and reactive responses "twist" the meaning of the on-screen dialogue, thereby introducing ironic distance that interrupts identification and has the effect, as I develop later, of "unsuturing" the film. However, a third class of actions performed by the audience can be identified that works in the opposite way. Simultaneous events are comments, movements, or actions that the audience performs in conjunction with the film. Simultaneous actions include the use of props, the *Rocky Horror* shadow cast, and the dancing and singing along with the movie that occurs at certain moments. Such actions can be referred to as empathetic. Rather than manifesting a desire to control the film, simultaneous empathetic actions demonstrate the opposing pull—the desire to "be" the film, to dissolve the boundaries between the cinematic world portrayed and the real world inhabited by the viewers and "submit" to the film.

Wood most clearly correlates audience response with what I call simultaneous empathetic acts, and significantly, as opposed to Siegel, he foregrounds the audience's nonverbal actions. He writes,

> The characteristics of the [*Rocky Horror*] audience's performance are generally well known. They typically throw rice at the wedding scene and toast at the banquet. They fire water pistols during the storm scene and ignite lights in the darkness. They dance the "Time Warp" . . . and they touch the screen during Janet's solo, "Touch-a, Touch-a, Touch Me." In short, even beyond specific performances, the audience asserts its physical presence and surrenders its anonymity, as if in obedience to the refrain in Frank-N-Furter's lyric, "Don't dream it. Be it." . . . To be "it," apparently is to be the film—or at least to be one with the film. (160)

I agree with Wood that it is through these simultaneous empathetic acts that the audience most clearly expresses its desire to be a part of the film, to enter into the filmic text to the fullest extent possible, yet it must be acknowledged that the use of props, although clearly exhilarating for audience members, inevitably can only foreground the audience's failure to achieve its desire by interrupting the viewer's absorption into the text. When one is struck by rice or returns to a wet seat, or perhaps most strikingly, when a role of toilet paper hits the screen, causing the projected image to ripple, imaginary identification with the filmic text is disrupted by reminding the viewer of the material conditions of spectatorship. The outward gesture of identification boomerangs around and returns to knock the viewer out of a state of absorption.[3]

The desire to be the film—as well as the inevitable failure of its realization—is perhaps most clearly evident during the *Rocky Horror* floor show. During the floor show, costumed actors (the shadow cast) against the backdrop of the movie screen alternate between performing simultaneous actions—doubling the actions that are taking place on the screen—and performing reactive gestures, such as groping Janet's breast during her "Touch-A, Touch-A, Touch Me" song. For the *Rocky Horror* "virgin," the moments during the floor show when the cast synchronizes its motions with those on screen—when the floor show actors "become" the movie—may be the most surreal or uncanny elements of the experience. Importantly, for audience members, the floor show is something to watch: an alternative, competing visual text, not something in which one participates, but perhaps something toward which audience members aspire.[4] In addition, the uncanny duplication of the screen action, although clearly an act of simultaneous empathetic identification for cast members, functions ultimately to alienate spectators from the experience of the movie itself. The ability of actors to synchronize their movements to the screen reveals the fixed, mechanical nature of the filmic substrate. The movements can only be mimed so precisely because the movie never changes, because what film theorist Jean-Pierre Oudart has called "the absent-one" has structured the text in advance. Rather than the illusion of a story in process being revealed as it occurs, the floor show reveals the plot to be one always already told, barring the subject forever from "being" or entering into the film.

What the audience's simultaneous empathetic actions materialize is the usually inchoate and unarticulated desire on the part of the audience of the classic plot-driven film to be absorbed into the film, to be a part of the experience to such an extent that boundaries between the narrative world and the real-life world of the audience dissolve. However, dance movements and the use of props "rematerialize" the viewing experience, ground the viewer in the bodily experience of spectatorship, and thereby disrupt psychic identification. In addition, the uncanny spectacle of the floor show further alienates the viewer by not only distracting the viewer from the filmic text but also revealing that text to be closed and unalterable.

Ironic Behavior

Previous analyses of *Rocky Horror* have suffered as a result of the failure to distinguish among different forms of audience response at the film. For the most part, critical attention to *Rocky Horror* has conflated all forms for audience response with mechanisms of identification that I have referred to as empathetic actions. For Kinkade and Katovich, for example, a primary characteristic of the cult film in general (of which for them *Rocky Horror* is the preeminent example) is that it allows for "narcissistic and empathic identification with subversive characters" (194). Telotte speaks of the audience investment in the cult film as a form of "love" that embraces a "comfortable difference" (5). As noted earlier, Wood associates the *Rocky Horror* audience's "performance" almost entirely with the desire to be the film, to dissolve boundaries between the world of the film and the world of the theater. This conflation, as I have suggested, leads to problematic assertions that *Rocky Horror* audiences treat the film reverentially or consider the script inviolate or sacred. However, what must be taken into consideration is the fact that the majority of the behavior exhibited by fans during *Rocky Horror* is not empathetic, but ironic; that is, rather than an effort to enter into the film or to be the film, the majority of interjections by audience members interrupt the narrative in ways that prevent absorption or identification. Signifiers are wrenched out of their embedded contexts and forced to signify differently—to say something (usually something crude) apart from their intended meanings. Furthermore, the comments are not neutral in tone but persistently debase the film and its characters. Although, to borrow from Telotte, this may be love, it is a sadistic form of love that continually insults and degrades the object of its affection. What I argue later is that ironic predictive and reactive interjections shouted by audience members demonstrate a desire running contrary to the empathetic desire to be the film—that is, they manifest the desire to control the film, to master it. In the process, they "unsuture" the film by preventing psychic identification and foregrounding the gaps in cinematic discourse. However, as with the desire to be the film, the desire to control the film also is inherently impossible, and the realization of this impossibility underlies both the audience's sadistic denigration of the film and the "repetition compulsion" manifested by *Rocky Horror* fans through obsessive viewing. Impotence to effect change or to establish a true dialogue with the film instantiates itself in insults and slurs and generates repetitive viewing in an attempt to master the experience. What I wish to emphasize here is that, as with the desire to be the film, this desire to control the film is not by any means something unique to *Rocky Horror* viewers. Rather, what *Rocky Horror* spectators exhibit in hyperbolic form is a general desire inherent in the cinematic experience (and in discourse in general): the desire to control discourse, to speak rather than to be spoken. To develop this idea, a brief summation of the notion of "suture" developed by film theorists adopting a psychoanalytic approach to viewership is necessary.

The influential model of cinematic spectatorship derived from Lacanian psychoanalysis emphasizes the way in which subjectivity is conferred on viewers—the manner in which viewers are "spoken" by classical cinema—through a process called suture. This process is exemplified for theorists such as Jean-Pierre Oudart and Daniel Dayan by the shot/reverse shot sequence. The shot/reverse shot dyad is a pairing of shots in which the second shot shows the field from which the first shot is presumed to have been taken.[5] As a result of this, "the gaze which directs our look seems to belong to a fictional character rather than to the camera" (Silverman 202). This sequence of shots in which the role of the camera in structuring what the viewer sees is obscured has been discussed in terms of both its affective and ideological ramifications. On the level of affect, according to Kaja Silverman, the viewer of the first shot initially experiences it as "an imaginary plenitude, unbounded by any gaze, and unmarked by difference" (203). The first shot is experienced as a "site of *jouissance* akin to that of the [Lacanian] mirror stage prior to the child's discovery of its separation from the ideal image which it has discovered in the reflecting glass" (Silverman 203). However, this pleasure is almost immediately interrupted when the viewing subject perceives its limitations and "discovers that he is only authorized to see what happens to be in the axis of the glance of another spectator, who is ghostly or absent" (Dayan 188). This absent controlling force, what Dayan, following Oudart, refers to as "the absent-one," and which Silverman calls "the speaking subject," "has everything which the viewing subject, suddenly cognizant of the limitations on its vision, understands itself to be lacking" (Silverman 204). This sense of lack, in turn, elicits a desire to see more.

The second shot of the shot/reverse shot dyad responds to this desire for more. By presenting a character who is assumed to be the owner of the glance corresponding to the first shot, the second shot, according to Dayan, closes or "sutures" over the "hole opened in the spectator's imaginary relationship with the filmic field by his perception of the absent-one" (189). A gaze within the film is presented that serves to conceal the controlling gaze outside the fiction (Silverman 204), a process of specular identification is elicited in which the viewing subject allows a fictional character to define what it sees, and "by means of suture, the film-discourse presents itself as a product without a producer, a discourse without an origin" (Dayan 191). What is concealed by this process of suture is the control an unrepresented outside force—the camera, the director, all the forces producing the film—has over the viewer's experience. The viewer therefore is being manipulated psychologically during the experience of the film in ways of which he or she remains unaware on a conscious level.

The ideological implications of suture revolve around the concealment of the forces that control and produce the filmic discourse. According to Silverman, what suture does is to encourage viewers to establish a relationship not with the apparatuses that produce the film but with their fictional representation (216). Drawing on Marxist philosopher Louis Althusser's notion of interpellation, Silverman explains that "The system of suture functions not only constantly to re-interpellate the viewing subject into the same discursive positions, thereby giving that subject the illusion of a stable and continuous identity, but to re-articulate the existing symbolic order in ideologically orthodox ways" (221).[6] Suture ultimately

> can be understood as the process whereby the inadequacy of the subject's position is exposed in order to facilitate (i.e. create the desire for) new insertions into a cultural discourse which promises to make good that lack. Since the promised compensation involves an ever greater subordination to already existing scenarios, the viewing subject's position is an extremely passive one, a fact which is carefully concealed through cinematic slight-of-hand. This sleight-of-hand involves attributing to a character within the fiction qualities which in fact belong to the machinery of enunciation: the ability to generate narrative, the omnipotent and coercive gaze, the castrating authority of the law. (231–32)

In effect, the viewing subject is "spoken" or constructed by the syntax or "code" of the film, but this code, which in Dayan's assessment "*produces an imaginary, ideological effect*," is hidden by the narrative. "Unable to see the workings of the code, the spectator is at its mercy. His imaginary is sealed into the film; the spectator thus absorbs the ideological effect without being aware of it" (188).

One last aspect of suture that it is necessary to highlight before turning back to *Rocky Horror* is the retroactive temporality of the constitution of meaning in film (or in any form of narrative communication). As with spoken language, the process of perceiving meaning in film is both retroactive and anticipatory, as each new shot modifies the meaning of the previous one and is dependent for its own meaning on the next. The result of this, according to Dayan, is that the "spectator is torn to pieces." He continues, "On the one hand, a retroactive process organizes the *signified*. On the other hand, an anticipatory process organizes the *signifier*. Falling under control of the cinematographic system, the spectator loses access to the present. When the absent-one points toward it, the signification belongs to the future. When the suture realizes it, the signification belongs to the past" (190).

The essential points of this discussion of suture for purposes of analyzing *Rocky Horror* fan response are the ideological interpellation and "speaking" of the viewer enacted by suture and the retroactive constitution of meaning inherent in cinematic syntax. What *Rocky Horror* fans do through predictive and reactive actions that establish ironic distance is to resist the "hail" of the film, so to speak—that is, to interrupt the process of suture and refuse to be spoken or interpellated by the film. *Rocky Horror* fans refuse to sit quietly and let themselves be manipulated by the obscured yet controlling mechanisms of the film's production. Rather, they attempt to control discourse through an act of verbal piracy that hijacks the film's intended meaning. To express this using the Lacanian, what *Rocky Horror* spectator behavior manifests is the desire to possess the "phallus."[7] It is through predictive actions that *Rocky Horror* fans demonstrate most clearly the desire to take control of the film, to wrench its significations out of their intended grooves and to redeploy them in new ways that they direct. Predictive verbal comments interrupt the retroactive constitution of meaning within the film by forcing actions and spoken lines within the film to signify in a dual capacity. The film is seemingly compelled to respond to the audience, whose omniscience allows it to "corner" the film and subvert the intended meaning by overlaying a secondary script that alters the meaning of the cinematic dialogue. The attempt to take control of the cinematic experience manifests itself even before the film begins, when excited audience members chant "Lips, Lips, Lips," and then, obedient to their wishes, the film begins and Patricia Quinn's now-famous brightly painted lips fill the screen.

The way in which the audience's secondary script subverts intended meaning is clearly evident in the following example of predictive audience participation, which occurs early in the film, when Brad and Janet first arrive at Frank-N-Furter's castle:

BRAD: Hi! My name is Brad Majors, and this is my fiancée, Janet Weiss. I wonder if you could help us. You see, our car broke down a few miles up the road. Do you have a phone we might use?
AUDIENCE: Look between Janet's legs!
RIFF RAFF: You're wet.
AUDIENCE: Hey Janet, are you a slut?
JANET: Yes . . .
AUDIENCE: What's the weather?
JANET: . . . it's raining.
AUDIENCE: No shit! Are you an asshole, Brad?
BRAD: Yes.

AUDIENCE: Are you on drugs, Riff?
RIFF RAFF: Yes. I think perhaps you better both . . .
AUDIENCE: Get lost?
RIFF RAFF: . . . come inside.

The insertion of audience commentary into the literal gaps of the cinematic dialogue here effectively "unsutures" the scene by preventing imaginary identification and bifurcating the meaning of each line such that, although each character is clearly responding to the preceding comment within the cinematic dialogue, he or she is also "forced" to answer the audience's question at the same time. The attempt to redirect meaning and to assume control of discourse reveals the desire to "master" the film, to speak rather than to be spoken. Predictive ironic actions demonstrate a desire inherent in cinematic viewing—the desire to control discourse, to master "the absent-one." However, this desire, similar to the desire to be the film, is destined to be thwarted, and its impossibility leads to the fetishization of interruption, repetitive viewing, and the sadistic debasement of the film through both predictive and reactive verbal interjections.

The sense of control felt by *Rocky Horror* audience members who effectively deploy predictive interjections is inevitably undermined by the inescapable awareness of their failure to direct the on-screen action or to prompt a response. No authentic dialogue is established with the screen, the film's characters remain forever oblivious to the presence of the audience, and spectators cannot force the film to deviate from its primary script. Indeed, for all their originality and occasional cleverness, audience exclamations remain bound to and directed by the primary script of the film. The apparent control manifested by predictive interjections is, at last, only illusory, and the senses of fullness and power felt by the spectator who presumes to redirect the significations of the film's dialogue ultimately is belied by an underlying sense of impotence.

One strategy by which *Rocky Horror* aficionados attempt to maintain the illusion of mastery and to ward off the distressing realization of disempowerment is the fetishization of interruption itself. What *Rocky Horror* fans do, again and again, is to interrupt the film in ways that reinforce their sense of mastery of the plot and dialogue. *Rocky* fans revel in their ability to predict what the characters will say and do and to subvert intended meaning through predictive interjections. Ironically, each "cut" enacted by the audience bolsters its own sense of plenitude: Each time the audience successfully redirects cinematic signification—turns the film back on itself—what is produced is humor and a sort of free-floating euphoria. The film appears powerless to resist the audience—it is subject to the audience's commands, and not the other way round.

The desire to maintain the illusion of mastery over the film—over discourse—is also manifested in the "repetition compulsion" many *Rocky Horror* fans demonstrate by viewing the film obsessively.[8] This is not to discount the powerful motivating factor that participation in a communal event provides. As commentators on *Rocky Horror* and cult films more generally have argued, what cult films construct are communities of viewers that reap psychic benefits from the shared experience of group identification—indeed, Mary Eden Minor's entire doctoral dissertation on *Rocky Horror* is premised on the idea that what *Rocky Horror* affords for those who regularly participate in its "cult" is a comforting sense of community and belongingness.[9] However, what I am suggesting here is that part of what is so rewarding about participating in the *Rocky Horror* event is the euphoria attendant on the empowering (but illusory) sense that one is in control of the film—that one speaks, rather than is spoken. Repetitive viewing develops out of and helps to repress the anxiety that one is not in control; each time the spectator views the film, he or she can imagine that he or she is one step closer to the impossible goal of "getting it perfect"—of directing the film, rather than being directed by it, of bending discourse to his or her will. *Rocky Horror* fans go again and again not just to experience the comfort of community but also to attempt to realize the impossible *jouissance* of plenitude.

However, as with the desire to be the film, the desire to master the film ultimately is unrealizable. Underlying the illusion of control is the awareness that, however provocative or prescient the audience interjection, the film will not yield or change. Its responses are mechanical and prescripted, and all attempts by audience members to "break into" the film and alter it fundamentally are in vain. It is a closed text, finished and sealed. Not only can it not be controlled, but it "refuses" to recognize the audience, and it is this knowledge that the audience's sense of empowerment is purely illusory that fosters aggression and turns love to hatred. Lurking beneath the fetishization of interruption and the spectatorial repetition compulsion is the repressed awareness of lack.

As I previously note, the vast majority of audience interjections—especially reactive ones—during *Rocky Horror* are comments that poke fun at or belittle the characters and debase the film. Every time Brad's name is mentioned, the audience shouts "Asshole!" Every time Janet's name is mentioned, the audience shouts "Slut!" The Narrator, Riff Raff, Magenta, Columbia, and even Dr. Frank-N-Further himself all are subject to the audience's playful yet disparaging remarks, as are the song lyrics and the scenery. Consider the audience's interjections into the following exchange between Brad and Janet just before their arrival at Dr. Frank-N-Furter's castle:

AUDIENCE: What's white and sells hamburgers?
BRAD: Didn't we pass a castle back down the road a few miles? Maybe they
  have a telephone we could use.
AUDIENCE: Castles don't have phones, asshole!
JANET: I'm going with you.
BRAD: Oh, no, darling, there's no sense in both of us getting wet.
AUDIENCE: Janet's already wet!
JANET: I'm coming with you.
AUDIENCE: That would be a first!
JANET: Besides, darling, the owner of the phone might be a beautiful
  woman . . .
AUDIENCE: He is!
JANET: . . . and you might never come back again.
AUDIENCE: You should be so lucky!

The audience here, through its interruptions of the dialogue, fore-grounds the couple's naïveté and mocks their sexual innocence. At the same time, the comments foreshadow Brad and Janet's encounter with the cross-dressing Frank-N-Furter and their subsequent sexual awaken-ings, thereby revealing the audience's awareness of the plot's development and its resignation to the inevitability of this progression. Foreknowledge turns to frustration, as the audience knows what will happen but is pow-erless to prevent it. The audience taunts the movie, attempting to goad it into a response. However, the limited empowerment developed through predictive interruptions transforms into aggressivity as this empowerment is revealed to be illusory, and this frustration is expressed through insults and debasing invective hurled at the screen. In its reactive commentary, the audience finally assumes the only authentic position it can occupy: that of critic. Despite its pretensions of grandeur, as it cannot fundamentally alter the on-screen action, it must resign itself to assessing what has transpired after the fact. The sadistic denigration of the film and its characters reflects the audience's failure both to be the film and to master the film. Its inability to realize either desire manifests itself in irreverent commentary that belies the audience's affective attachment to the film by fostering the impression that the movie is worth nothing.

To return to the beginning of this chapter, rather than a reverential experience of worship, what the *Rocky Horror* fan response demonstrates is a desire to displace God and to assume his position. However, despite a refusal on the part of *Rocky* fans to worship as anticipated or directed, what fans discover is that God—the Absent-One—cannot be unseated or even challenged. The audience joins together to abuse the priest but only succeeds in revealing its frustration over the fact that God does not hear or care.

My argument here has been that *Rocky Horror* audience behavior, rather than being anomalous, in fact embodies in hyperbolic form two fundamental desires inherent in the cinematic experience of conventional narrative film: the desire to be the film and the desire to control the film. The impossibility of realizing either of these desires ultimately manifests itself in interruption, debasement, and repetitive viewing of the film. The question remains, however, that if, as I claim, these are general desires inherent in cinematic spectatorship, what is it then about *Rocky Horror* in particular that elicits such vigorous viewer response? Although I don't have space to address this question fully here, I would like to suggest briefly that *Rocky Horror* fan behavior is a combination of the film's own comedic irreverence combined with historical contingency—that is, although I believe the film's own subversive iconoclasm, it's "nothing's sacred" attitude predisposes the audience to disregard conventional viewing practices, I suspect that, at bottom, entrenched forms of spectator behavior at *Rocky Horror* are primarily the product of chance. This is to say, although intrinsic qualities of the film do open up unusual spaces for audience engagement, many other films do as well and, given the proper conditions, could have catalyzed similar audience response.

Works Cited

Corrigan, Timothy. "Film and the Culture of Cult." *The Cult Film Experience: Beyond All Reason.* Ed. J. P. Telotte. Austin: U of Texas P, 1991. 26–37.

Day, Richard R. "Rocky Horror Picture Show: A Speech Event in Three Acts." *Sociolinguistics and Language Acquisition.* Ed. Nessa Wolfson and Elliot Judd. Rowley, MA: Newbury House Publishers, 1983. 214–21.

Dayan, Daniel. "The Tutor-Code of Classical Cinema." *Film Theory and Criticism: Introductory Readings.* Ed. Gerald Mast, Marshall Cohen, Leo Braudy. 4th ed. New York: Oxford UP, 1992. 179–91.

Grant, Barry Keith. "Science Fiction Double Feature: Ideology in the Cult Film." *The Cult Film Experience: Beyond All Reason.* Ed. J. P. Telotte. Austin: U of Texas P, 1991. 122–37.

Hoberman, J., and Jonathan Rosenbaum. *Midnight Movies.* New York: Da Capo, 1991.

Kawin, Bruce. "After Midnight." *The Cult Film Experience: Beyond All Reason.* Ed. J. P. Telotte. Austin: U of Texas P, 1991. 18–25.

Kinkade, Patrick T., and Michael A. Katovich. "Toward a Sociology of Cult Films: Reading *Rocky Horror.*" *The Sociological Quarterly* 33.2 (1992): 191–209.

Lee, Jonathan Scott. *Jacques Lacan.* Amherst: U of Massachusetts P, 1990.

McDonald, Bruce. "Semiology Goes to the Midnight Movies." *Etc.: A Review of General Semantics* 37.3 (1980): 216–23.

Michaels, Scott, and David Evans. *Rocky Horror: From Concept to Cult*. London: Sanctuary Publishing, 2002.

Minor, Mary Eden. "The Folklore of Mass-Mediated Celebration: Audience Participation at *The Rocky Horror Picture Show*. Diss. University of Southwest Louisiana, 1995.

Piro, Sal. *Creatures of the Night II: More of* The Rocky Horror Picture Show *Experience*. Livonia, MI: Stabur, 1995.

Samuels, Robert. E-mail to the author. March 21, 2005.

Siegel, Mark. "*The Rocky Horror Picture Show*: More Than a Lip Service." *Science-Fiction Studies* 7.3 (1980): 305–12.

Silverman, Kaja. *The Subject of Semiotics*. New York: Oxford UP, 1983.

Telotte, J. P. "Beyond All Reason: The Nature of the Cult." *The Cult Film Experience: Beyond All Reason*. Ed. J. P. Telotte. Austin: U of Texas P, 1991. 5–17.

Wood, Robert E. "Don't Dream It: Performance and *The Rocky Horror Picture Show*." *The Cult Film Experience: Beyond All Reason*. Ed. J. P. Telotte. Austin: U of Texas P, 1991. 156–66.

Notes

1. For example, one of the most inescapable forms of verbal audience participation throughout the film is the shouting of "asshole!" each time the character Brad's name is spoken and "slut!" each time the character Janet's name is mentioned.

2. Importantly, what I call predictive behavior differs from what I call anticipatory behavior. Predictive behavior derives from confident knowledge of what will come next based on familiarity with the filmic text. Anticipatory behavior expects something to happen on the basis of various cinematic cues but remains defined by uncertainty. An example of the latter would be the horror movie viewer who anticipates an attack and covers his eyes on the basis of familiarity with the genre and cues generated by the movie, such as soundtrack changes and camera shots from the monster/killer's perspective, and so on.

3. There is a striking parallel here with Timothy Corrigan's assertion that what characterizes cult films in general is "the debris and excess that defines characters and environments" (28). What the audience is left with at the end of any showing of *Rocky Horror* is literal debris in the form of a theater strewn with rice, newspapers, hotdogs, and so on. The audience here produces and leaves behind its own debris, which not only explains why many theaters are reluctant to show *Rocky Horror* but foregrounds the material conditions of spectatorship.

4. Unlike what I have referred to as the primary and secondary *Rocky Horror* scripts, it is difficult with the floor show shadow cast to establish a primary and secondary text. When the two are synched, one goes back and forth between them, and it is difficult to say which is primary and which is secondary. During moments when the floor show innovates—for example, when I saw

floor show cast members pile on top of one another to "fuck" the Narrator's chin cleft—the floor show clearly becomes the main attraction.

5. As summarized by Kaja Silverman, the first shot shows a space that may or may not contain a human figure. The second shot "locates a spectator in the other 180° of the same circular field, thereby implying that the preceding shot was seen through the eyes of a figure in the cinematic narrative" (202).

6. Interpellation, according to Silverman, "designates the conjunction of imaginary and symbolic transactions which results in the subject's insertion into an already existing discourse" (219).

7. Distinct from a physical organ, Lacan's notion of the phallus signifies "all of those values which are opposed to lack" (Silverman 182–83). According to Jonathan Scott Lee, "The phallus then serves to signify . . . that fullness of being, that complete identity, the lack of which is the fact of our ineluctable want-of-being" (67). For Lacan, to have the phallus is impossible. Human beings are born into culture and language that precedes and situates them—they are spoken. To have the phallus would mean to control discourse rather than to be controlled by it.

8. At the top of the list here is *Rocky Horror* "superfan" Sal Piro, who, in 1995, claimed to have seen the film over 1,500 times (Adler in Piro, "Foreword").

9. In addition to Minor, for attention to the cult film's development of community, see Day, Grant ("Science Fiction"), Hoberman and Rosenbaum, Kawin, Kinkade and Katovich, McDonald, Siegel, Telotte, and Wood. It should also be pointed out here that another way in which spectators attempt to assert their authority and to "control discourse" is through the development of what Robert Samuels terms a "rigid social order that disciplines anyone who does not replicate the group actions in the proper manner." Although I do not have space to pursue this idea in this chapter, what is suggested by this is that although the group actions enact an ironic distancing from the film, *Rocky Horror* fans hail and interpellate others into their own nonironic apparatus.

5

Mocking the Mirror

Film Spectatorship as Hypperreal Simulation

Heather C. Levy and Matthew A. Levy

Movie houses blacken out the light and quiet audiences to direct and intensify the individual's experience of the film. Psychoanalytic approaches to film theory tend to reinforce this taming of the audience by describing the audience primarily as individual spectators and ignoring their social performance—performance that is more blatant at cult films but is also important in traditional film venues. The spectators at *The Rocky Horror Picture Show* challenge the norm by misbehaving: They actively participate with the film in a physical way, transforming the show by adding elements of improvisatory live theater. Incorporating their bodies and voices into the viewing experience, the spectators defy the boundaries and limitations placed on them by a darkened theater designed for viewing pleasure only.[1]

The dominant psychoanalytic model of film fails to account for the excesses of these audiences because it begins with the concept of a developing individual psychological subject rather than with the concept of a complex social situation. As we explain, *Rocky Horror* performances and rituals cannot be explained as "mirror-stage identification," a central concept of Lacanian film theory. Nor do *Rocky Horror* fans move (in Freudian fashion) from voyeurism (sexual enjoyment of seeing) to exhibitionism (sexual enjoyment of being seen) because of some kind of rule of cognitive development of the perversion of individuals. When *Rocky Horror* audiences refuse to obey the etiquette of passivity before the screen, they reveal the false opposition that structures much spectator theory. Against this opposition between the active screen object and the passive spectator subject, the *Rocky Horror* audience "asserts its physical presence and surrenders its anonymity, as if in obedience to the refrain in Frank-N-Furter's lyric, 'Don't dream it. Be it'" (Wood 160). *Rocky Horror* players perform seeing and being-seen as one and the same social gesture: They are (at) a party. So, although the question "How do individuals come into being?" is an interesting and fruitful one, in the context of film theory it has been counterproductive, making it more difficult to see the many different forms spectatorship can take and how spectators perform in context.

There Are Some People Who Say that Life Is an Illusion[2]

If this extraterrestrial sex farce were ever amenable to traditional psychoanalytic interpretations of spectatorship, the addition of a floor show with constantly evolving audience scripts would render those models obsolete. Although some attending *Rocky Horror* choose to sit and try to enjoy the film in the traditional way (sitting at the back of the theater, not participating), if a floor show is going, the emphasis remains on displays of voyeurism (pleasure in seeing) and exhibitionism (pleasure in being seen). Because, as in theater, living actors perform a floor show, the audience itself is gazed on by the performers. The gazes of the spectators turn from the screen to the spectator-subject-turned-object. Most *Rocky Horror* spectators enter the theater expecting to be looked at and listened to and often hoping to be incorporated into the floor show. They bring the appropriate props for certain scenes to function at once as extended technical crew and extras. They shoot water guns during rain scenes while holding newspapers overhead and throw rice during a wedding. When the floor show and props release the audience from the singular hold of the screen, gazes multiply in a feeding frenzy of visual desire.

Audience participation at *Rocky Horror* screenings reveals a falsifying opposition between viewer and viewed that continues to vex psychoanalytic models of film spectatorship. Even sophisticated Lacanian approaches to film commonly maintain a foundational passive-subject-spectator versus active-object-screen opposition. This problem has been dealt with by Lacanians themselves as a problem of misinterpretation and misapplication of Lacan's theoretical works. Spectator theory must be adjusted, they say, "Making it even more Lacanian."[3]

As fruitful and compelling as Lacanian film theory may be, viewing it as "The Theory"[4] has only limited attempts to understand film spectatorship. We can move beyond the opposition that Lacanian theory has questioned but not escaped by turning to French postmodernist Jean Baudrillard's theory of simulation and description of the postmodern hyperreal. Baudrillard's theory of simulation explores the psychological and sociological effects of technological progress that have made it possible to represent, replicate, and redesign so much of nature. He writes, "The very definition of the real has become: that of which it is possible to give an equivalent reproduction.... The real is not only what can be reproduced, but that which is always already reproduced: that is the hyperreal ... which is entirely in simulation"—a copy of an original that never was (Baudrillard, *Simulations* 146).

Our capacity to copy, reshape, and redesign human experience sometimes provides a sense of control. At the same time, the feeling that that everything is manipulated and processed—from the places we live to the foods we eat to our culture and politics—can produce a nostalgia for the real thing. (Ever wonder why Coke decided to market itself as "the real thing"?) Ironically, we begin to use our great powers of fabrication to produce a feeling of authenticity—a process that works in part by producing a picture of the "normal way things used to be" that really never was. This nostalgia can be dangerous when it justifies enforcing conformity to codes of normality and punishing or even bashing those who are perceived to be different. The preoccupation of spectator theory with the relationship between individual viewing subjects and the screen-as-viewed-object prevents film theorists from observing how the filmic experience functions within our culture of simulation, sometimes in a vain attempt to create an authentic state through simulation and sometimes accepting, foregrounding, and experimenting with our simulated state. *Rocky Horror* spectators see that their world is fake and decide to have fun with it rather than to despair or to act desperately to make things authentic again (as if that were possible). The content of the *Rocky Horror* play—aliens and gender bending—goes together perfectly with this attitude toward simulation. *Rocky Horror* enactors accept that life is illusion and use that fact as a way to create a radically inclusive social space. This argument will be clearer after a review and discussion of Lacanian spectatorship theory that we hope will show the need to account for the active and collaborative nature of spectatorship—a problem overcome by Baudrillard's discussion of hyperreal simulation.

"Double Feature": The Dualistic Nature
of Psychoanalytic Models of Spectatorship

The concept of spectatorship permeates the study of film, but the specific ways in which a film's audience finds meaning has particular relevance to the psychoanalytic branch of film theory. In the description provided by theories of spectatorship, "traditional" filmic spectators passively direct their gaze only at the action on the screen. According to the widely accepted model outlined by Laura Mulvey in "Visual Pleasures and Narrative Cinema," this cinematic ritual serves to objectify women, who are represented either as "the lack" or as a fetish object on screen. Essentially, this means that women are depicted in degrading or highly sexualized ways to satisfy a psychological purpose for men (primarily). Mulvey describes three types of gazes: the camera's gaze as it records an event, the spectator's gaze as the film is shown, and the gazes characters exchange on screen. Mulvey's second gaze—the gaze of the spectator—relies on the more Freudian aspects of the Lacanian model of the cinema (Mulvey 16–17). Of central importance is Lacan's idea of the mirror stage, in which a prelinguistic child held up to a mirror by his mother (or some sort of baby chair) recognizes the reflection as his own (Lacan describes the child as male in his explanation of the mirror phase). Importantly, this recognition is a misrecognition: The child sees himself as a separate self but does not recognize the fact that he remains utterly dependent on the mother or the device that supports him in front of the mirror. In the dominant version of Lacanian film theory, the spectator's relationship to the screen is analogous to the baby's relationship to the mirror. The viewer identifies with the image on the cinematic screen, ignoring the technology that makes the fantasy possible. Mulvey holds, with Lacan, that this fantasized relationship between the fixed passive spectator (subject) and the reflected image (object) produces the illusion of fulfilled desire, bringing us back for more.

Mulvey's spectators can enjoy either direct "scopophilic" contact with the desired object or fascination with the image of his or her own likeness, which results in a feeling of control over the object. According to the cause-and-effect reasoning that Mulvey adapts from Freud and Lacan, scopophilia precedes exhibitionism. First I see, then I want to be seen. The subject begins by seeking pleasure from an extraneous object and enjoys seeing it. Then the pleasure is turned inward, causing the scopophiliac to want to be seen also. At this point, another subject is required to play the role of scopophiliac.

At first glance, this model seems especially helpful for a reading of *Rocky Horror* in which the spectator/subject's desire is not fulfilled by simply watching the film but only satisfied when he or she becomes an exhibitionist-object.

These ideas of cause and effect and subject and object are appealingly simple. First, according to this model, we have our Self. Then, when we want to show it off, we need another person to admire it. This explanation, however, requires that we accept that a Self can precede the existence of others. In *Ways of Seeing*, John Berger suggests that looking at others is crucial to the very formation of identity: "Soon after we can see, we are aware that we can also be seen. The eye of the other combines with our own eye to make it fully credible that we are part of the visible world" (Berger 9). Thus, the psychological formation of selfhood (like that of the body) does not precede but follows and depends on those who precede the self and support its existence—not merely its genetic parents but also the social body that provides its "ways of seeing" as well as its way of being. Mulvey's theory does not account for the shape this interdependence takes in the context of the cinema, and it ignores the social crosshatchings of desire that fill a room and make social life possible.

The *Rocky Horror* spectacle challenges Mulvey's model of spectatorship because its spectators are not passive and the screen does not monopolize the audience's gaze. Although Mulvey's spectators repress "their exhibitionism" and project this "repressed desire onto the performer," the live cast and crew of *Rocky Horror* compete with the screen for attention, actively enhancing their objectification and blurring the status of subject and object (Mulvey 17).

Paul Willemen adds a fourth gaze to Mulvey's list to account for the gaze that sees the other viewers in the darkened theater (216). This imagined look (of others watching us watch) is signified by the reflection of light bounced off the screen onto the audience, making us visible in the otherwise dark theater: "As the viewer has to confront his/her sadistic voyeurism, the presence of the imagined look in the field of the other makes itself increasingly felt, producing a sense of shame at being caught in the act of voyeurism. By this time, the viewing subject has become the exhibitionist. The scopic drive has turned back on the subject and the active aim had become a passive one, delegating the role of actively viewing sadist, in a displacing gesture, onto the camera" (Willemen 216). Willemen's fourth look recognizes the presence of other spectators and thereby turns the voyeuristic spectator-subject into a nervous exhibitionist object—but still in the setting of a traditional theater constrained by Lacanian splits. Where Mulvey focuses on the bliss of seeing one's distorted reflection, the fourth gaze recognizes the pleasure in providing one's self as an object that can serve as the mirror for the distorted reflection of another. If this description is making you feel like you are at the county fair in a hall of mirrors, that is only fitting. As complicated as this "I see you seeing me see it" situation gets, however, this mirror metaphor continues to require that some element in the subject-object relation be passive in a given encounter—no one has agency. The mirror metaphor creates a closed model of the cinema that prohibits the possibility of some middle state that would escape the psychoanalytic economy of sadistic and masochistic gazes.

Christian Metz addresses a problem with Mulvey's model that the addition of a fourth gaze does not: Mulvey's use of the mirror stage. How can the mirror stage be used to explain the adult experience of subject-spectators who experienced the mirror stage long ago, as children? Furthermore, "there is one thing, and one thing only that is never reflected in it: the spectator's own body" (Metz 45). That is wholly unlike a mirror, in which we view our selves. Although Metz rejects the characterization of cinematic spectatorship as an instance of the mirror phase—an important distinction within the context of Lacanian film theory—his use of the concept of "identification" preserves the force of Mulvey's gesture, which defines the viewer as a passive spectator-subject. Metz downplays the importance of the viewer's identification with the characters onscreen (crucial for Mulvey) in favor of self-identification as "a pure act of perception" and a concomitant identification with the eye of the camera (Lapsley and Westlake 83). In other words, the main pleasure is not seeing a reflection of our self but seeing the other and feeling powerful over that other as a result. As previously explained, in the mirror stage, the child recognizes himself as a distinct and complete being in the mirror in a moment of bliss in which he does not recognize his state of dependence on others and artifacts. Likewise, Metz's spectator identifies himself or herself as a completely adequate viewer—a feeling of confidence that leaves the spectator more susceptible to the power of the cinematic apparatus to limit the field of vision and to manipulate the spectator through the representation of absent objects. Thus, although Metz says that the mirror stage does not really apply to spectatorship, his description is substantially the same in that he maintains the subject-object split. He maintains this subject-object split as part of a larger political understanding, shared with Mulvey, that envisions a subject that is simultaneously autonomous (in the sense of being individually motivated by an interior economy of desire) and passive (the subject is susceptible to the tricks of the cinema—or, in the jargon of the Theory, the subject's desire is motivated by a lack that is temporarily sutured by the fantasy projected on the screen).

In all fairness, Metz does attempt to account for the characteristics that distinguish the cinema from other environments; for instance, he points out how the cinema differs from live theater: "The film is not exhibitionist. I watch it but it doesn't watch me watching it. . . . The visible is entirely confined to the screen" (Metz 95–96). Of course, in *Rocky Horror*, the presence of audience members mimicking the actions and lines of the characters in the film while spectators handle props complicates Metz's argument not only by injecting the live theater into the cinematic event but also by erasing the borders between spectator, performer, and show. Further challenging Metz's theory, *Shock Treatment*, the sequel to *Rocky Horror*, contains satiric depictions of audiences that could be taken as barbs at *Rocky Horror*'s own obsessive audiences. This would suggest that although Metz is right that the screen itself has no eyes, the cinema-at-large does see and react to its audiences. After all, producers decide which movies to make and distribute in large part based on assumptions about which movies will make money. Films are audience tested and changed based on audience reactions.

There's a Light (Over at the Frankenstein Place)

There is no universal theory accepted for film or spectatorship; however, psychoanalytic models dominate film theory to an extent that, in a way, theorists have created their own "monster." The psychoanalytic view of the subject can be explained by the development of psychoanalysis within the context of one-on-one clinical relations between analyst and patient in which the transference between the two interlocutors is of primary importance. On the one hand, the patient is the subject and the analyst is the object of the patient's gaze and, in a certain sense, his or her mirror. On the other hand, the analyst is also a subject for whom the patient/object serves as a kind of mirror, as the analyst projects ideas about psychology onto the patient. In the more complicated social setting of *Rocky Horror*, at any time the audience (as one or many), the cast of the floor show, the screen, or the camera could be identified as subject or object, depending on whose gaze is directed where. Furthermore, these assignments of subject-hood and object-hood tell you little about what actions are taking place. In the decades of Lacanian psychoanalytic rereadings and reinterpretations, there have been occasional attempts to attribute some power to the specta-tor/subject; however, Lacanian discourse never escapes the subject-object binary but only complicates it by equating the subject to the object or by using symmetries to multiply dualities (as we previously saw in the list of possible viewer-viewed pairings in the complicated social situation of *Rocky Horror*).

The binary model that Freud developed while dealing with individual patients does not translate well into the cinema, and the ramifications of subject-object splits in general extend well beyond a failure to understand cinema. Binary thinking creates a concept of the viewing subject that ignores the fact that we all see differently based on our situations and experience. It hides the fact that we all have bodies and emotions that affect how we observe the world. It creates a concept of the thinking mind as a disembodied eye, floating somewhere in space, from which it can observe objects in a completely objective, disinterested way. As Slavoj Žižek writes, "It is this very desubstantialization which opens up the empty space (the 'blank surface') onto which fantasies are projected, where monsters emerge" (Žižek 136). Unsurprisingly, this powerful Enlightenment eye (which Freud was not the first or last to imagine he was using) has historically been associated with those in power, and as such, it becomes a justification for all kinds of abuse. For instance, men have been considered the thinking *subjects* and thought to be capable of science and rational thought, whereas women, the emotional *objects*, have been associated with nature. This same sort of objectification has been applied to minority groups by majority groups and to indigenous groups by colonial powers. This subjectification and objectification would seem too simplistic for people to believe, except for the fact that history shows it happening over and over again. Remedying this error in Western thinking (and, ostensibly, its ethical consequences) is supposed to be one of the major motives of Lacanian theory; however, as we have seen, even as Lacanians criticize the subject/object split, they continue to employ it. To the extent to which this binary opposition helps in naming an oppressive relationship, its use is just; however, we contend that thinking in those terms has become habitual in film theory to an extent that it blinds theorists to what happens in the living spaces around them.

Lacanian analysis performs a postmortem on the apparatus of the cinema, breaking down its parts and situating the spectator's gaze as a feature of a cinematic system; however, according to Todd McGowan in "Looking for the Gaze: Lacanian Film Theory and Its Vicissitudes," "the primary problem with 'the Theory' is that Lacanian concepts have been applied to the cinema without regard for the specifics of the cinematic experience itself" (27). McGowan suggests that Lacanian film theory exposes itself to easy criticism because the theorists have been "too modest" and do not explore the true intricacies of Lacan; however, arguably, Lacanian theorists such as Žižek explore the intricacies of Lacanian film theory in a not so modest way (27). McGowan suggests that many have ignored the particulars of the cinematic encounter (44), and he also suggests that those critical of Lacanian film theory mainly find fault with the lack of empirical data to back up the Theory as applied to the cinema: "In short, traditional Lacanian film theory goes too far in its claims and extrapolates too much from its theoretical presuppositions.... It is my contention, however, that traditional Lacanian film theory became a target for these attacks not because of the grandeur of its claims but because of its modesty. The proper response, therefore, is to expand Lacanian analysis of the cinema" (McGowan 28–29).

Toward this purpose, McGowan describes the appeal of giving oneself over to cinematic fantasy: "One reduces the object to the level of an ordinary object, eliminating its Real, traumatic dimension. Fantasy is thus a way of avoiding the Real of the gaze" (36). This "Real of the gaze" refers to the trauma of the other looking back. If you stare at another person and he or she looks back at you, you may feel compelled to look away in embarrassment. You can stare at a screen with impunity, giving you a feeling of power. McGowan is correct that the spectator's gaze needs further and deeper evaluation, and his use of face-to-face encounters makes more sense than the mirror stage for describing the psychology of adults; however, our reevaluation of spectatorship need not remain reverently entrenched in Lacanian film theory. As we see again and again in psychoanalytic approaches, McGowan's description of the spectator's traumatic face-to-screen meeting with the Real once again reasserts the subject–object split.

Those who believe that the Theory provides an adequate description of film psychology and culture err by discounting Baudrillard's theories of simulacra, simulation, and the hyperreal, which allow us to ask the question, "What if there is no 'Real' at *Rocky Horror*?" As we now explain, the spectators' experience can be better understood using Baudrillard's vocabulary of hyperreal simulation because it helps us to recognize the spectators' own acts of creation that contribute to the cinematic experience as well as the entire technology and culture of simulation supporting that experience.

It's So Dreamy, Oh Fantasy Free Me![5]

Lacanians and Marxists have attacked Baudrillard's arguments regarding hyperreal simulation as dystopic, nihilistic, and excessive.[6] Nevertheless, modern critical theory and psychoanalysis cannot accurately describe the postmodern spectator's experience without accounting for how developments in technology and the resulting culture of simulation have transformed our lives. Whereas Baudrillard's hyperbolic style can rightfully be criticized for leaving much of the difficult empirical work to others, it is too much to claim that his theory "rests on some shaky theoretical premises, especially concerning the role of the media" (Kellner). Baudrillard's descriptions, although admittedly delivered in a prophetic style that sometimes conceals their influences, provide a constructive approach to the problem of understanding media.[7]

The postmodern cinematic experience, defined by hyperreality—a symptom of postmodern culture and the condition left after the implosion of images and reality—is more real than real. This Baudrillardian wordplay refers to the elimination of the boundary between the actual and the virtual that sustains the very notion of the real. We can only speak of something being "real" in a meaningful way as long as we can reasonably believe it is distinct from simulation: The real supposedly comes before and is only copied by art; however, we know that our participation in simulation actually produces "real effects." Technology, including the cinema and other media, transforms the earth (and its inhabitants) in an imaginative process; as a result, the real can no longer be said to be truly distinct from the fake. For example, the stock market has become a virtual space in which investors buy and sell symbols that represent pieces of companies almost entirely using communication technologies. What happens in this "nowhere" space transforms our actual physical landscape as economic projects are funded and defunded and buildings go up and shut their doors. One could sensibly ask where individuals live their lives—in those "real" buildings? Or in the virtual mental spaces where we do most of our thinking? What happens on screen—the make believe—has real consequence to us.

Exploring the spectator-as-hyperreal[8] means viewing the space of spectatorship as a space in which people "imitate and instantiate hyperreal simulation models" (Kellner). Anne Friedberg explains Baudrillard's notion of hyperreality as a "representation of the thing replacing the thing—and extends it into a mise-en-abîme of the 'hyperreal,' where signs only refer to signs. Hyperreality is not just an inverted relation of sign and signifier, but one of receding reference, a deterrence operation in the signifying chain" (Friedberg 178). *Rocky Horror* exemplifies this space of signifiers where there is an "escalation of the true, of lived experience, resurrection of the figurative where the object and substance have disappeared. Panic-stricken production of the real and of the referential, parallel to and greater than the panic of material production" (Baudrillard 7). Baudrillard here explains that the demands for authenticity and reality that we find everywhere—for instance, in the safely reproduced "American" scenes of Disneyland—only show we already know existence is "tainted" by simulation. Part of the attraction of an intense simulation is that it can "deter" us from seeing how fully simulation has affected our world. Simulation allows us to believe we can leave it and return to a life of normality; however, normality is structured by simulation. You can turn off your computer, but try turning off the Internet. We demand the real specifically because we suspect that these demands cannot be met. Out of this psychological motive, we fake the authentic.

Let There Be Lips[9]

We don't have to read all cultural performances in such negative terms. The do-it-yourself aspect of *Rocky Horror* and other cult film experiences encourages us to understand participation not as denial or false consciousness of the simulated nature of contemporary reality but as a means of coping with simulation by engaging with it creatively: "Specifically, the postmodern urge to create facsimiles of the self or images perceived as emphatically tied to the self inspires a consciousness of images sensed as unreal, but treated as 'real in their consequences.' Thus, attention to cult movies draws attention to the arcane dress codes associated with the event. People often dress as carefully and elaborately for cult films as for a job interview, perhaps even more so. In both contexts, a proper impression entails attention to an imaginary self" (Katovich and Kinkade 195–96). Cult filmgoers like *Rocky Horror* fans provide an admirable exception to the rule of simulated nostalgia. They do not fake the authentic; they celebrate the monstrous and the fantastic. When psychoanalytic theorists rush in to describe the self-consciously kinky *Rocky Horror* behavior as fetishistic and pathological, they completely miss the point. For example, Henkin quotes a *Rocky Horror* fan who speaks of identification, but engages, rather, in hyperreal simulation: "If you're an enthusiast, you can relate to the characters. I feel quite comfortable relating to Frank on a one-to-one basis. The movie is a takeoff on all the monster and rock 'n' roll and science fiction films. Every type of fantasy personality is in the movie. So it appeals to a wide range of people. Then there's the sheer fun of dressing up and going to the theater" (119). It is hard to conceive of this fan's relationship to *Rocky Horror* as one of simply unconscious identification, either in Metz's sense of self-identification as all-knowing spectator or in the sense of outwardly projected self-wholeness. Instead, the fan dresses up and performs along with the movie, entering a relation of parody with parody. The expanded *Rocky Horror* cast does not pass between states of subject- and object-hood but unsettles those terms altogether to don their getups and thereby become part of the hyperreal simulation. As Kyle Tyson writes, *Rocky Horror* has become a "Bakhtinian carnival—demonstrating that the meaning of texts produced for mass consumption can be appropriated and subverted" (qtd. in Faigley 223). *Rocky Horror* fans again exceed the explanatory capacity of the Theory when they take control of the language of the film by shouting (often in unison) added lines to the film. These acts of agency were even remarked upon in a 1978 *National Review* article: "These night folk surely do want some credit, input, and billing, and to acquire it they've taken one of the most creative steps live theater has seen in years. Audience response to the movie is widespread and often spontaneous. Although certain elements of the audience script remain identical from one location to another, other elements are unique to specific regions, theaters, and even performances. No one knows for certain how talking to the screen developed" (Henkin 12). *Rocky Horror* fans attend the show not just to join the spectacle but also to inject their own punch lines into the show. Their repetitions of the scripts shape the audience as a sort of congregation that continually revises its service by injecting new lines: "Cult filmgoers' paradoxical perspective holds 'nothing is sacred' on the one hand, and 'our film is sacred' on the other" (Katovich and Kinkade 192). Its evolving script relies on the social context of the viewing experience—the theater with its local flavor and the larger social backdrop of current events—and frequently contains political and cultural criticism. Understanding film as a paradigm of hyperreal simulation helps explain the public's desire to view a film multiple times (at the theater, at home, or in another space) or to encounter the same themes, storylines, and myths again and again. In the case of *Rocky Horror*, the repetition gives fans a chance to make their own additions to the Frankenstein myth that has been appropriated through hundreds of films, commercials, and other media.

The hyperreal simulation cannot be missed when one attends a midnight "mass." First, the carefully rehearsed floor show simulates every move, facial expression, and emotion of *Rocky Horror*'s characters. Dressed exactly like the cast member's character, the floor show performer *becomes* the character. Discussing his role as Frank-N-Furter, a cast member told us, "When I am performing, I am not me. I *am* Dr. Frank-N-Furter. When he dies at the end of the film, I am myself again." Tim Curry, in an interview in *Oui* magazine in 1978, says that Frank was an entirely separate, simulated being: "In the film I ended up looking like a rather crazed Bianca Jagger." Speaking of his character as though he is a real individual, Curry says, "Frank loved it; he thought he was finally a movie star" (qtd. in Whittaker 137). Members of the audience who dress in costume do so as an escape from the normalcy and the banality of everyday life, which is not real enough. They, too, simulate the characters they play, seeking acceptance, approval, and praise from the cast members and the film itself in a sort of reverence to the institution. Finally, even uninitiated spectators usually begin simulating as well by jumping up to learn and perform "The Time Warp" along with the Transylvanians on screen (Twitchell 74). Quickly, one learns to shout "Bitch!" or "Slut!" upon hearing Janet's name and "Asshole!" when hearing Brad's. Regulars sell or lend props to virgins so that all can actively and more fully simulate the film.

Although *Rocky Horror* remains a unique and enduring example of how audiences have transformed the cinema, we believe that *Rocky Horror* brings to light what the Theory ignores in typical spectatorship as well—aspects that perhaps could never be expressed under the rubric of spectatorship, which tends to emphasize a dualistic paradigm of subjectivity. Unlike at *Rocky Horror*, spectators do not plan the eruptions of applause and cheering for Sylvester Stallone in the Rocky films (that other *Rocky*), nor do they expect to sob uncontrollably during *The Bridges of Madison County* and *Casablanca*, but nevertheless they do—repeatedly. Spectators desire their involvement, their hyperreal simulation, even when it causes them anxiety and sadness, again and again. Even after multiple viewings of the same horror film, someone will tell a character, "Don't open that door!" Has that participant really forgotten they are not watching a "real" event? Has he or she really forgotten she is at the movies? Or, does the spectator engage in simulation like a fan of *Rocky Horror*? Does it matter? Internal and (sometimes) external dialogues, common at *Rocky Horror*, exist for every spectator during both marginalized and mainstream film. Just because a spectator chooses to follow a theater's rules regarding silence does not mean he or she escapes the involvement of simulation. Even though we know *Apollo 13* returned to Earth, we sit on the edge of our seat during the Tom Hanks film, hoping that "we" return home safely. A man viewing *Titanic* exclaims urgently, "Slow down! You are going to kill everyone!" In these moments, we literally forget ourselves, and our status changes from that of spectator to that of hyperreal simulation, "merging with the film" (Katovich and Kinkade 196):

> This insatiable hunger for shows and the increasing reliance on mediated rather than real experience marks off what Baudrillard terms an "ecstasy of communication" that defines postmodern life and culture. And this ecstasy is "obscene," he maintains, "because today there is a pornography of information and communication, a pornography of circuits and networks, . . . of the visible, the all-too-visible, the more visible than visible." This is the age of simulations and the simulacra, of mediated representations and reproductions, images and signs that have taken up the place of objects and commodities in the fabric of social, everyday life. (Kokonis)

The engaged spectator at *Titanic*, similar to engaged spectators of any film or film-like medium, believes the inevitable to be preventable. Although if one pretends to watch from the outside, this spectator may seem ridiculous, the psychological commitment to simulation of the shouting filmgoer only reflects the degree to which signs constitute our environment. In a culture of simulation, more is at stake in "suspended disbelief" than merely the ability to take a fictional ride. The spectator's choice to enter the theater and play along can equally represent the desire, on the one hand, to enter a fictional space to pretend that the rest of life is authentic, or on the other hand, to allow one's simulated identifications to go down with the fictional ship.

Film simulation does not contain itself within the movie house. Many films allow corporations to capitalize on the spectators' desire for hyper-real simulation. *Evita*, for example, launched a line of cosmetics allowing women to *become* Madonna's Evita before leaving home, and lightsaber toys became available at stores very early in the life of the *Star Wars'* franchise. This is not simply Halloween but the human-become-simulacra—the spectator simulating an imaginary original. Film can still be escapist, but does the audience seek to escape reality, or the reality that there is now only simulation? Or, does the audience use film as a means to embrace the simulated nature of postmodern life, as those things that we choose to simulate together we might also choose to simulate differently? Every subculture testifies to the possibility of bringing into being a different way of being, whether by holding fast to an earlier technological state like the Amish or by attempting to bring filmic technology to life, as with the Trekkies.

Conclusion: Removing the Cause But Not the Symptom[10]

Baudrillard's explanations allow us to recognize the audience's role in the enactment of *Rocky Horror* as a proactive, creative—even ethical—means of coping in a simulated society. In the film and in the ritual of the film, the dualistic nature of gender, power structures, master/slave relationships, and distinctions between virgin and whore are literally blown up. *Rocky Horror* spectators mark this implosion during the last moments of the film with relative quiet as their simulated "Christ"/Frank and "Adam"/Rocky lie dead, and the "Church"/Castle no longer exists. The apocalyptic finale mocks the nostalgic panic accompanying the breakdown of the binaries that prop up not just oppressive structures but also the Theory that ostensibly means to question them: "And crawling on the planet's face, some insects called the human race. . . . Lost in time and lost in space and meaning," *Rocky Horror*'s conclusion evokes Baudrillard's concept of implosion in which the dualities that have provided the traditional source of meaning collapse. For the fans who have found in *Rocky Horror* a socially inclusive space, however, one wonders whether this orgy of simulation that collapses inward does not contain some utopian hope for a larger collapse. After all, *Rocky Horror* and film in general have a greater meaning than merely as a commodity circulated within a larger capitalist system. As we learn from Baudrillard, the capitalist system itself can be fruitfully understood as the enactment in everyday life of filmic (hyperreal simulated) reality. The simulation within the movie house and the simulation of the greater economy may be of different orders, in that people place greater stake in the value of virtual Enron than they do in the meaning of a movie. However, signification is a slippery business: Meanings fall away, and with them value.

Though *Rocky Horror* is shown in "classic" movie houses where "shhh!" has been the law and focus has resided on the screen, it is performed through creative imitation and deviance with the screen as a psychological-theatrical setting. *Rocky Horror* is not best described as a cooperative effort of subjects who become objects as they watch it and each other. It is not something *seen* so much as a *scene*—a playground of interacting desires. This *Rocky Horror* play has serious consequences for film theory. It tells us that Lacanian film theory provides a sorely incomplete description of what is really going on at the movies, and it shows us this by magnifying the spectators' active and collaborative role in simulating film and other media. Although unique in its specific character, *Rocky Horror* is not an exception to the rule of spectatorship. *RHPS* and other cult films should be seen as exaggerations that showcase the roles played by the postmodern spectator. Thus, although we agree that "*The Rocky Horror Picture Show* does a superb job of unveiling the hidden dynamics of the committee of the unconscious mind" (Ruble 163), in recognizing this inner committee—the multiple forces that act within each of us—we should not forget the "outer committee"—the social scene that people are born to encounter and often go out to find in the evenings, such as at *Rocky Horror*.

Works Cited

Banash, David. "Reading Baudrillard." 89.1 (2003): 123–29.

Baudrillard, Jean. *Simulacra and Simulation*. Ann Arbor: U of Michigan P, 1994.

———. *Simulations*. Trans. Paul Foss, et al. New York: Semiotext(e), 1983.

Benjamin, Walter. "The Work of Art in the Age of Mechanical Reproduction." 15 Feb 2004. http://www.marxists.org/reference/subject/philosophy/works/ge/benjamin.htm (accessed March 8, 2005).

Berger, John, et al. *Ways of Seeing*. London: BBC and Penguin-Allen Lane, 1972.

Burgyan, George. "The Rocky Horror Picture Show Movie Script." 3 May 1993. http://www.alwaysontherun.net/rhps.txt (accessed March 17, 2005).

Faigley, Lester. *Fragments of Rationality: Postmodernity and the Subject of Composition*. London: U of Pittsburgh P, 1992.

Friedberg, Anne. *Window Shopping: Cinema and the Postmodern*. Berkeley: U of California P, 1993.

Henkin, Bill. *The Rocky Horror Picture Show Book*. New York: Penguin, 1979.

Katovich, Michael A., and Patrick T. Kinkade. "Reading Rocky Horror." *The Sociological Quarterly* 33.2 (1992): 191–209.

Kellner, Douglas. "Boundaries and Borderlines: Reflections on Jean Baudrillard and Critical Theory." *Illuminations: The Critical Theory Project.* http://www.gseis.ucla.edu/faculty/kellner/Illumina%20Folder/kell2.htm (accessed March 17, 2005.

Kokonis, Michael. "Postmodernism, Hyperreality and the Hegemony of the Spectacle in New Hollywood: The Case of the *Truman Show*." http://genesis.ee.auth.gr/dimakis/Gramma/7/02-kokonis.htm (accessed March 17, 2005).

Lapsley, Robert, and Michael Westlake. *Film Theory: An Introduction.* New York: St. Martin's, 1988.

McGowan, Todd. "Looking for the Gaze: Lacanian Film Theory and Its Vicissitudes." *Cinema Journal* 42.3 (2003): 27–47.

Metz, Christian. *Film Language: A Semiotics of the Cinema.* New York: Oxford UP, 1974.

———. *The Imaginary Signifier: Psychoanalysis and the Cinema.* Bloomington: Indiana UP, 1977.

Mulvey, Laura. "Visual Pleasure and Narrative Cinema." *Visual and Other Pleasures.* Bloomington: Indiana UP, 1989. 14–25.

Richter, Richard P. "Baudrillard, Jean. *Simulacra and Simulation.* May 5, 2004. http://webpages.ursinus.edu/rrichter/baudrillardone.html (accessed March 8, 2005).

Ruble, Raymond. "Dr. Freud Meets Dr. Frank N. Furter." *Eros in the Mind's Eye: Sexuality and the Fantastic in Art and Film.* Ed. Donald Palumbo. New York: Greenwood, 1986. 161–68.

Skal, David J. *The Monster Show: A Cultural History of Horror.* New York: Faber and Faber, 1993.

Twitchell, James. B. "Frankenstein and the Anatomy of Horror." *Georgia Review* 37 (1983): 41–78.

Whittaker, Jim. *Cosmic Light: The Birth of a Cult Classic.* Altoona, PA: Acme Books, 1998.

Willemen, Paul. "Voyeurism, The Look, and Dwoskin." *Narrative, Apparatus, Ideology: A Film Theory Reader.* Ed. Phillip Rosen. New York: Columbia UP, 1986. 210–18.

Wood, Robert E. "Don't Dream It: Performance and *The Rocky Horror Picture Show*." *The Cult Film Experience: Beyond All Reason.* Ed. J. P. Telotte. Austin: U of Austin P, 1991. 156–66.

Žižek, Slavoj. *Enjoy Your Symptom!: Jacques Lacan in Hollywood and Out.* New York: Routledge, 1992.

Notes

1. In David J. Skal's *The Monster Show: A Cultural History of Horror*, he points out that audience participation, specifically in the horror genre, is not a new phenomenon, as "surrealists were fond of disrupting films like *Nosferatu* with shouted litanies of the kind that decades later would attend *The Rocky Horror Picture Show*" (54).

2. See script, section 80 (Burgyan).

3. Todd McGowan holds that psychoanalytic film theory primarily analyzes the spectator's master gaze, which he claims to be a misreading of Lacanian theory. McGowan, who is primarily concerned with the spectator's gaze, claims the gaze is an occurrence of the *objet petit a*—the moment where the "object looks back . . . a traumatic encounter with the Real, with the utter failure of the spectator's seemingly safe distance and assumed mastery" (McGowan 29).

4. McGowan points out that "David Bordwell and Noël Carroll simply label Lacanian film theory 'the Theory'" (27).

5. During the performance of the "Time Warp," Magenta exclaims, "It's so dreamy, oh fantasy free me / So you can't see me, no, not at all / In another dimension, with voyeuristic intention / Well secluded, I see all." Richard O'Brien's lyrics here suggest Magenta's turn to the fantasy as discussed in this essay.

6. This is in reference to an online review of Julia Witwer's *Reading Baudrillard: The Vital Illusion* by David Banash.

7. Frankfurt School author Walter Benjamin's 1936 "The Work of Art in the Age of Mechanical Reproduction" offers a Marxist precursor to Baudrillard's idea of simulation. Benjamin states, "In principle a work of art has always been reproducible. Man-made artifacts could always be imitated by men. . . . Mechanical reproduction of a work of art, however, represents something new. . . . Even the most perfect reproduction of a work of art is lacking in one element: its presence in time and space, its unique existence at the place where it happens to be. . . . The presence of the original is the prerequisite to the concept of authenticity." Richard P. Richter addresses the Frankfurt School's influence on postmodernity as well: "Baudrillard . . . may be seen at the task that the Frankfurt School set for itself years before: to analyze social reality so closely that the analysis will burst it from within and reveal a new and better arrangement. Baudrillard belongs in the first rank of critical theorists because of the intention that his tone unmistakably identifies" (Richter).

8. Anne Friedberg explains Baudrillard's notion of hyperreality as a "representation of the thing replacing the thing—and extends it into a mise-en-abîme of the 'hyperreal,' where signs only refer to signs. Hyperreality is not just an inverted relation of sign and signifier, but one of receding reference, a deterrence operation in the signifying chain" (178).

9. Before the film begins, *Rocky Horror* spectators chant, "A long time ago, in a galaxy far, far away, God said: 'Let there be lips,' and there were. And they were good." This audience comment merges the beginning words of *Star Wars* with language from *Genesis*, seriously and comically placing their ritual on the same level as a blockbuster film and a religious text.

10. Dr. Frank-N-Furter addresses the suburban virgins, Brad and Janet, in the song "Sweet Transvestite." He suggests the cause for their arrival at the "Frankenstein Place," a blown tire, doesn't matter. Their symptoms (the need for the implosion of gender dualities, the need for sexual liberation, and the need for escape from a restrictive suburban structure contained neatly within a white picket fence) would have freed them from their naïve view of the world eventually regardless.

6

Wild and Untamed Thing

The Exotic, Erotic, and Neurotic
Rocky Horror Performance Cult

Michael M. Chemers

Is not the most erotic portion of the body where the garment gapes?

—*Roland Barthes, The Pleasure of the Text*

Whatever happened to Fay Wray?
That delicate, satin-draped frame?

—*Frank-N-Furter, "Don't Dream It"*

Barthes' question, simply asked and simply answered, provides a fertile field of inquiry for *The Rocky Horror Picture Show* performance cult; Frank's query, in contrast, is startlingly complex. The cult is a phenomenon, apparently unique in American history, which by definition exists at a perceived "edge" of our culture, on that slender dividing line between the forces that regulate our cultural consumption and those that seek its destruction, like the edge of a garment as it falls away from naked flesh. The cult is the flaw, the crack where the façades of pop counterculture and bourgeois conservatism meet and sometimes painfully mingle, a gap

This project was generously supported by a postdoctoral research fellowship from the Center for Arts in Society at Carnegie Mellon University.

through which flows a narrative of liberation, both sexual and social—fresh enough to keep its devotees weird decades after our initiations into its sacred mysteries—and like all sacred mysteries, the clearer it becomes, the more tenuous and precarious is its existence. Born outside the light and familiar warmth of popularity and success, the cult gestated and grew in the twilight zone—as do all states of bliss, ever on the edge of collapse. Ironically, it may prove that those forces that seek most strongly to preserve the cult will contribute most mightily to its dissolution, as they endow the new rituals established by the cult—subversive and therapeutic surrogates for the conformity rituals they assaulted—with the very authority they originally struggled so desperately to subvert.

What Charming Underclothes You Both Have

> Neither culture nor its destruction is erotic; it is the seam between them, the fault, the flaw, which becomes so. The pleasure of the text is like that untenable, impossible, purely *novelistic* instant so relished by Sade's libertine when he manages to be hanged and then to cut the rope at the very moment of his orgasm, his bliss.
>
> —*Roland Barthes, The Pleasure of the Text*

Barthes locates the origin of erotic desire neither in total nudity nor total coverage but in the intermittent state, the flash of flesh at the edge of a low collar, or the sweet sensual gap of a bare midriff between shirt and pants. This, too, is *Rocky Horror*'s eroticism: the rhythmic revelation of fishnet stockings, the allure of supple flesh rippling along the harshly rigid upper rim of a merry widow. It is, very specifically, an eroticism drawing from the performative tension between the known and unknown, the explored naked flesh and the forbidden skin concealed by the clothing. *Rocky Horror*'s creator Richard O'Brien, actor, playwright, cross-dresser, in a recent interview, linked the supremacy of bourgeois morality to the decline of the sensuality of royal court dress and the rise of the repressive dark suit of the Victorians ("Cast Interview: Richard O'Brien"). This sense of clothing as therapy was present long before the film was made, during the tumultuous period of the show's onstage existence. Patricia Quinn reported that Tim Curry was unable to "find" the character of Frank until he stepped into his platform shoes; "The high heels did it for Tim," she reported ("Cast Interview: Patricia Quinn"). Meat Loaf walked out of rehearsals at the Los Angeles Roxy when he learned he had to appear in fishnets; cajoled back into the cast, he ultimately experienced a faith healing concurrent with his character's, Dr. Scott's, when the crowd erupted in celebratory laughter as he revealed the leggings beneath his conservative lap quilt ("Cast Interview: Meat Loaf Aday"). The eroticism of *Rocky Horror* has a great deal to do with the clothing of the characters: Preppy protagonists Brad and Janet are stripped of their bourgeois pretensions as they are stripped of their middle-class clothing and, naked, are reclothed in the liberated transsexual getup of the floor show; Riff Raff sheds his stooped posture and hunchback even as he trades his servant's rags for a futuristic transvestite military uniform, in which he appears rail-straight during his personal minirevolution (see Figure 6.1). However Frank-N-Furter's goals in the film are not merely to satisfy his superhuman lust but to rebuild Brad and Janet, as he did Rocky, in his own image—an ambiguous body, even a freakish one, one in which the breaking down of sexually repressive boundaries could begin.

Whether O'Brien had internalized the lessons of Michel Foucault's *History of Sexuality* is not expressly clear, but his dress-up-play-*qua*-social-therapy program worked. Of the play's London staging, O'Brien reported that "Our first reviews revealed to us that we'd done something exceptionally right. Somehow or other, perhaps by chance or accident, we'd done something very clever of which we were never aware. It was a very interesting sociological kind of footnote; it was that a man wearing fishnet stockings and high heels was turning on the *women* in the audience" ("Cast Interview: Richard O'Brien").

Accident it may have been, but in the late '70s, as the United Kingdom and the United States witnessed the triumphs of proto-neo-conservatism in the persons of Maggie and Ronnie, it was a happy, happy accident for

Figure 6.1

those of us aching for some kind of alternate mode of being. The erotic transgression that began in Frank's sweet transvestite, transsexual body and spread like a luxuriating disease to Brad's and Janet's classically rigid bodies would not stop until it had blurred boundaries that would extend to the very tradition of audience spectatorship.

Of course, in the final analysis, it is that performance cult that snatches *Rocky Horror* from B-movie oblivion. Robert E. Wood notes in his 1991 article "Don't Dream It" that the exuberant rise of the performance cult succeeded where the general tradition of neo-avant-garde theater spectacles of the 1970s had failed in their attempts to trigger an emotional and spiritual liberation of the theater audience (156–66).[1]

Sponsored by the sacerdotal class of intellectuals and artists who set themselves up as the prophets of a modern cultural revolution only they themselves could understand, the neo-avant-garde had a tendency to descend into a sort of perverse sadism that appeared desperately to need to humiliate and confound its audience: The turn-of-the-century goal of the avant-garde to *épater le bourgeois* in a Dionysian ecstasy of dissolving boundaries manifested itself only too often as a sort of quasi-aesthetic *schaudenfreude*.

Wood's point is well taken, but he fails to observe concerning the phenomenon that the success of the *Rocky Horror* cult, as compared with the theatrical avant-garde, was, fundamentally, its love. Whereas the neo-avant-garde described the desire to assault and shock its audience, the *Rocky Horror* cult seemed to want only to embrace it. The cult became the sexual fetish that desired the fetishist, the *fumisme* that turns its laughter on its own *fumistes*. Because of this self-consciousness, the cult, unlike most events developed by the avant-garde theater, offers surrogate rituals to replace those it undermined, creating a new sense of *communitas* that exists not within the mainstream aesthetic, and not within the radical deconstruction that seeks to destroy that aesthetic, but balanced precariously as a dream on the sensual, erotic, liminal, theatrical space that adumbrates both conformity and its opposite—an ecstatic gestalt of the total utterance. That is the erotic appeal of *Rocky Horror* and her wild cult, the delicious combination of sexual repression and its subversion, the permissible and the forbidden, the revealed flesh and the concealed.

This kind of ambiguous erotic aesthetic lends itself well to ecstatic cult behavior because it emphasizes the ambiguity of the human body itself. Mikhail Bakhtin observes in *Rabelais and His World* that such ambiguity is the font, refuge, and excuse for total freedom of thought and action in a personal as well as social sphere. The most liberatory aspect of the body is its very grotesqueness; the body is unclassifiable, not least because it is always in the process of *transforming* into something else. The hierarchy of normal society cannot contain or explain this wonder, and so that hierarchy is revealed to be an imperfect construct of limited utility: "Such concepts as becoming, the existence of many seeds and of many possibilities, the freedom of choice, leads man towards the horizontal line of time and of historic becoming. Let us stress that the body of man reunites in itself all the elements and kingdoms of nature, both the plants and animals. Man, properly speaking, is not something completed and finished, but open, uncompleted" (Bakhtin 364). This is the body element in its most utopian aspect; undeniably erotic, an ecstatic union of separate selves into a single grotesque but communal entity of multiple bodies orgiastically manifested in Frank's swimming pool: a single body, wearing a single costume, housing multiple merged people, arms, legs, mouths, breasts, genitalia.

Elsewhere, Riff Raff's hunchback becomes indicative of a pregnant belly, swollen with his own rebirth as dominator—a grotesque echo of the round perfection of Janet's hitherto-unmolested breasts. Rocky's monstrous, hypersexualized, hyperconditioned body possesses its own grotesqueness[2] in opposition to the irresistible fat rock and roll sensuality of Meat Loaf's Eddie, with whom he shares a single brain. Even the classically sexy Columbia and Magenta are rendered celebrationally grotesque during the climax of "Touch-A, Touch-A, Touch Me," when we, the audience, vicariously experience taking the submissive position as Janet, to be fucked missionary-style by all the film's characters. In addition, the Transylvanian conventionists, who appear as the lineup of a nineteenth-century ten-in-one freak show (a long-honored tradition of the performance of erotic boundaries and their subversions), include a person of short stature, a skeleton-dude, obese persons, and several persons who appear hermaphroditic. The conventionists are, we ultimately discover, their own avantgarde—the first wave of an invasion of Earth by a species of transvestite aliens from a distant galaxy, where "transsexual" is not a lifestyle choice but a galactic identity and tribal marker.

Frank-N-Furter, of course, has the most transgressive and ambiguous of all the film's bodies. Modeled in Richard O'Brien's words, on "a combination between Eisenstein's Ivan from *Ivan the Terrible Part One*, and the Wicked Queen from Snow White" ("Cast Interview: Richard O'Brien"), Frank is, as Amittai F. Aviram observes in his 1992 article, a sort of postmodern Dionysus, a transformational—indeed, in some ways, transcendent—figure that can switch genders and sexualities as it suits his whims and schemes.[3] Similar to Dionysus in Euripides' *The Bacchae*, Frank's body encompasses the sacred and profane, native and alien, animal and human, human and divine, divine and demonic, subject with object (of desire), the living with the dead, male and female, sub and dom, sadist and masochist; in all, a Bakhtinian bursting forth of Hell in a sensual, even sexual, cornucopia of abundance. Frank lives on Barthes's erotic edge, like Dionysus—at once a thing and its opposite, yet never wholly either. It is this ambiguity that gives him his seductive power over Brad and Janet, mired in their static, hierarchical eroticisms. However, Brad and Janet's bodies are equally grotesque; through the unique practice of the cult in performance the abnormal is rendered commonplace and the idealized, bourgeois bodies of Brad and Janet become understood by the cult as diseased. They are outcast, and the cult is instructed to affix on them the labels of their diaspora from Frank's polymorphous polyamory: "Asshole!" and "Slut!" Denton is Hell, and Frank, the medical genius, has the only cure: rendering their hierarchical, seemingly finished and closed bodies into open, transcendent ones by penetrating them (literally and figuratively), creating orifices of pleasure where once only senseless, mechanical organs existed.

Admittedly, of the four participants in the floor show who have ostensibly been "liberated" by Frank's healing hypersexual energy, only Janet appears to be able to handle it; the others complain of the "trouble and pain" engendered by their lack of control (Columbia's loss of faith in Frank, Rocky's uncontrolled heterosexual libido, Brad's infantile longing for his lost bourgeois innocence condensed into his plaintive cry: "Help me, Mommy!"). Janet's refrain, in contrast, is an unqualified celebration:

> I feel released
> Bad times deceased
> My confidence has increased
> Reality is here.
> The game has been disbanded
> My mind has been expanded
> It's a gas that Frankie's landed
> His lust is so sincere!

One of my students suggested that Janet gains the most from Frank's program of sexual liberation precisely because she is, after all, a slut. In any case, her song of thanksgiving to Frank invokes the queening alien's temporary apotheosis as a transvestite RKO radio demigod, manifested in a song about Fay Wray's dress in *King Kong*. It is, as Janet observes, the sincerity of his lust—unbounded and, like the *logothete* de Sade's, encompassing repression and transgression in one omnivorous appetite—that she appreciates.

However, for Bakhtin, Barthes, and O'Brien alike, the ecstasy is temporary—its inevitable catastrophic implosion adding savor, all the more seductive for its very impermanence. Even Frank's new sexually open miniverse must fall prey to the new order sponsored by Riff Raff's jealousy, three-pronged antimatter dildo/pistol ("that's hard to come by," quips the cult), and quasi-militarist quasi-conservatism, leaving our newly liberated characters in their smeared makeup and lingerie writhing on the ground in the exhaust of the castle-spacecraft like spent lovers, worrying about how, or perhaps if, they can ever return to the sexual conformity nightmare that is Denton.

It's the sincerity of its lust, I argue, that engendered the *Rocky Horror* performance cult and nurtured it through thirty years. It's a sincerity only rendered more sincere by its fragility and ephemeral nature, and only its consistent association with a lack of sincerity of lust could undo it.

It's Not Easy Having a Good Time

The success of *Rocky Horror* came out of the failure of *Rocky Horror*. I think that if *Rocky Horror* had come out and been moderately successful it might be gone today. The fact that it failed and we had to look for an alternative way of exhibiting it was added to what became the phenomenon.

—Lou Adler, "VH-1: Behind the Music"

Mad I cannot be, sane I do not deign to be, neurotic I am.

—Roland Barthes, *The Pleasure of the Text*

It seems that the failure/success *pas de deux* that *Rocky Horror* dances is primarily a result of the facility with which the film lends itself to *subversion* of conventional boundaries, but not entirely to their *dissolution*. *Rocky Horror*'s dance is on the commercial edge of failure/success as much as it is on the erotic edge of safe/forbidden sexuality. As was true for the theatrical avant-garde, official success and critical acclaim for *Rocky Horror* would have destroyed the performance cult before it could ever be born. It requires no stretch of the imagination to understand *Rocky Horror*'s underground counterculture success, as Adler describes, as a function of its failure in the "official" bourgeois commercial film universe. In fact, it does not seem out of bounds to suggest that the very eroticism of *Rocky Horror*, which is the basis of its cult success, is derived in no small part from the film's illegitimacy and rejection by all things elite and hierarchical. Of course, of all the subversive qualities of *Rocky Horror*, none is so interesting as its subversion of audience behavior conventions; perhaps what Twentieth Century Fox has failed to understand is that the new traditions of eroticism and boundary breakage that the *Rocky Horror* cult generated are intensely fragile, surviving only so long as they can maintain that razor's edge ballet on the rim between radical revolution and corporatized officialization: One step too far in either direction, and they must shatter.

Robert E. Wood's conclusions notwithstanding, the historical theatrical avant-garde and *Rocky Horror* actually have much in common: primarily their shared predilection for redefining the boundaries that separate the spectator of the art piece from the producer. I say predilection rather than desire, for the *Rocky Horror* cult was never designed; to attribute an aesthetic motive to the cult's activities would be at once a gross overstatement and a callow injustice to the cult's most salient feature: its spontaneous, autochthonous self-generation. In the first step of the proposed avant-garde cultural shock therapy, the audience would be jolted out of their dependence on bourgeois aesthetic rituals, which throughout the past two centuries or so have cultivated a sense, even in the theater, of isolated, individual reflection on art, negating the older, more atavistic desire for a communal experience of shared wonder and spiritual growth. Thus, the spectator would, with theater's help, emerge into a new, liberated and self-determined identity, arrived at through the action of participation in performance. It is performance, of course—in this case that of living cultists—that provides *Rocky Horror*'s most striking and long-lasting radical innovations.[4]

It is, however, the surrogate rituals that interest us—those that the film and cult generate to replace the stodgy conventions they subvert. Some are recognizable (the predictable patterns of science fiction and horror films remain intact; the couple in the car, the dark road, the forbidding castle, the monster running amok, etc.), and some are innovated (the Time Warp and elbow sex, for instance). Most significant to this study is the subversion of the bourgeois aesthetic ritual of passive cinema spectatorship, which is utterly annihilated in the *Rocky Horror* cult performance and replaced with something rich and strange—an audience with no spectators and a cast of living actors that brings the hitherto-unalterable images of the silver screen down to earth, where they can be manipulated for the end goal of liberating each participant.[5] This subversion works because it rejects nothing: Similar to the film's sincere, all-inclusive lust, the cult's monstrous creativity loves the repressive as well as the rebellious elements of its multifarious construction.

In the best traditions of *fumisme*, and with enough vandalism to the theater to satisfy even Marinetti, the cult adores even as it mocks. The stuffy Criminologist is the paragon of the normal, hierarchical body, stuffed into a rigid gray suit that echoes only faintly the stiff corsets of sexual liberation later in the film. His sophisticated good looks are markers of classical, normative beauty. For the cult, however, Gray's prominent cleft chin, classically a coveted marker of masculine beauty, becomes a vaginal opening to be titillated and finger-fucked by a cast member, who caresses it with his hands as he will later to do Janet's screen-image breasts. Gray's neck vanishes into his Victorian armor, a source of endless running gags from the congregation. For the Criminologist, as the film's bourgeois moral center who holds himself up as an "authority" on deviance, is reserved the iciest of the congregant's vicious play: They even trick him into describing his own testicles as "heavy, black, and pendulous." Every piece of information he delivers is rendered ridiculous, superfluous, and fatuous, but not negated, by the actions of the congregation, who change his (and everyone else's) power to mean what they mean:

> CRIMINOLOGIST: And so, by some extraordinary coincidence, fate, it seems, had decided that Brad and Janet should keep that appointment with Dr. Everett [Scott].
> CONGREGATION: (over) [Snot!]
> CRIM: But it was to be in a situation which none of them could have possibly foreseen.
> CONG.: Was it a picnic?
> CRIM: And just a few hours after announcing their engagement, Brad and Janet had both tasted [forbidden fruit.]
> CONG.: (over) [Frank's furter] at a picnic.
> CRIM: This in itself was proof that their host was a man of little morals . . .
> CONG.: No morals!
> CRIM: And some persuasion.
> CONG.: BOTH persuasions!
> CRIM: What further indignities were they to be subjected to?
> CONG.: A picnic?
> CRIM: And what of the sonic transducer and floor show that had been spoken of? What indeed? From what had gone before, it was clear that this was to be . . .
> CONG.: A picnic?
> CRIM: No picnic.
> CONG: (Coda) Awwwwwwwwwwwwwww.[6]

However, the Criminologist's representative power, callously ripped from him by the cult's actions, is later returned to him when his sudden halting of a spinning globe sends cast members who had been riding it careening headlong around the stage. His power to mean is returned to him: His final word is "meaning," and the cast responds ritualistically, singing "me-eee-ning" as the film ends. The Criminologist is a *teacher*—he instructs the congregation on how to do the Time Warp and does it himself standing on his desk with such childlike enthusiasm that goes a long way toward recouping the cult's adoration. The pattern is equally true of Asshole Brad and Janet the Slut:

A windscreen wiper working under strain. Torrential rain on the windscreen.
  Brad concentrating on visibility. Janet eating chocolates and listening to the car
  radio playing Nixon's resignation speech.
  [During this shot, the cast pretend to move the wipers back and forth. Some of
  the congregants will start spraying water around prematurely.]
  CONG.: Only virgins squirt too soon.

Objects become rendered into their own subjects, and the cast hovers
between objectivity and subjectivity, player and that which is played on.

  CONG.: Hey, Dick, have you ever been a quitter?
  NIXON: I have never been a quitter.
  CONG.: Bullshit!
  NIXON: To leave office before my term is completed goes against every instinct
    in my body.
  CONG.: You call THAT a body?
  NIXON: But as President . . .
  CONG.: You call THAT a President?
  NIXON: I must put the interests of America first.
  CONG.: What does America need, Dick?
  NIXON: America needs a full-time President.
  CONG.: Is that all?
  NIXON: And a full-time Congress. Especially at this time . . .

This is no ordinary presidential speech: This is the nadir of presidential
speeches, the speech that by its very utterance unspeaks every other presidential utterance. This is the most subversive presidential speech in American history, and the *Rocky Horror* cult consumes it, devours its poison like
eager coprophiliacs at a banquet. The scene continues:

  A motorcycle roars past them.
  JANET: Gosh, that's the third motorcyclist that's passed us. They certainly take
    their lives in their hands. What with the weather and all.
  BRAD: Yes, Janet. Life's pretty cheap to that type.
  CONG.: Yay, that type!

Here, the freaky conventionists appear for the first time, springing whole
from the darkness like hellspawn monsters from the womb of chaos itself.
The road is closed: They can only have come from the abyss of outer space.
Cult practice elevates these characters to the level of minor gods to be wor-
shipped: They are cheered and mimicked by the congregation multiple
times, even from this first ambiguous appearance. Their presence changes
everything and derails the bourgeois quest of Brad and Janet to secure a

marriage blessing from their high school science teacher Dr. Everett Scott, whom, we have earlier learned, began their romance by urging Brad to "give [Janet] the eye and then panic." It's a stupid quest, but then, Brad's an asshole, and he is now confronted by the limits of his abilities and scope in the form of a blocked road.

> *The car slows to a halt.*
> JANET: What's the matter Brad darling?
> CONG.: Make a sound like a cow!
> BRAD: Mmmmm . . . I think we took the wrong fork a few miles back.
> CONG.: Asshole!
> CAST: But then where did that motorcycle come from?
> JANET: But then where did that motorcycle come from?
> CONG.: *(hums the theme from "Twilight Zone.")*
> BRAD: Hmmmm. . . . Well, I guess we'll just have to turn back.
> CONG.: Don't turn back, Asshole!
> *Car reverses. Brad puts his foot on the accelerator. The wheel skids and explodes.*
> JANET: What was that bang?
> CONG.: A gangbang, Slut!
> BRAD.: We must have a [blow-out].
> CONG.: (over) [Blow-job!]
> CAST: Right here in the car?
> JANET: Oh . . .
> BRAD: Dammit!
> *The congregation claps once together.*
> BRAD: I knew I should have gotten that spare tire fixed.
> CONG.: Asshole.
> BRAD: You just stay here and keep warm while I go for help.
> JANET: But where will you go? We're in the middle of nowhere.
> CONG.: They're in Utah!

Regionalisms abound, making each performance of the cult at once comfortingly familiar and startlingly unique. The cult also encouraged a tendency for regionalisms to be picked up and spread. Sal Piro, President of the Rocky Horror Fan Club, discovered that innovations of his own had been picked up by cults across the country, and I myself was startled to hear innovations I knew were specific to my home congregation in Salt Lake City repeated years later in New York and Chicago:

> CAST: What's white and sells hamburgers?
> BRAD: Didn't we pass a castle back down the road a few miles?
> CONG.: [cheers]

It is worth mentioning that Susan Sarandon's entrée into the world of serious dramatic acting would eventually follow her role as a waitress at a "White Castle"–inspired burger chain who seduces an uptight preppy Brad-type in the critically acclaimed film *White Palace*.

Passive spectatorship is eliminated from the film event in a manner very specifically hostile to and, at the same time, very loving of bourgeois conventions and sexual ideologies. Nixon's resignation, Brad's elitism, and Janet's antifeminism are hyperbolized and assaulted by the congregation, but later, so is Frank's oversexed behavior, Riff Raff and Magenta's incest, and Columbia's exposed nipples. The new cult dialogue is, then, actually a conjunction of the traditional and the transgressive, obscenely liberating and highly sexually charged. The film's counterculture moral center, exemplified by the song "Don't Dream It, Be It" (another referent to the sexual liberation power of clothing, a corporate slogan lifted by O'Brien from a Frederick's of Hollywood lingerie catalog), strives for a moment of Dionysian ecstasy when the stultifying self-negation of conformity to socially constructed barriers is transcended in the pleasurable sexualized healing of O'Brien's deranged, boundary-blurring high-heel fetish *communitas*.

Rocky Horror cult performance is subtle, despite its raucous front. It is not really attempting to annihilate the conventions it ridicules but is creating a dialogic relationship embracing warmly both social hierarchies and those forces that seek their dissolution. Just as Frank's sexual paradise consumes itself until it becomes vulnerable to Riff Raff and Magenta's fifth-column sabotage, the *Rocky Horror* cult embraces both the tyrant and the rebel. Barry Bostwick, at the twentieth anniversary convention, asked the assembled Rockyphiles in a self-deprecating way to admit that few of them played the asshole Brad in their home theaters, and he appeared genuinely surprised when a significant portion of the crowd gave forth with an enthusiastic cheer ("VH-1"). Bostwick, whose own response to the performance cult was, by his own admission, Brad-like (he complained, "Wait! You can't hear the movie, dammit! Wait a minute! They're shouting over my lines! Why are they calling me 'asshole?'" ["Cast Interview: Barry Bostwick"]) seemed reluctant to accept that the cult, the fetish that loves the fetishist, would be as ready to embody its own beloved sluts and assholes as it would its groovy gender-bending aliens. But it is . . . or, rather, was.

Whatever Happened to Saturday Night?

Nothing has stopped it. Three administrations at Fox couldn't kill it, and Ronald Reagan couldn't kill it. I don't see what could stop it.

—*Lou Adler*

I think it's time, in a way, to hang up your mesh stockings and high heels and move on. . . . Just don't build your lives around acting out on Saturday night, you know? Life's too short.

—*Barry Bostwick*

At the time of this writing, *Rocky Horror* is dying, vanishing from American cinemas, and the glorious, monstrous reconfigurations of its exuberant cult are vanishing along with it. Traveling in the country in the mid-1980s, when I was a regular participant in *Rocky Horror* performance, it seemed that every town large enough to have a cinema had a *Rocky Horror* performance cult. While researching this article between 2000 and 2003, I discovered a vibrant community of self-proclaimed Rockyphiles in three midsized American cities (Seattle, Des Moines, and Pittsburgh) but was informed in each case, with some scratching of heads, that the midnight movie no longer regularly played. A search of the "official" *Rocky Horror* Web site at http://www.rockyhorror.com reveals that many of the listed casts no longer assemble, or even maintain a Web site. What forces could conspire to remove the performance cult from the vast popularity it once enjoyed, when critical and authoritative derision only sustained the tradition for nearly three decades?

From the perspective of the avant-garde theater, one might be able to trace a causal connection between the cult's decline and the renewed attempts by Twentieth Century Fox to "officialize" the event. The company hosted a grand and wildly popular Twentieth Anniversary convention in 1995, where Tim Curry got a massive ovation for saying "It's so comforting to know there are so many people in the world sicker than I am. I think I'm the only person in this room that doesn't look like me." Five years later Fox released a very flashy and exquisitely produced two-disk DVD set with "official" biographies and filmographies of the cast and crew (emphasizing their post–*Rocky Horror* successes and accolades), behind-the-scenes cuts, a featurette in which an aging Richard O'Brien performs an "unplugged" version of the "Time Warp" (lacking, I'm sad to say, Riff Raff's simmering resentment and leering sexuality), and a feature that includes the recording of an "official" audience participation aspect of the performance that "contains members of one of RHPS's finest audiences interacting with the movie as only veterans can." Unfortunately, the call-and-response is utterly lost in a sea of noise. The DVD also has a "participation prompter" feature that purports to "inform you when it's time to misbehave."

Following this release, *Rocky Horror* in its original stage form was revived on Broadway, on the stiletto heels of a delightfully perverse revival of *Cabaret*. This trend suggests less that Broadway is morally loosening up than that the borders of what art bourgeois aesthetics renders acceptable for consumption are expanding to envelope territories once forbidden— territories that can no longer provide a refuge for avant-garde artists.

From the point of view of the historical avant-garde, nothing could be more disastrous for this cult performance event that can exist only at the fringe of a culture than to be "officialized" by the very systems of bourgeois aesthetics that it ostensibly was created to ridicule and subvert. It seems unlikely that the participants in the event would fail to see these incidents, as I do, as an attempt to co-opt and commodify the performance cult not for the purposes of preservation but to secure more control over the cult's money-making potential for Fox. Even if that is not the case, the acceptance of the film and play by the bourgeois mainstream certainly robs the rebellious and revolutionary savor from the cult for all but the most die-hard congregants. Although I do not begrudge Sarandon her great success, I do not particularly relish the knowledge that the woman I knew as Janet, for instance, is now a famous honoree of the Academy of Motion Picture Arts and Sciences, a fiscally motivated edifice of bourgeois aesthetics that once turned up its nose at *Rocky Horror*. Such recognition rather takes the subversive antibourgeois, sexually liberating *jouissance* out of cult participation, especially if you have an expensive DVD at home telling you "when it is *time* to misbehave." Ho-hum. This is tantamount to trying to add to Fay Wray's electric sensuality in *King Kong* by removing the satin dress entirely and having the ape carry her up in the nude. It wasn't just her delicate frame that attracted Frank to transvestism, as he explains in the bridge of "Don't Dream It," it was the dress clinging to her thigh.

I loved *Rocky Horror*. I will always remember my initiation into its mysteries as a celebratory abandonment of an innocence I suddenly understood as naiveté; the film helped me to recognize that I had no use for it. The *Rocky Horror* cult made me weird, and I still feel weird. I played Riff Raff in theaters all over the United States when I was a teenager. Am I, then, in my incarnation as a professional historian, a hapless stepchild of the lecturing Criminologist, to drive the final nail into *Rocky Horror*'s cult coffin? Even writing about the event as a professional scholar, as I have done here, for an anthology of critical scholarship on *Rocky Horror*, citing much of my evidence from the very DVD I neurotically despise and treasure, is likely to contribute to its demise. I'm sensitive to this irony.

The *Rocky Horror* cult, similarly neurotic, has found a new existence in American living rooms, perhaps gaining a renewed sense of purpose in bringing life to a room long deadened by the omnipresence of television. As Aviram wrote more than a decade ago, though, "There is a deep irony in the celebration of this cult privately at home, however, an irony which would seem powerful enough a reason to have forestalled distribution of the *Picture Show* on video hitherto. The irony is that the Rocky Horror Cult ought to be celebrated in public spaces, late at night in the dark, and not trivialized by suburban solitude and trips to the kitchen for beer" (183). It's difficult not to be seduced by Aviram's Dionysian sensibilities. It is *Rocky Horror*'s eroticism that engendered its cult, and *Rocky Horror*'s eroticism is an extension of its ability to straddle discursive boundaries, to be at once one thing and another, yet never wholly either. The more this cultural product is officialized, the more private the performance cult, the less erotic it feels. The increasing commercialization of *Rocky Horror* comes to resemble the paradoxical slope Baudrillard observes in relation to science: To live, its object must die, and like Orpheus, it is doomed always to turning around too soon to watch in helpless horror as the thing it desires most plunges backwards into Hell (Baudrillard 7). Similar to de Sade's autoerotic libertine, we are in danger of being strangled by the very source of our pleasure. The official/forbidden cult performance at the Midnight Movie felt transgressive and exciting; officially sanctioned cult performance in your living room is just pathetic. Even as I write this closing, though, I can already hear the truly die-hard fans calling down the wrath of the postmodern Dionysus on my head, insistent that their own group maintains the traditions in the most time-honored, public, sex-drenched ambiguous style—that *Rocky Horror* will never *truly* die.

More power to you, you twisted freaks.

Works Cited

Aviram, Amittai F. "Postmodern Gay Dionysus: Dr. Frank-N-Furter." *Journal of Popular Culture* 26.3 (1992): 183–92.

Bakhtin, Mikhail. *Rabelais and his World.* Trans. Helene Iswolsky. Bloomington: Indiana UP, 1984.

Barthes, Roland. *The Pleasure of the Text.* New York: Hill and Wang, 1975.

Baudrillard, Jean. *Simulacra and Simulation.* Ann Arbor: U of Michigan P, 1997.

Fischer-Lichte, Erika. *The Show and the Gaze of Theater: A European Perspective.* Iowa City: U of Iowa P, 1997.

Grant, Barry. "Science Fiction Double Feature: Ideology in the Cult Film." *The Cult Film Experience, Beyond All Reason.* Ed. J. P. Telotte. Austin: U of Texas P, 1991. 122–37.

Harding, James. *The Rocky Horror Show Book*. London: Sidgwick and Jackson, 1987.

Harding, James M. "Introduction." *Contours of the Theatrical Avant-Garde*. Ed. James M. Harding. Ann Arbor: U of Michigan P, 2000.

Hoberman, J., and Jonathan Rosenbaum. *Midnight Movies*. New York: Harper, 1979.

"Cast Interview: Barry Bostwick." *The Rocky Horror Picture Show* DVD. Dir. Jim Sharman. [1975]. 20th Century Fox, 2000.

"Cast Interview: Meatloaf Aday." *The Rocky Horror Picture Show* DVD. Dir. Jim Sharman. [1975]. 20th Century Fox, 2000.

"Cast Interview: Patricia Quinn." *The Rocky Horror Picture Show* DVD. Dir. Jim Sharman. [1975]. 20th Century Fox, 2000.

"Cast Interview: Richard O'Brien." *The Rocky Horror Picture Show* DVD. Dir. Jim Sharman. [1975]. 20th Century Fox, 2000.

Lindsay, Cecile. "Bodybuilding: A Postmodern Freak Show." *Freakery: Cultural Spectacles of the Extraordinary Body*. Ed. Rosemarie Garland-Thomson. New York: New York UP, 1996. 356–67.

McDonald, Bruce. "Semiology Goes to the Midnight Movie." *Et Cetera, A Review of General Semantics* 37.3 (1980): 216–23.

Minor, Mary Eden. *The Folklore of Mass-Mediated Celebration: Audience Participation at the Rocky Horror Picture Show*. Diss. Lafayette: University of Southwestern Louisiana, 1995.

Piro, Sal. "It Was Great When It All Began." *The Rocky Horror Fan Club Home Page*. March 3, 2004. http://www.rockyhorror.com/history/howapbegan.php.

Senelick, Lawrence. "Text and Violence: Performance Practices of the Modernist Avant-Garde." *Contours of the Theatrical Avant-Garde*. Ed. James M. Harding. Ann Arbor: U of Michigan P, 2000. 15–42.

Studlar, Gaylyn. "Midnight S/Excesses: Cult Configurations of 'Femininity' and the Perverse." *The Cult Film Experience, Beyond All Reason*. Ed. J. P. Telotte. Austin: U of Texas P, 1991. 138–54.

"VH-1: Behind the Music." *The Rocky Horror Picture Show* DVD, 2000.

Wood, Robert E. "Don't Dream It: Performance and the *Rocky Horror Picture Show*." *The Cult Film Experience: Beyond All Reason*. Ed. J. P. Telotte. Austin: U of Texas P, 1991. 156–66.

Notes

1. For a lengthier survey of the aspirations and shortcomings of the theatrical avant-garde, please consult Harding, Senelick, and Fischer-Lichte.
2. On the grotesque attraction of bodybuilding as a relocated freak show, see Lindsay.
3. Aviram's analysis, although deeply provocative and resonant, does raise a few eyebrows. Aviram makes several minor errors in the events of the film and their sequence, and I would certainly take exception to the notion that the *Rocky Horror* performance cult restricts its liberating sexual energy to homosexuality.

Rocky Horror's sensibilities, as O'Brien previously notes, have proven equally effective on heterosexual eroticism; I argue that it is the movement between the two, represented by Frank's omnivorous bisexuality, that makes the cult seductive to all of its audience—straight, gay, and bi—and progressively equalizes all forms of lust in a nonhierarchical orgiastic soup, permitting the one to play in (and with) the other; as it were, a dalliance along the edge of the safe and the forbidden, as along Barthes's unclothed and clothed body. This reading is not inconsistent with Aviram's observations and traditional readings of Dionysian cult worship, regarding Maenadism. Therefore, the deeply positive, affirmative erotic fallout from *Rocky Horror* and its cult need not be limited to the gay sub/counterculture in modern America: Straights can be weird, too.

4. *Rocky Horror* critics and scholars have already described the many filmic and bourgeois rituals that the film alone is designed to complicate through the employment of such Bakhtinian notions as carnival, grotesquerie, and billingsgate, as well as gender role subversion and semiotic reconfiguration. The film contains a wedding, a proposal, an academic lecture, a presidential speech, a formal party, a medical theater, a formal dinner, a floor show, a faith healing, a class revolution, and a picnic. However, the wedding becomes a homosexual one, the speech is Nixon's resignation, the party is part of an alien invasion, the medical theater devolves into a Frankensteinian monster creation, the dinner is cannibalistic, the floor show and faith healing turn out to the sexual liberation of the film's stodgiest characters, the class revolution is conducted by space aliens, and there is, ultimately, no picnic (see also the following: Studlar, Telotte, Grant, Hoberman and Rosenbaum, McDonald, and Minor).

5. The origin of the audience participation tradition of the cult is dubious. Certainly the tradition began during the play's stage life in London, where audience members as elite as Mick and Bianca Jagger might have thrown Kit-Kat bars at the stage (see Harding). Meat Loaf relates that Carole King appeared at the Roxy performances in Los Angeles dressed as Magenta ("Cast Interview: Meat Loaf Aday"). How the audience participation transferred over to the showing of the film is likewise murky. Individuals like Louis Farese, Jr., or Sal Piro and the Waverly Cinema group may claim to have "invented" or innovated certain aspects of the *Rocky Horror* phenomenon (see Piro), but by no stretch of the imagination could these individuals be imagined to be responsible for the proliferation of the cult and the persistence of this phenomenon on a nationwide scale for the best part of three decades with very, very few instances of, or even attempts at, overt promotion or officialization. During the late '70s and throughout the '80s and '90s, a traveler could find a welcoming community of initiates on a Saturday midnight in almost any American township, just as an ancient devotee of Dionysus would find welcome in communities of initiates anywhere in Hellas he might have roamed. Tracing the evolution of the cult would require an extraordinary historical effort, as regional innovations have been transmitted and diffused around the country into the multitudes of performance communities. I myself have played Riff Raff in six cities, welcomed by the locals with open arms each time,

and found the event to be replicated in startling uniformity between communities, apart from regional variance (in Salt Lake City, for instance, the congregants responded to Riff's threat to Frank: "Say goodbye to all of this and hello to oblivion" with a choral cry of "helloooooo Utah!"). The *Rocky Horror* performance cult is also subversive of traditional economic relationships that exist between a producer and a consumer of art. Influential avant-garde theatrical producer Max Halbe believed such subversion was a critical first step in destabilizing the aesthetic superstructure that rests on the base of commodity exchange: No free aesthetic could exist so long as it remained lashed to the wheels of commerce and market demand (see Senelick 23–24). To the extent that *Rocky Horror* casts do not pay for admission, that the cult tends to trash the theater (requiring cleanup costs), and that the projectionists takes his cue to begin the film from the *cast* and not from the theater manager, traditional commercial relationships are undermined.

6. All screenplay quotes in this text are from Jim Sharman and Richard O'Brien's *The Rocky Horror Picture Show, a screenplay.* Cast and congregational additions are my own additions, taken entirely from memory of personal experience and not from the "official" DVD audience participation feature.

7

"What We Are Watching" Does Not Present "Us with a Struggle"

Rocky Horror, Queer Viewers, and the Alternative Cinematic Spectacle

Nicole Seymour

From its advent, the film medium has had a complex relationship with its audience. As Miriam Hansen summarizes, "in [the late nineteenth and early twentieth centuries], cinema figured as part of the violent restructuration of human perception and interaction effected by industrial-capitalist modes of production and exchange" (362). In this early period, multitudes of people would crowd into neighborhood music halls and storefront nickelodeons to see moving trains, chaotic city streets, and other dynamic images of the newly industrialized world (Belton 350). For the average American, then, the turn-of-the-century film experience was inextricably

---

As Alexander Doty writes, "I am using the term 'queer' to mark a flexible space for the expression of all aspects of non- (anti-, contra-) straight cultural production and reception.... Various and fluctuating queer positions might be occupied whenever *anyone* produces or responds to culture" (338). To the term "straight" I would like to add capitalist, normative, mainstream, and so on; in troubling many norms of film exhibition and film viewing, the alternative cinematic spectacle benefits queer people in particular, and those uninterested in the status quo film experience in general.

connected to both "spectacularism" and capitalism; film itself was a reflection and a producer of those particular social features.[1]

Several decades later, a cultural anomaly that I have dubbed the "alternative cinematic spectacle"—a participatory event in which the film text plays just one part, though an indispensable one—speaks to the same obsessions, but with important differences: The *presentation* of the film, not its content per se or even the act of moviegoing itself, becomes the main spectacle, and these presentations particularly trouble the capitalist system that normally inheres in moviegoing. With this specific formula in mind, I argue that, despite not necessarily being homosexually inflected or even advertised as such, alternative cinematic spectacles such as *The Rocky Horror Picture Show* midnight screenings, *The Sound of Music* Sing-a-Long-a events, and the Cinespia film screenings at Los Angeles's Hollywood Forever cemetery constitute queer experiences.[2]

Although Alexander Doty warns that an emphasis on "notions of audience and reception leaves you open to the kind of dismissive attitude that sees queer understandings of popular culture as being the result of 'wishful thinking' about a text or 'appropriation' of a text by a cultural and/or critical special interest group" (4), I show that the queerness of these alternative cinematic spectacles does not simply emanate from their content or from individuals' "wishful thinking" about that content—be they filmmakers, viewers, or exhibitors. Rather, the queerness inheres in a set of transgressive acts both encouraged and allowed for by the spectacle, including inscribing oneself into the film text, purging internalized norms of film-watching (norms that either render one an alienated entity or demand one's complicity in an ideological project), and the perpetuation of a recursive, alternative film economy. Thus, to rephrase Tamsin Wilton's complaint about "film, by and large," these cinematic spectacles do not categorically force the queer or otherwise marginalized viewer into an ideologically, psychologically, or morally depleting struggle (353).

In 1975, the film version of Richard O'Brien's hit rock musical *The Rocky Horror Show* (retitled *The Rocky Horror Picture Show*) debuted to abysmal reviews and minimal box office returns. Over thirty years later, the film has a rabid cult following and continues to spawn everything from CD box sets and books to its own *Guinness Book of World Records* entries.[3]

Queer viewers have long been part of this following—as Scott Michaels and David Evans report, the movie's second run was launched at two Manhattan theaters "frequented by gays, students and punks" (9)—but I argue that this has less to do with *Rocky Horror*'s specifically homosexual content than with the radical "viewing/survival" strategies that viewers typically deploy during the movie's screenings. These strategies developed out of and continue to speak to the outsider status of the audience members, and they have found their way into other alternative cinematic spectacles such as Sing-a-Long-a and Cinespia for similar reasons. Despite their characteristic location in pointedly alternative events, these strategies also suggest productive ways for queer and marginalized viewers to approach and read the average, mainstream film text; the innovation, creativity, and spontaneity they exemplify indicate that filmgoing need not always be a passive, rote experience, nor a solely analytical one devoid of personal enjoyment.

One might call the secondary *Rocky Horror* "script" the most famous example of such a strategy. Prompted by dialogue or action, audience members hurl various insults, comments, and interjections at the screen—this is no "reception in a state of distraction," to quote Walter Benjamin (240). Many of these comments are now classic, but they are by no means regulated or regularized—Liz Locke's essay "'Don't Dream It, Be It': The Rocky Horror Pictures Show as Cultural Performance" notes how the script shifts over time and depending on place, with new comments popping up in different contexts.[4]

Of course, even if the audience comments have taken on the form of ritual to some degree, their very existence speaks to a fundamentally radical move on the part of the alternative cinematic spectacle: simultaneously undermining the "authority" of the film text and shattering its highly fictive nature. For example, when Barry Bostwick and Susan Sarandon's characters first appear onscreen, audience members shout out "slut!" and "asshole!" Doing the same in a regular movie theater would not simply disturb others but would demolish the much-needed illusion that, in the darkened theater, we are privy to some real conversation, some actual interaction that we are quietly and submissively to observe. Yelling "asshole!" at a character means stepping out of one's normally occluded and subordinate place in the audience and exposing the reality of what Christian Metz calls the theater's "segregation of spaces" (217). In speaking at or toward the screen, the attendees of alternative cinematic spectacles make it clear that they know the film to be a fiction; although it may be open and inscribable in a certain sense, as I discuss below, it is also impervious to the degree that the actors cannot hear us, and we are thus free to "talk back" to them. Such a recognition of film's falsity has even further liberatory implications for the queer viewer: Being hyperaware of film's fictional nature means knowing the filmic exclusion of the queer subject to be merely incidental, though it may be personally troubling.

Although the audience's verbal actions—following a participation "script," singing along, booing and cheering, and making spontaneous remarks and imperatives (e.g., yelling "kiss him!" to Rock Hudson's character in *Written on the Wind*, which was screened at Hollywood Forever in August 2003)—presuppose a fictive, artificial text, they do much more by penetrating that text in a transgressive, empowered/empowering manner. By adding a nondiegetic soundtrack, so to speak, audience members can comment on the film, insert new meanings into it, and inject sexual—often homosexual—innuendo where there was little or none before. The audience thus renders the film a malleable, living text, one at the mercy of their whims, perspectives, and particular cultural position(s).[5] In Roland Barthes's terms, the films at the center of these cinematic spectacles are "writerly texts," meaning that the audience does not "simply consume the text but 'writes' it in their act of reading" (Hollows, Hutchings, and Jancovich 193). Even though nothing indicates that the filmmakers intended the "sutures" of these films to be opened, however, the audience can and does open them.[6] In fact, we could refine Barthes's theory to say that the "writerliness" of a text does not depend on the text itself—or, rather, on any antimainstream machinations by the screenwriter, director, cinematographer, and so forth. Instead, it depends on the audience being committed to rendering the text as such. Coming from a disenfranchised and underrepresented vantage point, the queer viewer may be particularly inclined toward, or even well-versed in, this kind of cultural reinterpretation—as Wilton writes, "queer consumers (and producers) of culture [may be] so accustomed to self-consciously inhabiting contradictory viewing/reading positions as to make us preeminently skilled deconstructionists" (348). More important, queer viewers in the alternative cinematic spectacle may ultimately find more pleasure and reward in verbally penetrating or deconstructing a film than either Barthes or Wilton seem to expect; they have a unique and public opportunity to write their personal experience into a film that may have otherwise lacked familiar representations.[7]

If verbal participation represents one way of disrupting the normative film-viewing process and writing oneself into the text—thereby ameliorating or precluding the alienation that the queer viewer typically experiences in mainstream film—physical participation represents another. *Rocky Horror* and *Sound of Music* viewers bring various props that are launched, disseminated, or sometimes just displayed at certain points in the films' trajectories. For example, *Sound of Music* Sing-a-Long-a attendees wave bunches of fake white flowers during Julie Andrews' and Christopher Plummer's rendition of "Edelweiss"; *Rocky Horror* attendees dance the "Time Warp" along with the Transylvanian conventioners and squirt water from water guns or spray bottles when it rains onscreen. By thus mirroring the actions of the soundtrack, actors, or plot, viewers of the alternative cinematic spectacle can put themselves *inside* the screen as well as reposition the screen's boundaries to include the world immediately *outside*. Either way, they give film viewing a more democratic angle, rather than accepting it as a hierarchical system in which they occupy the passive and unrepresented bottom rung.

Rocky Horror actually takes this participation ethos one step further by having separate live casts (or shadow casts) simultaneously act out the story in front of the screen (after a famous line in the film, these performances are known as "the floor show").[8] These participatory actions cause the usually hermetic categories of "audience" and "actors" to break open and bleed into one another, in a tumultuous reworking of Metz's aforementioned "segregation of spaces" (217). Although a theater production unfolds in the same space and time in which the audience exists, just from a different perspective, Metz says films are from another dimension altogether—a dimension necessarily removed from the audience because the production period has since passed. Although the era in which Rocky Horror was shot has indeed passed, the employment of a separate live cast certainly troubles the idea that a film necessarily becomes sealed-off and "done" once it has been committed to the negative—that it becomes detached from an authentic "aura," per Walter Benjamin (221). (In fact, if audience participation can be said to show that the cessation of studio production does not necessarily make a film complete, then perhaps no discrete "original" exists to be depreciated in the first place, to play off of Benjamin's terminology.) Together, the floor show cast and the physically participating audience prove that a film need only be a jumping-off point for creative (re)inscription—not a finalized or univocal object that necessarily oppresses certain viewers when it neglects to represent them.

Physical participation in the alternative cinematic spectacle also troubles another definitive idea about narrative cinema: the doubly false nature of film posited by Metz's "Imaginary Signifier" essay.[9] For example, when one watches cowboys chase Indians across the plains in a Western, not only are the cowboys and Indians physically absent from the theater but these men are actually just actors on a set. In other words, the average film captures an event that is simultaneously intangible and unreal. However, the alternative cinematic spectacle has the potential to disturb this "double falsity" on both counts while simultaneously preventing its internalization. In the cases of Sound of Music and Rocky Horror, the mimesis of the audience, the inclusion of physical props that both mirror and simulate the onscreen action, and the machinations of live actors make the film's action physically as well as visually present. The film's story, and even aspects of its physical setting, are thus real by virtue of the fact that they are respectively happening and existing inside the theater. The two most basic tenets of the regular narrative film experience—fake action and inorganic presentation—have thereby been dismantled, and the contents of the film text have been externalized, rather than internalized by a passive audience.

Aside from the verbal and the physical, the external mise-en-scène of audience costuming also allows attendees to "see" or "write" themselves into the film text. The majority of attendees at these special *Rocky Horror* and *Sound of Music* screenings dress up as characters from the films and often participate in costume contests. Although dressing up as a film character confers a certain degree of reverence on him, her, or it, such an act still has particularly queer radical potential.[10] First, in the case of *Rocky Horror*, both the floor show cast members and the regular audience members dress up as characters in the film. This multipositional, multidirectional transvestitism creates a complex network of identification and power that disturbs the hierarchical relationships between the filmed body and the live body, the performing body and the nonperforming body: relationships that are intrinsic to the mainstream film-viewing experience as well as that of theatergoing. It also complicates the normally sound designations of "cast members" and "audience members." Add to this the possibility of literal transvestitism, and participation via clothing has an even more radical, and queer, dimension. For example, in the *Sound of Music* sing-along screenings, children, women, and men alike dress as nuns, and in *Rocky Horror*, both men and women reenact Tim Curry's transvestite role as Dr. Frank-N-Furter—which further disrupts the supposedly stable categories of gender and sexuality on which cinematic identification so often depends.[11]

In fact, the highly performative nature of the alternative cinematic spectacle—that is, people are not just performing songs and dramatic parts but also exposing the fact that everything from normative film viewership to gender is a performance of sorts[12]—means that attendees are getting closer to a true identification with the film text than one usually has the chance to become, especially if one is queer. Although Benjamin writes that the film actor "lacks the opportunity of the stage actor to adjust to the audience [and,] consequently, the audience's identification with the actor is really an identification with the camera" (228), a completely different scenario takes place in the alternative cinematic spectacle. In the case of *Rocky Horror*, stage actors actually exist alongside screen actors. Furthermore, in their mimetic and parodic movements, the regular audience members in both *Rocky Horror* and *Sound of Music* can also be called actors in their own rights. By specifically positioning themselves in the clothing of certain characters, and with their particular accoutrements and mannerisms, all of these attendees are more likely, and better enabled mentally, to cut out that mediating camera and locate themselves on the screen and vice versa. The "mental machinery" that has "adapted [spectators] to the consumption of films" (Metz 213)—a machinery that rests on the supposition that one has to identify with at least one film character even if none of them looks like you, lives like you, or loves like you—has now begun to operate in a wholly different, and less alienating, manner.

At this point, the cultural contexts of the films that these alternative cinematic spectacles revolve around should be considered. As a classic family film devoid of any explicit discussion of sexuality whatsoever, *Sound of Music* does not offer any obvious overtures to the queer community or "underground" society as such. The films screened at the Hollywood Forever cemetery also tend to be classics (*Sunset Boulevard* [1950], *Strangers on a Train* [1951], etc.) with no overt "queer credentials," aside from possibly having camp cachet in their outdated language and depictions. Nonetheless, the staging of both of these spectacles creates an alternative space to which queer people are attracted—more than simply being "abnormal," the events transgress the norms set by an obvious and present exemplar of wholesome, mainstream culture. The event thus becomes highly charged, and even eroticized, by the prospect of inserting a perverse element into a revered text—a prospect that the participant can instantly make real. As the Web site for the Prince Charles Theatre in London proclaims, "this special screening [of *Sound of Music*] comes equipped with subtitles to all the songs, allowing you the pleasure of experiencing an incestuous, exhilarating bonding session with a few hundred other fruitcakes as you sing-along to such classics as Climb Every Mountain, Do Re Mi, and of course, Edelweiss [*sic*]." Costumes and spontaneous vocal participation aside, the fact that *Sound of Music* sing-along has been framed in terms of incest and "fruitcakes" fundamentally alters the film text and its possible meanings. Indeed, attendees heeding such advertising may be even more inclined to read queerness into or onto the text than they would have before.

Unlike *Sound of Music* and the films of Cinespia, of course, *Rocky Horror* was anything but "classic" or revered from its first appearance. Nevertheless, O'Brien's music, visuals, and dialogical references situate it solidly in the tradition of the mainstream blockbuster, nodding to *The Wild One* (1953) here, spoofing *Frankenstein* (1931) there, and so on. The opening song itself, "Science Fiction/Double Feature," actually provides a catalog of noteworthy horror and science fiction films ranging from the 1930s to the 1960s:

And *Flash Gordon* was there in silver underwear
Claude Rains was *The Invisible Man.*
Then something went wrong
for Fay Wray and *King Kong*
they got caught in a celluloid jam.
Then at a deadly place *It Came From Outer Space*
And this is how the message ran.

Although not necessarily respected by critics—or even all audience members—most of *Rocky Horror*'s and science fiction's referents are well-known, modern American movies that have become ingrained in the popular consciousness for one reason or another.[13] Science fiction movies often featured a straight, masculine hero and a corresponding feminine love interest—images that still figure into social expectations and pressures years after the films themselves began to look outdated. By drawing on such a weighty and substantial cultural heritage, the bizarre and often hilarious plot of *Rocky Horror* manages to upend cinematic conventions of storyline, characterization, gender roles, and sexuality, lampooning both the mainstream Hollywood film and mainstream morality. In building a cult around such a film, fans not only endorse its critiques but also perform the same cultural work, though of course with an added level of mediation. So whereas O'Brien was immediately responding to and playing off of an established film tradition, *Rocky Horror* devotees enthusiastically respond to this response and participate in the warping (and queering) of the classic/popular narrative film by way of the 1975 pastiche.

Although these alternative cinematic spectacles manage to take an average film—or, in the case of *Rocky Horror*, a patchwork of somewhat canonical film and literary texts—and rework its content, they are perhaps most radical in their subversion of politics as usual. Simply put, participation in one of these spectacles does not implicate the viewer in the film market in the same way that simply "going to the movies" does. This would seem to be a distinct boon for the queer viewer, who often faces the decision of either boycotting mainstream films because of their heterocentric, heterosexist, or even homophobic nature (a choice that alienates them from the rest of the filmgoing populace) or viewing them anyway and feeling at least financially, if not philosophically, complicit in their ideology. In fact, identity issues momentarily aside, film viewing often seems to be part of a circular, inescapable pattern of reinforcing the ideological/ political status quo—Metz discusses how paying for admission "makes it possible to shoot other films" (213), and Jean-Luc Comolli and Paul Narboni state that, "as a result of being a material product of the system, [a film] is also an ideological product of the system, which in France [and, we could add, just about everywhere else] means capitalism" (197). Thus, attending a film not only perpetuates the production of further films but also further perpetuates capitalism, which in turn both dictates and inheres in film production. If, then, capitalism rules the day, issues that do not immediately concern those who govern the modes of production (e.g., queer representations and sensibilities) necessarily drop out of the film economy altogether.[14]

Alternative cinematic spectacles both remedy and circumvent the aforementioned pitfalls. Although they can never take the place of "going to the movies"—primarily because they literally center on the same old films most of the time—they pointedly do not set up the dead-end choice between seeing and complying or avoiding and being alienated, the choice that the queer viewer usually faces at the cinema. Moreover, they also circumvent what Wilton envisions as a more attractive third option for the marginalized viewer. She writes of her "queer-chameleon ability to adopt an alien reading position for the night," to go on "queer holiday" when watching a movie (351–52). Although this may be more adaptive or immediately gratifying as a viewing strategy, it still reeks of a defeatist or even voluntary collapsing of critical distance, a lá Jennifer Hammett—a move that radical queer theorists and feminist critics such as Mary Ann Doane would certainly lament.[15] In any case, this third option simply does not apply to an alternative cinematic spectacle: Although a classic or otherwise mainstream film might be its focus, the very fact that it has been presented as something of a "special event" immediately introduces a level of critique and critical distance into its reception while simultaneously exhorting the viewer not to take the film so seriously in the first place. In this light, Doane's distinction between "submission and critique" (Hammett 247) becomes irrelevant, as these positions are no longer mutually exclusive. To use Hammett's own terms, the alternative cinematic spectacle does not pose or construct an "ideological impediment," first because the event has been staged as participatory rather than submissive, and second because participation and commentary have been staged as entertainment. Moreover, the queer viewer no longer has to take an evaluative position organized around whether or not a film immediately applies to him or her. As alternative cinematic spectacles do not "expect" or encourage viewers to leave themselves or their interests at the door and "just enjoy," the enjoyment actually comes from bringing oneself and one's interests along and writing them into the text.

The alternative cinematic spectacle also subverts politics as usual in a specifically socioeconomic sense. *Rocky Horror* mainly plays at art houses and independent movie theaters, a phenomenon that, in many cases, indirectly underwrites the exhibition of nonmainstream and, often, queer films. Moreover, Robert E. Wood explains that, even in its initial run, *Rocky Horror*'s (relative) success depended on "repeat business" (162), rather than on wide appeal to a large number of one-time viewers—as is the case with most films. Ironically, such repeat business manages to subvert the cultural state of things spelled out in works such as Benjamin's "The Work of Art in the Age of Mechanical Reproduction." In that essay, Benjamin expresses concerns about the fascist potential and capitalist nature of contemporary art, writing that "the technique of reproduction detaches the reproduced object from the domain of tradition," substituting "a plurality of copies for a unique existence" (221). Although *Rocky Horror* is surely no exception to the phenomenon of mass reproduction—VHS and DVD copies of the film are widely available—the nature of its public exhibition ensures that even identical prints of the film will not have the same "life." The unpredictable and ever-changing nature of the spectacle, resulting from new audience members, slightly differing and never-static "scripts," different staging choices, and so on, ensures that a given film print will enjoy a "unique existence," even though it may not be the only one of its kind, and even if it never leaves the confines of one particular theater.

The Sing-a-Long-a series also changes the typical process of film exhibition by virtue of being, essentially, a brand-name product. Acting as the intermediary between the film company and the theaters, Sing-a-Long-a secures the rights to a film, including the right to run the lyric captions on the screen, and then farms the event out to various host theaters. The films are then marketed as "Sing-a-Long-a *Sound of Music*" or "Sing-a-Long-a *Wizard of Oz*," and so on, which immediately marks them as alternative or altered versions. Tickets are sold directly through the company, as well as through booking agents and the theaters themselves, which also tend to be independent or historical venues; thus, no regular "box office" exists, or at least not one in which the Sing-a-Long-a films are evaluated or judged alongside current releases. The cinematic spectacles that Cinespia hosts at Los Angeles' Hollywood Forever cemetery—which, of course, has no real theater to begin with, a fact that fundamentally changes the aesthetics of the viewing experience—also incorporate film prints that have to be specifically procured for the occasion. In fact, many of the prints that Cinespia shows are rare ones that first require restoration—a fact that provides the very film print with an almost literal aura.[16]

All of the previously mentioned instances speak to the fact that the alternative cinematic spectacle does not, as Metz says, "ensur[e] the auto-reproduction of the institution" (213). Although some of the prints involved in these alternative cinematic spectacles may have been purchased or rented from a mainstream film company, the fact remains that they are not circulating in the same institutional economy in which most movie releases exist. For example, *Rocky Horror*'s exhibition trajectory (not to mention its financial history) has been wildly unpredictable: As Sal Piro explains in *"Creatures of the Night"*: The Rocky Horror Picture Show *Experience*, "the film was considered a failure and did not get a wide release and was shelved. Then, on April Fool's Day, 1976, Tim Deegan, a young advertising executive at 20th Century Fox ... persuaded Bill Quigley to replace the midnight show at the Waverly Theater with [*Rocky Horror*]" (1). Moreover, "long after its initial run, the film continues to be distributed and promoted by its producers ... far more widely than was ever planned" (Wood 157). Importantly, unlike the typical filmgoing state of affairs, the (potential) popularity of particular alternative screenings does not perpetuate the institutional cycle that produces new films—which would thereby constitute a "reproduction of the system." Rather, such popularity extends to, and potentially enacts, the restaging of the *same* film. As Gregory A. Waller explains, the spending power of "midnight moviegoers . . . becom[es] a directly determining factor, since the films they patronize will be booked—revived—again and again, so long as 35 millimeter prints are available and the films turn a profit." In contrast, "the paying customers at a first-run multicinema can in part determine how many weeks a particular film might be booked, but not whether the film will be repeatedly revived after its first run" (180). In fact, Waller's idea that midnight movies constitute a genre suggests that the aforementioned patronization actually has the power to determine the cultural placement of a given film.

Taking all of the above into account, we might consider Comolli and Narboni's claim that "no film-maker can, by his own individual efforts, change the economic relations governing the manufacture and distribution of his film" (197). This statement that may look different in our age of digital video, the Independent Film Channel, and so on, but it essentially holds true in a capitalist society. However, the alternative cinematic spectacle proves that at least certain events can upset these relations by changing the normal distribution and consumption pattern—and by placing viewers, not just filmmakers, in the position of changing the economic (and social) relations referred to previously. More than just constituting alternatives to the mainstream cinematic economy, these events set up their own microeconomies in which the central texts are involved in radical self-reiteration. In fact, if we consider that the reproduction of social and economic relations is a key concern in much Marxist criticism,[17] we might say that such events present us with a truly queer version of reproduction: an unpredictable process of reinstantiation that refuses to replicate normative social structures.

Although these central texts are restaged in ways that circumvent the normative film economy, *Rocky Horror* attendees explicitly play out this idea of radical self-reproduction among themselves. The *Rocky Horror* spectacle includes (or, as some might even argue, centers around) the "devirginizing" ceremony: First-time attendees are usually branded with a "V" in lipstick or marker on their foreheads and brought onstage for a mock group sex ritual, during which other audience members may yell insults, encouragement, or (homo)sexual comments at them. (The very fact that "virgins" are singled out from the larger crowd indicates that most attendees have seen *Rocky Horror* before and actually see it on a fairly regular basis—which again echoes the idea of the same film being transmitted and transacted over and over, yet with a difference each time: the uniqueness of the particular setting, the composition of the audience, and so forth.) *Rocky Horror* fans thus beget other *Rocky Horror* fans in a sort of nonsexual, though highly sexualized, mode of reproduction. In a mythological sense, this ritual seems to hearken back to the colloquial ideas about "homosexual reproduction" that modernist Djuna Barnes affectionately lampooned in *Ladies Almanack*—a mock epic about how lesbian seductions produce new lesbians, obviating the need for them to go outside their circle (i.e., to men) to reproduce. However, although the *Rocky Horror* experience is often particularly homosexual in nature, it would more accurately be described as "homosocial" in the sense that attendees—whether there for their first time or their hundredth time—share a particular queer sensibility that attracts them to the spectacle and bonds them together in it.

Read in light of works such as Walter Benn Michaels' *Our America*, the folk concept of homosexual reproduction and the *Rocky Horror* tradition itself seem to operate on a similar basis to the nativist family. In *America*, Michaels describes that family as a cultural space passionately policed and maintained by its members, with homosexuality, incest, and sterility as the only possible expressions of sexuality (12–14). In fact, such incestuous, insular impulses have fueled the recent uproar over Sing-a-Long-a's acquisition of the rights to show *Rocky Horror* on a limited-run basis in the United Kingdom. *Rocky Horror* fans and floor show cast members have publicly stated on a now defunct Web site that this move undermines the entire viewing culture that has grown up around the film and also potentially threatens individual theaters' and floor show casts' rights to exhibit the film as they choose and as they have long done.[18] (Some also fear that, if the Sing-a-Long-a *Rocky Horror* does well, Twentieth Century Fox might enter into an exclusive distribution contract with the company.) This uproar further implies that although Sing-a-Long-a also provides a democratic and queer-friendly viewing experience, it may paradoxically end up doing so at the expense of the cinematic spectacle that spawned it.

However strongly its fans hold on to the idea of membership and "insiderness," though, the fact remains that *Rocky Horror* and most other alternative cinematic spectacles exhibit democratic, rather than exclusive, ideals at their very core. The participation ethos, the destruction of various hierarchies that structure normal moviegoing, and the grassroots level at which *Rocky Horror* floor show casts search for theaters and organize screenings speak to its very egalitarian nature.[19] Beyond this, there are even more specific, literal ways in which attendees of alternative cinematic spectacles have more authority and control than filmgoers usually do. Richard R. Day notes how *Rocky Horror* attendees begin shouting "Lips! Lips! Lips!" after the audience has assembled for a screening in a call for the actual projection to begin. As "the houselights dim and the movie begins

[and] the shouting reaches the threshold of pain," he writes, a tiny onscreen image finally comes into focus and "acquires meaning" (216): It is a pair of disembodied lips, out of which Richard O'Brien's voice begins singing the "Science Fiction/Double Feature" theme song. In a very real way, the audience's chant has set the physical film itself in motion, and in a very symbolic way, this chant has "caused" the lips to appear and the overall spectacle to begin unfolding.

However, the film does not go on to unfold in a wholly continuous manner—depending on the floor show cast's decisions and the staging of extrafilmic events (costume contests, the devirginizing ritual, etc.), the person in charge of projection will stop and restart the film at various points. The doggedly teleological process of film exhibition has thus been disrupted. More important, the floor show cast members, not a professional projectionist, theater owner, or member of the film industry, have disrupted it. (Although a professional projectionist may be employed, of course, he or she is instructed when to stop and restart the film.) In a sense, *Rocky Horror* attendees have fundamentally disobeyed the original filmmakers' implicit instructions, as well as the informal instructions that most people internalize over many years of watching movies in the theater: As a discrete object with certain boundaries and certain systems of logic, a publicly exhibited film must be (and, in the normal cinematic situation, can only be) watched from beginning to end without interruption. By establishing these wildly different rules for viewing, *Rocky Horror*'s audience members control the *physical* film as well the public experience of it. Although they are necessarily alienated from the now-bygone modes of production, as a Benjaminian-Marxist interpretation might assert, they are no longer alienated from the processes that govern consumption.

Another aspect of democratic audience control exists in the level of extratextual understanding that the alternative cinematic spectacle allows for—or perhaps even encourages. As previously mentioned, the exhibited Sing-a-Long-a films are never first- or even second-run movies, and some date back as far as 60 years. Viewers have had ample time to memorize the action and dialogue of the films, and they have also had the chance to familiarize themselves with the background histories, details, and minutiae, thus becoming privy to various inflections in and influences on the text. As Alexander Doty states, certain "elements of queer reading" develop from "knowledge of extra-textual behind-the-scenes gossip" (340)—in other words, ways of penetrating the text and finding spaces for pleasure within it often depend on the viewer's particular knowledge of what to "read in" and where to do it. In fact, a particularly acute reading can produce the kind of *jouissance* or bliss of which Roland Barthes speaks. Writing of his first time seeing *Sound of Music* Sing-a-Long-a production, one gay viewer says that, when Uncle Max approached the children about singing in the Salzburg Festival, "his cry of 'I have an announcement! Surprise, surprise!' led to someone shouting out, 'I'm gay!' [. . . which] was especially funny since Max was played by Richard Haydn, who was a homosexual" (Kenrick, para. 9). The alternative cinematic spectacle thus allows the queer or otherwise-marginalized viewer to negotiate his or her film-watching experience in an expert manner, becoming distinctly empowered in comparison to the average filmgoer. Not only can he or she master the art of what to say and when/where to say it but he or she can become master of both the fundamental and the external elements of the text.

For queer or otherwise-marginalized viewers, these cinematic spectacles present a good alternative to mainstream filmgoing, while simultaneously modeling a widely applicable, radical mode of viewership. Some of the tactics involved in these spectacles would never be appropriate under any other circumstances, but the ways of watching that they suggest—seeking the inscribable spaces, consciously recognizing falsity, refusing to internalize the system's norms, and so on—can be applied in everyday reception. Moreover, these spectacles develop and strengthen a particular queer sensibility. Regardless of whether or not the "beneficiary" is actually queer, this sensibility precludes one from taking the defeatist route of viewership, from deeming a film or other artistic work devoid of potential if one cannot immediately relate to or find obvious inroads to it. One of the last songs in *Rocky Horror* actually seems to urge the viewer to adopt such a queer sensibility: In "Don't Dream It," Frank tells his audience not to "dream it," but to "be it," and to also "give [themselves] over to absolute pleasure." While participating in *Rocky Horror*, singing along to *Sound of Music*, or picnicking "above and below the stars" during a classic Cinespia screening are distinctly pleasurable, escapist acts, they are not apolitical in the way that Wilton would imagine—they subvert the normative reproductive capitalism of the film industry and fundamentally uproot the often-exclusionary and alienating norms of traditional moviegoing. Therein lies the real "absolute pleasure": escaping the struggle or "ideological impediment" that the cinema usually presents, without having to shed one's identity or interests first.

Works Cited

Belton, John. *American Cinema/American Culture*. New York: McGraw-Hill, 1994.

Benjamin, Walter. "The Work of Art in the Age of Mechanical Reproduction." *Illuminations: Essays and Reflections*. New York: Schocken Books, 1968. 217–51.

Butler, Judith. *Gender Trouble: Feminism and the Subversion of Identity*. New York: Routledge, 1990.

Comolli, Jean-Luc, and Paul Narboni. "Cinema/Ideology/Criticism." *The Film Studies Reader*. Ed. Joanne Hollows, Peter Hutchings, and Mark Jancovich. New York: Oxford UP, 2000. 197–200.

Coupland, Douglas. *Generation X: Tales for an Accelerated Culture*. New York: St. Martin's, 1991.

Day, Richard R. "Rocky Horror Picture Show: A Speech Event in Three Acts." *Sociolinguistics and Language Acquisition*. Ed. Nessa Wolfson and Elliot Judd. Rowley, MA: Newbury House Publishers, 1983. 214–21.

Dayan, Daniel. "The Tutor-Code of Classical Cinema." *The Film Studies Reader*. Ed. Joanne Hollows, Peter Hutchings, and Mark Jancovich. New York: Oxford UP, 2000. 219–25.

Doty, Alexander. *Flaming Classics: Queering the Film Canon*. New York: Routledge, 2000.

———. "There's Something Queer Here." *The Film Studies Reader*. Ed. Joanne Hollows, Peter Hutchings, and Mark Jancovich. New York: Oxford UP, 2000. 337–47.

Guinness Book of World Records 2001. London: Guinness World Records, 2001.

Hammett, Jennifer. "Epistemology, Feminism and Film Theory." *Film Theory and Philosophy*. Ed. Richard Allen and Murray Smith. New York: Oxford UP, 1997.

Hansen, Miriam Bratu. "America, Paris, the Alps: Kracauer (and Benjamin) on Cinema and Modernity." *Cinema and the Invention of Modern Life*. Ed. Leo Charney and Vanessa R. Schwartz. Berkeley: U of California P, 1997. 362–402.

Hollows, Joanne, Peter Hutchings, and Mark Jancovich, Eds. *The Film Studies Reader*. New York: Oxford UP, 2000.

Kenrick, John. "The Sing-Along Sound of Music." Sep. 2000, 25 Nov. 2003. http://www.musicals101.com/singsound.htm.

Locke, L. "'Don't Dream It, Be It': *The Rocky Horror Picture Show* as Cultural Performance." *New Directions in Folklore* 3 (1999). 12 Aug. 2004. http://www.temple.edu/isllc/newfolk/rhps1.html.

Metz, Christian. "The Imaginary Signifier." *Screen* 16.2 (1975): 14–76.

Michaels, Scott, and David Evans. *Rocky Horror: From Concept to Cult*. London: Sanctuary Publishing, 2002.

Neale, Steve. "Extract from *Genre*." *The Film Studies Reader*. Ed. Joanne Hollows, Peter Hutchings, and Mark Jancovich. New York: Oxford UP, 2000. 98–101.

Piro, Sal. *"Creatures of the Night": The Rocky Horror Picture Show Experience*. Redford, MI: Stabur Press, 1990.

Rocky Horror Picture Show "Interactive Theater List." 8 July 2008. http://pages.towson.edu/jbaker/rockytheaters/theater.html.

Singer, Ben. "Modernity, Hyperstimulus, and the Rise of Popular Sensationalism." *Cinema and the Invention of Modern Life*. Ed. Leo Charney and Vanessa R. Schwartz. Berkeley: U of California P, 1997. 72–99.

Waller, Gregory A. "Midnight Movies, 1980–1985: A Market Study." *The Cult Film Experience: Beyond All Reason.* Ed. J. P. Telotte. Austin: U of Texas P, 1991. 167–86.

Wilton, Tamsin. "On Not Being Lady MacBeth: Some (Troubled) Thoughts on Lesbian Spectatorship." *The Film Studies Reader.* Ed. Joanne Hollows, Peter Hutchings, and Mark Jancovich. New York: Oxford UP, 2000. 347–55.

Wood, Robert E. "Don't Dream It: Performance and *The Rocky Horror Picture Show.*" *The Cult Film Experience: Beyond All Reason.* Ed. J. P. Telotte. Austin: U of Texas P, 1991. 156–66.

Notes

1. Douglas Coupland's novel *Generation X* defines spectacularism as "a fascination with extreme situations" (50). Critics such as Ben Singer have discussed how such a fascination has figured into film's development, stating that "from very early on, the movies gravitated towards an 'aesthetics of astonishment,' in . . . both form and subject matter" (90).

2. The Sing-a-Long-a company operates sing-along events in Canada, the United States, and the United Kingdom. *Sound of Music* was their first and remains their most popular screening. The independent group Cinespia screens films on a mausoleum wall at Los Angeles' famous Hollywood Forever cemetery. (Their respective Web sites are located at http://www.singalonga.net and http://www.cinespia.org/cinespia.html.) Though many other alternative film events take place throughout the world, I have selected these three to show how dissimilar events can make for powerful reworkings of the film experience, with particular benefits for traditionally underrepresented audience members.

3. Among other records, the 2001 *Guinness Book* reports that 4,446 children performed the film's famous song-and-dance number "The Time Warp," at the National Exhibition Centre in Birmingham, England.

4. Various scripts posted on the Internet include references to O. J. Simpson and Rodney King, for example, whereas Richard R. Day's 1983 article "Rocky Horror Picture Show: A Speech Event in Three Acts" records a contemporaneous reference to a series of Miller Lite commercials.

5. The film seems like even more of a "living text" considering how certain references generated by the audience—both sexual and nonsexual in nature—change over time. The *Rocky Horror* of five years ago is not the same as the one of today, nor is the *Rocky Horror* screened in Los Angeles the same as the one screened in New York. Although the reception of any given art object always depends on time and place, the average, mainstream film text appears static in comparison to those screened at alternative cinematic spectacles.

6. Daniel Dayan writes of the "system of the suture," the highly ideological language system that "speaks" the film, in his essay, "The Tutor-Code of Classical Cinema."

7. Steve Neale's "Extract from *Genre*" selection quotes Barthes as saying that the "writerly text" (alternately called the "text of *jouissance*") "unsettles . . . historical, cultural, psychological assumptions" to the point that the reader may be discomforted or even bored (99).

8. These casts have their own names, from Belfast's Lip Service to the Satanic Mechanics of the University of Maryland, and they are often in charge of planning and scheduling the screenings themselves. The spectacle thereby becomes even more dynamic and democratic: The screening dates, times, and locations, as well as the existence of a screening to begin with, depend on the work of self-motivated, nonprofessional lay people.

9. Metz actually says that "what unfolds [on the screen] may . . . be more or less fictional, but the unfolding itself is fictive: the actor, the 'decór,' the words one hears are all absent, everything *is recorded*" (214). I thus extrapolate the principle that nondocumentary films are fictive in their unfolding as well as fictional in their content.

10. As evidenced by screenings of *Star Wars* films and the like, fans are not necessarily—and in fact rarely—trying to be irreverent by dressing up as film characters. However, the intimate relationship that such homage presupposes disrupts the normative economy of identification—a film protagonist should be an emblematic figure, not an inhabitable space, and audience members should be interpellated by a film, not attempt to interpellate it or its characters.

11. Although Teresa de Lauretis and other critics and contemporaries of Laura Mulvey have suggested that women must be mentally "cross-dressed" to take pleasure in narrative cinema, all manner of people are voluntarily cross-dressing in *Rocky Horror* and are actively taking pleasure in their viewing experience.

12. See Judith Butler, *Gender Trouble: Feminism and the Subversion of Identity*; although she had a more sustained notion of "gender-as-a-performance" in mind—drag often, rather erroneously, gets tagged as the exemplary, or at least easiest, application of the concept—I do believe that *Rocky* attendees are at least subconsciously exploiting her theory to some degree.

13. The exhaustive annotated version of the lyrics at http://www.rockymusic.org/sfdf/ also looks at the source stories for some of these films, tracing one back as far as Shakespeare. *Rocky Horror*, then, exists as a complex amalgamation of cultural influences, both literary and cinematic, and must be considered in the context of wider popular culture, not just the seminal world of "midnight movies."

14. Many queer theorists would—and have—called homophobia a particular feature of capitalism, not just a by-product.

15. Although Hammett seems to doubt that "we" (feminist viewers to her, though queer or other minority viewers certainly fit into her schema) can escape the ideology of the film system. As Doane and Mulvey et al. see it, however, her prescription to "give up the epistemological ambitions of feminist film theory, and pursue feminist critical and political goals unencumbered by fears of the

alienating effects of representation" seems overly simplistic and even flippant (246).

16. Cinespia often advertises its screenings based on the rarity of the print it has procured, which obviously speaks to the (supposedly) unique tastes of the viewer, as well as to his or her eagerness to experience an atypical cinematic event.

17. See, for example, Louis Althusser's 1977 essay "Ideology and Ideological State Apparatuses."

18. While the "singalongasucks" Web site is no longer active, other sites to exist that critique Sing-a-Long-a's production of *Rocky Horror*. For example, a United Kingdom fan site has a forum at http://www.timewarp.org.uk/sing/index.htm where fans can weigh in on the Sing-a-Long-a's version. Most posts are very critical and say that Sing-a-Long-a's production pales in comparison to the cast-based stage shows run by fans.

19. The *Rocky Horror* "Interactive Theater List" (http://pages.towson.edu/jbaker/rockytheaters/theater.html) has a state-by-state listing of active theaters, defunct theaters, and "Active Casts without Theaters." This odd cataloguing suggests not only that the Rocky Horror phenomenon is larger than the film itself but also that a floor show cast's *raison d'etre* is to bring the spectacle experience to the masses.

8

"Don't Dream It, Be It"

Cultural Performance and Communitas at *The Rocky Horror Picture Show*

Liz Locke

Liminality, marginality, and structural inferiority are conditions in which are generated myths, symbols, rituals, philosophical systems, and works of art. These cultural forms provide men with a set of templates or models which are, at one level, periodical reclassifications of reality and man's relationship to society, nature, and culture. But they are more than classifications, since they incite men to action as well as to thought.

—*Victor Turner, The Ritual Process: Structure and Anti- Structure*

As a popular form of religious life, movies do what we have always asked of popular religion, namely, that they provide us with archetypal forms of humanity—heroic figures—and instruct us in the basic values and myths of our society. As we watch the characters and follow the drama on the screen, we are instructed in the values and myths of our culture and given models on which to pattern our lives.

—*M. Darrol Bryant, "Cinema, Religion and Popular Culture"*

Milton Singer's phrase "cultural performance," adopted by social scientists as a unit of analysis for circumscribing "plays, concerts, and lectures ... but also prayers, ritual readings and recitations, rites and ceremonies, festivals, and all those things we usually classify under religion and ritual rather than with the cultural and artistic" (71), can be productively applied to many of the quasi-cultic creations and recreations enjoyed by many young Americans in the early years of the twenty-first century. Singer's search for a unit of analysis ended when his Indian friends suggested that if he wanted to understand "who we are," he should attend local performance events in which what was on display for all to see was "who we are not." In the same spirit—from skate boarding to eroticons, from goth costuming to online gaming, and from fan fiction to poetry slams—the current generation of adolescents and postadolescents have devised/discovered myriad forms of performative self-expression and group identification that allow for the instantiation of "who we are" via the always temporary category "who we are not."

The Rocky Horror Picture Show—a film that spawned a participatory cult involving about thirty thousand people at its peak (Piro and Hess)—is a unique example of just such performative group expression. On a weekly basis, in theaters across the United States, Europe, and Australia, people gather up props, put on stage makeup, outfit themselves (often in drag), and attend an event at which they shout instructions, comments, requests, mockeries, rhetorical questions, and appreciative catcalls at light flickering on one end of a darkened room. Some dress as closely as possible to the costumes of the film's characters and stand in front of the projection screen facing the audience, reciting every memorized line in sync, mimicking each gesture, turn, and facial expression of the actors behind them. Some have enacted this scene, whether seated in the audience or as local "cast members," more than a thousand times (Piro, *Creatures of the Night*; Sharman). Many of the film's showings are prefaced by preshows involving the initiation of "virgins," costume competitions, trivia bowls, parodies of beauty contests, or skits incorporating material from other movie cults.

When the evening is over, the heightened sense of community provoked by the event and the intensity of the audience's unabashed confidence in itself and in the vivid world of *Rocky Horror* dissipates. Most of the participants then resume their conventional roles as high school students, librarians, e-workers, and accountants. They have experienced a temporary transformation but will show no outward signs of any permanent change in their lives. They have simply, in the words of *Rocky Horror*'s narrator, had a "night out they will remember for a long, long time." For others, however, the event will become a weekly rite in which the preshows, weekly ceremonials, and the film itself will act as catalysts for personal and social transformation.

Rocky Horror performances are characterized by individual and collective transformation and embodiment and are marked by a high degree of reflexivity on all levels, from the content of the film to the weekly creation of the participatory theater event. The phenomenon is especially well accounted for by Victor Turner's work on liminality and communitas. After a sketch of Turner's ideas, I draw on Julia Kristeva's term "intertextuality" and discuss the relevant elements constituting what Lee Haring (borrowing from Kristeva) calls "interperformance." Haring's checklist, designed for application to folkloric performance events, frames a discussion of the intertextual content of *Rocky Horror* and the interperformances created by its audiences and audience-casts.

Liminality and Communitas

Following Arnold van Gennep, Victor Turner notes three stages in what have come to be known as rites of passage (*rites du passage*), those "rites which accompany every change of place, state, social position, and age" that occur in every human society (94). It was Turner's particular contribution to anthropology to investigate closely what van Gennep identified as the middle phase of these processes: the liminal or threshold stage. Liminality may not be productively divorced from the structural phases that precede and follow it—separation and reincorporation (or schism)—however, the intervening antistructural period in which "the characteristics of the ritual subject . . . are ambiguous" (94) will serve as the initial route for understanding the transformational value of *Rocky Horror*.

"Communitas" is Turner's neologism for the collective spatial and temporal dimension occupied by liminal personae. His characterization of communitas fits well with reports of what people experience at *Rocky Horror* performances, and his description of liminal entities holds for virtually every agent typically or necessarily associated with them. Turner writes,

> Since this condition [of liminality] and these persons elude or slip through
> the network of classifications that normally locate states and positions in cultural space . . . their ambiguous and indeterminate attributes are expressed
> by a rich variety of symbols. . . . [L]iminality is frequently likened to death,
> to being in the womb, to invisibility, to darkness, to bisexuality, to the wilderness. . . . [N]eophytes in initiation or puberty rites . . . may be disguised as
> monsters, wear only a strip of clothing, or even go naked. . . . [They may possess]
> nothing that may distinguish them from their fellow neophytes or initiands.
> Their behavior is normally passive or humble; they may obey their instructors
> implicitly, and accept arbitrary punishment without comment. (95)

Although Turner's focus as an anthropologist was on traditional societies, he wrote that "the collective dimensions, communitas and structure, are found at all stages and levels of culture and society" (113). He continues, "Communitas breaks in through the interstices of structure, in liminality; at the edges of structure, in marginality; and from beneath structure, in inferiority. It is almost everywhere held to be sacred or 'holy,' possibly because it transgresses or dissolves the norms that govern structured and institutionalized relationships and is accompanied by experiences of unprecedented potency" (128). I return to the various elements that he identifies as characterizing liminal states and persons in the context of the *Rocky Horror* experience. Later, Turner continues, "The kind of communitas desired [by initiands] is a transformative experience that goes to the root of each person's being and finds in that root something profoundly communal and shared" (138) that "emerges where social structure is not" (126). What Turner calls "normative communitas," an experience that falls within the domain of structured social life, will first figure tentatively and then decisively in this analysis, both for the film and for *Rocky Horror* performances; however, it is the experience of "existential or spontaneous communitas" (132), a temporary state of "betwixt-and-betweenness" (138) that simultaneously collectivizes and transforms social entities, that will concern us at the outset.

The *Rocky Horror* phenomenon creates the experience of communitas by embodying textual and performative elements that can only be called religious. Ron Rosenbaum tells us that he experienced it as "a mutant form of organized religion . . . , a midnight mass that was less satanic than sophomoric, but utterly serious for all that. The prescripted lines the audience called out were like the responsive readings of a congregation to a holy text. The absurdity of the passion play on screen was less important than the state of ecstatic communion the audience worked itself into while watching" (87). *Rocky Horror*'s sacred dimension is diffuse insofar as it has the potential to arise wherever and whenever the film is viewed, yet it is also highly structured and contained insofar as viewing of the film and the audience participation that accompanies it is bounded by time and space. The existential communitas that arises in the carnival atmosphere of the theater will be maintained on the street at a lower pitch by certain audience members who will gather outside to talk or go out for breakfast after the show, but these groups are small, however central they have become in the ongoing performativity of liminality-as-identity within the *Rocky Horror* context.

Inter-, Meta-, and Hyperperformance

Turning now to Haring's elements of "interperformance, the first to lend itself to an analysis of the *Rocky Horror* cult phenomenon is "transmodalization," his term for a form of variation that denotes a shift in genre from one performer to another (371). *Rocky Horror* audiences and cast members shift the performances of the on-screen actors to themselves, the generic frame of the event from cinema to drama, and the theatergoing experience itself from film-as-object to film-as-relationship. Haring also discusses "transvalorization"—a "change in the value explicitly or implicitly attributed to an action or set of actions"—as a variant of interperformance. The most readily noticeable shift of performative value during a successful *Rocky Horror* performance occurs in the speech of the audience: It provokes the lips of the opening sequence to appear, it engages in dialogue with a filmed image, it evokes the creators of that image by calling their names, and most important, it smashes the convention that keeps theatergoers together in a state of normative communitas, characterized by passivity and silence.

Umberto Eco makes a case for *Casablanca*, arguably one of the most enduring cult films of all time, that "it is not *one* movie. It is *movies*" (208). He posits that a cult film "must display certain textual features, in the sense that, . . . it becomes a sort of textual syllabus, a living example of living textuality" (199). In the same way, intertextuality, in the strict sense, serves as *Rocky Horror*'s primary framing device on all levels of the experience. Originally, the initial sequence was scripted not with dark red lips but with a montage of scenes from the ten classic science fiction films mentioned in the opening song (Henkin 194). *Rocky Horror* not only cannibalizes the science fiction and horror genres but borrows motifs and conventions from Mae West and Elvis Presley movies, Roger Corman's biker flicks, gothic romances, Kubrick's *Dr. Strangelove*, striptease and cabaret shows, the myth of Psyche and Eros, 1960s-style happenings, and soap operas. In tacit agreement with Eco, Irene Oppenheim writes, "Taken in disparate parts, it's all too contrived and too familiar; but stuck together, *Rocky*, while not altogether different, emerges with something of its own. There's a clumsy good-natured innocence about this stew that (in the right circumstances) can seem redeeming" (28).

Rolf Eichler discusses the intertextual elements in Shelley's *Frankenstein*, which he identifies as the template for all subsequent literary and cinematic treatments of the Promethean theme of "man's [sic] desire to perfect himself through others" (99). He then goes further than most critics to point out "the effect of intertextuality on a work's reception." In the case of *Frankenstein*, Mary Shelley's readers were in an excellent position to understand the social and moral conventions that held sway in the novel's narrative present. Hence they were also in position to grasp why and when these norms were being challenged and undermined. "The more time that elapses between creation and reading, the more texts will have interposed themselves between work and reader—a fact that becomes the more significant for *Rocky Horror* since so many texts, plays, and films have now erected a background that is bound to give a new appearance to the author's subject matter" (Eichler 99–100).

This interposition of texts is not limited to those directly concerned in a comparative discussion of *Rocky Horror* and Shelley's bricolage monster, nor even to those genres mentioned earlier. The makers of *Rocky Horror* also extended "intertextual space" (Kristeva 225) to include a wide variety of icons from elite culture. They give us Grant Wood's *American Gothic*, first reproduced in tableau (in the wedding scene), then as a reproduction of the painting (next to the mummy case), and finally parodied in tableau (Riff Raff beside Magenta with a three-pronged laser gun). The Criminologist's scrapbook contains a "Whistler's Mother" signed by Meatloaf and a reproduction of Da Vinci's *Last Supper*. The *Mona Lisa* and *David* appear, first facing right and then left, making us hyperaware of their reproducibility (Eichler 112), and hence their incorporability into mainstream culture. *The Creation of Adam*, signed by Michelangelo, is painted on the bottom of Frank-N-Furter's swimming pool.

But the audience has taken all this yet further. Having no fear of transgressing even the shattered generic conventions exploited by its creators, *Rocky Horror* fans drag in literally everything they can think of. If an intelligible remark is covered by "Grice's four maxims of conversation: be relevant, informative, brief, and truthful," and Day's addendum: "Be witty" (Day 217–18), it will elicit a positive response from the *Rocky Horror* audience in the form of being repeated at subsequent shows; it may even be incorporated into *Rocky Horror* liturgy (see Piro, *Creatures of the Night*; Henkin; Day; Duranti). Obviously, the creators were fully conscious of their *own* intertextual manipulations, but they could not have anticipated what their audiences would do with the result. In the eight-minute preface to the 1992 video edition, Richard O'Brien, who wrote the play, music, and lyrics, says to the camera, "People come over and say to me, 'Hey, have you seen what they're doing with your movie?' Well, I finally went to see it. It was the best piece of theater I've ever seen. It encapsulated live action with filmed image with audience participation. And three out of three . . . ain't bad" ("Interview").

Another variant of interperformance, which Haring calls "allusion," is also in play here. Citing Susan Stewart, he writes, "In folktale as in literature, an allusion is a brief reference to something the interpretive community will recognize from its existing knowledge. Few situations in life, in fact, do not make use of allusion in that sense" (366). We can see allusion at work when considering audience responses to Frank's preparation for his "last supper." Magenta stands holding a huge gong and says in an exaggerated southern accent, "Dinnah is prepared!" Audiences in 1979, alluding to a television commercial for Shake-'n-Bake, yelled, "And I helped!" When Riff Raff hurls the roast onto the dining table, the audience groaned, "Oh, no, Meatloaf again?" referring to the actor/rock star who plays Eddie and who Frank mercy-butchers with an ice pick. ("You sure know how to pick your friends!" quips the audience.) Frank reaches for an electric knife to carve the roast at dinner, and the audience cheerfully supplied, "Always reach for a Hamilton Beech!"

It is clear that the audience uses intertextuality to create interperformance. However, in the process of remarking on audience responses and behaviors, it also creates "meta-performances"—performances that comment on earlier performances and ensure a high standard for responses in much the same way as traditional storytellers "ensure excellence in folktales" (Haring 368) by using the operation Alan Dundes called "metafolklore," or "folkloristic statements about folklore" (506). For example, when overenthusiastic audience members use their spray bottles too soon—before the on-screen Brad and Janet actually step into the rain—veterans shout, "It doesn't rain in cars, assholes!" Haring's element of "tradition" is also relevant in this regard. He writes, "What is most relevant to the notion of interperformance is that the rules for narrative performance are 'traditionalized.' Thus, if a narrator is perceived as conforming to the rules, he can imitate or even parody a predecessor" (366). *Rocky Horror* shadow casts—practiced performance groups comprised of fully made-up and costumed fans who parallel the action of the film—have taken the participatory aspect of the event farther than any midnight movie cult has ever gone (Hoberman 19).

The concept of "hypertextuality" as developed by Gerard Genette refers to "the transformations which change one story into another, for instance when a prose narrative is versified" (Haring 369). I extend the term to include the concept of "hyperperformance" to describe what happens at a *Rocky Horror* event. Over the years, Double Feature, San Francisco's Strand Theater cast, The Celluloid Jam of the Oriental Theater in Milwaukee, Voyeuristic Intention of the Rialto in South Pasadena, the Eighth Street Players of the Eighth Street Playhouse in New York, and countless other shadow casts formally and informally constituted (see Piro, *Creatures of the Night*) have transformed a film into a live performance event, a movie into a celebratory festival, film buffs into drag queens, theater aisles into dance floors, and cinema houses into unrestrained, yet safe and (usually) sober, late night parties. In other words, "hyperperformance" as executed by the audience and casts of *Rocky Horror* parallels Haring's interrelated notions of "situation" and "tradition." Citing Richard Bauman's and Dell Hymes's work in folklore studies, Haring writes, "The specific conditions in which stories are told actually constitute the *event* as the meaningful context for artistic communication. . . . When societies adopt borrowed plots and characters, they bring to them certain 'pre-existing cultural emphases' which determine how the borrowed stories are adapted into a new setting. Responding to specific situations, storytellers demonstrate their creativity" (366). The fact that an audience for a film demonstrates *any* creativity is in itself noteworthy, but that an audience would go to such lengths actively to bring its "pre-existing cultural emphases" into the open and into dialogue with a film is virtually fantastic.

The last element of Haring's interperformance model that I consider here is what he calls "quotation." This is obviously related to what I have called *Rocky Horror*'s primary framing device—intertextuality; it is also connected to the notion of metaperformance insofar as the audience is repeatedly engaged in quotation of its own previous response lines. I have already noted the *Mona Lisa* and *David* as examples of intersemiotic quotation; however, the most famous visual quotation occurs when Rocky carries Frank, dead without having satisfied his wish to be dressed like Fay Wray, draped across his tanned, muscled back up a model of the RKO Radio Tower, shaking his fists and growling over his shoulder at his attacker.

It is also possible, however, to discuss recognizable reentextualized quotations from spoken discourse. For example, Frank-N-Furter has told us that he's "making a man with blonde hair and a tan." Thrilled with his creation, he sings, "In just seven days, I can make you a man." The allusion here, of course, is not only to the famous Charles Atlas fitness regiment but also, more loosely, to Genesis 1:26–27. A lesser-known and more direct quotation is spoken as the ultimate call to "absolute pleasure" and serves as the cathartic mainspring of the movie: "Don't dream it. Be it" was an advertising slogan for Frederick's of Hollywood lingerie (Corliss 23).

Working in the opposite direction, *Rocky Horror* performance is the source of one-liners that occasionally crop up in conversations far removed from their original context. I've heard more than one fan express a divergent opinion by saying, "I didn't make him for *you!*" And "What charming underclothes you both have" is a remark I heard from a friend while watching MTV. Oppenheim cites several examples: "This week . . . I received a potpourri catalogue from the Midwest that featured loungewear emblazoned with 'Creature of the Night,' a memorable phrase in the *Rocky* song, 'Touch-a Touch-a Touch-a Touch Me.' The line, 'Don't Dream It. Be It,' has rhythmically entered the language in places as far afield as the sign language text *Survival Sign*, with its cover quote: 'Don't say it. Sign it.' [I] created a T-shirt with my own favorite *Rocky* quote: 'Madness takes its toll.' I still like that one" (29).

Over at the Frankenstein Place

Having said that the liminal is, according to Turner, "almost everywhere held to be sacred," it is my intention now to show that *Rocky Horror* is no exception. Oppenheim makes the connection: "I'm surprised theologians haven't paid more attention to *Rocky*. For there are, I think, religious implications in both the film and its rituals. Certainly among the reasons *Rocky* has endured is that beneath its surface silliness the film tells a tale about initiation into a dangerous world; about surviving lost innocence; about deviance and acceptance; about creation, forgiveness, death, and regeneration" (29). Referring to Turner's characteristics of threshold people already cited, we find death and the womb (the wedding-funeral), darkness and sexuality, and the wilderness (Frank's castle is "in the middle of nowhere"). The range of liminal attributes encapsulated in *Rocky Horror*'s star, Tim Curry as Frank-N-Furter, is impressive. Similar to Victor Frankenstein, his literary near-namesake, Frank is a scientist who creates life in a laboratory. Lou Adler, *Rocky Horror*'s producer, explains the resonance of the archetype: "You need not have seen *King Kong* to recognize the ape in *Rocky Horror*'s final climb. You need not have heard of Mary Wollstonecraft Shelley or seen Boris Karloff's monster to know the legend of Frankenstein. Certain themes and cinematic images have become part of us" (Henkin 131).

Reversals of normative convention in *Rocky Horror* are compiled from life as they were for Shelley, but also from Shelley's story itself. Tim Curry's scientist is no recluse—his castle is a site of revelry in the form of a convention and party for his guests from home, the planet Transsexual in the galaxy of Transylvania. Mark Siegel notes,

> [Brad and Janet's] entrance onto the castle grounds is an appropriately marked transition from the profane world of daily life to the sacred world of ritual. The transitional ground of the forest, the warning sign on the gate, the Transylvanian flag, and the massive ornamental door are all normal ceremonial aspects of rites of separation and transition [liminality], emphasized in the film by Janet's singing "Over at the Frankenstein Place." Their entrance into the castle is further marked by what Van Gennep calls "purifications," rituals that mark the individual's separation from the profane world.... Frank notes that their nakedness makes them "vulnerable," and this is precisely the act [of disrobing them]'s ritual significance. (309)

In other words, the liminal phase is disorienting by definition. Other instances include Frank draping himself, blasphemously pieta-like, over a throne as he presides lasciviously at the "Annual Transylvanian Convention," paralleling his ministerial role at the Happschatt wedding. Later, his newest playmate, Rocky, will sing about his dread of imminent death immediately upon his emergence from the birth vat. Rocky then runs from the embrace of his mother-father-lover-exploiter to seek the sympathy of the alien "unconventional conventionists," who meet his distress with elated dancing and choruses of "That ain't no crime!" Meanwhile, Eddie, the presumably frozen donor of half of Rocky's cerebral tissue, comes roaring out of the walk-in freezer on a motorcycle (his sax-drenched rendition of "Whatever Happened to Saturday Night" is proof that you can have more fun than anybody in the movie with only half a brain), and Janet reverses her position on male musculature while a sullen Brad holds Eddie's gleaming saxophone, iconic of all that Brad is not.

The normative image of the scientist is still our most cherished projection of inviolate, objective masculinity. Even when our scientists are female, they are caricatured as sexlessly dispassionate, but Frank is not only "a sweet transvestite" from another planet, he's bisexual, narcissistic, exhibitionistic, insensitive, rapacious, rude, and hot as hell. He struts around in a black corset with fishnet stockings, sometimes covered by a green lab coat (sporting a pink triangle), abetted by stiletto heels and pearls. He obviously spends hours on his makeup but isn't at all concerned when he smears it for effect. In short, he is what every repressed, sexually anxious, outcast intellectual male or female sees as a self-reflection in her or his wildest dionysiac nightmares. Frank is "the underbelly, the dark side of creation; and it should come as no surprise to us when he suffers satanic ruin. . . . He is the richly charactered magus who dies for our imagined sins, and redeems our fantasies as he lives out our hidden dreams" (Henkin 53–55).

Early critics of Curry's portrayal invariably described it in terms of combined personae: "half Auntie Mame, half Bela Lugosi," "a cross between Greer Garson and Steve Reeves," and "part David Bowie, part Joan Crawford, part Basil Rathbone" (Henkin 133). Frank has ambiguous and indeterminate attributes, but he is indisputably male. He succeeds in winning our hearts to such an extent that even when he whips his "faithful handyman" until he cries for mercy, abuses Janet, shoves Brad to the ground, and kills Eddie, we the audience and his on-screen groupies not only forgive him but emulate him—more than we ever emulated Clint Eastwood or John Wayne. They never really knew us like Frank does. Perhaps more to the point, his abusiveness reminds us of another characteristic of liminal personae: "they may obey their instructors implicitly, and accept arbitrary punishment without comment" (Turner 95).

Gaylyn Studlar gets it but is obviously not a fan: "Dr. Frank-N-Furter represents a gender transformation that borrows from perverse possibilities but safely recuperates the revolutionary promise of homoerotic hedonism through the sexual politics of masculine aggression" (8). Frank, whose sexual generativity appears to reside only in the lab, makes himself a man. The reflexive is deliberate. Although he can entertain his homoeroticism with Rocky Horror, he has complete, and completely masculine, power over him. "I made you and I can break you just as easily." He accomplishes his act of creation through asexual (scientific) means, but by accident—the same route taken by Brad and Janet to reach his castle and, thereby, their own sexual awakening. Frank's creation speech may be interpreted on both levels, that of complete control and that of serendipitous accident: "Paradise is to be mine! It was strange in the way it happened. Suddenly you get a break. All the pieces seem to fit together. What a sucker you've been! What a fool! The answer was there all the time. It took a small accident to make it happen. An accident! And that's how I discovered the secret, that elusive ingredient, that spark that is the breath of life." He is the wise fool, the perpetrating sucker; it was an accident, but Frank made it happen.

And even before Frank was, he—well—*was*. As the lips close back into the central point on the screen, they are overlain by a Celtic cross on the top of a church steeple. The doors of the church open and a wedding party pours out onto the steps. Frank, in his guise as God's celebrating minister, stands at the door flanked by the custodial Riff Raff and Magenta in *American Gothic* mode. After a photo is taken of "just the close family," Frank is gone from the scene. Brad and Janet move from the graveyard into the church to celebrate their engagement. Riff Raff and Magenta spin the wedding bouquets on the pews to reveal funereal blooms. Just as Brad suggests that he and Janet should "visit the man who began it," ostensibly meaning Dr. Everett Scott, the staff carries in a coffin. The camera moves from the coffin backgrounded by an American flag, to Brad and Janet on their knees in naive bliss, to a stained-glass cross.

Frank's divinity is campy but efficient. Brad carries the emblem of Eddie's free spirit, and Janet, coy with one male character after another under the spell of Frank's unbridled lustiness, confesses her fascination aloud. The power of redemptive sexuality and its concomitant costs are implicit even before Frank touches Janet or Brad. He "offers" to initiate them into their own sensuality by telling them that he'll "remove the cause, but not the symptom." For the final floor show, Frank decorates each character with identical makeup and clothes, corsets, fishnets, feather boas, and stiletto pumps. Recall that "[Initiands possess] nothing that may distinguish them from their fellow neophytes or initiands. Their behavior is normally passive or humble" (Turner 95). Of masking, Turner says, "Rituals of status reversal . . . mask the weak in strength and demand of the strong that they be passive and patiently endure the symbolic and even real aggression shown against them by structural inferiors" (177).

Frank, of course, is not masked, and what he "patiently endures" is listening to his "creations" (a term used by fashion designers of their clothing) say what they really think about him and about themselves. Columbia admits she was only able to fulfill her role as "a regular Frankie fan" by using drugs. Rocky Horror tells us that he suffers from a lack of trust in anything but his own libidinous satisfaction. Brad and Janet admit that they have been transformed. Brad is still shaky about it and, paraphrasing Jesus in Gethsemane, begs "Mommy" to "take this dream away from me," but Janet is "released": her "confidence has increased," and her "mind has been expanded." She is unequivocally grateful to have entered the liminal phase and undergone initiation.

The final transformation effected during the floor show is confirmed in the pool. Frank invites his new friends to join him, to "swim the warm waters of sins of the flesh." We know it's all over because Frank is lying in a life preserver emblazoned "USS Titanic." (Alluding to a toilet-bowl cleanser commercial, the audience response is "Come look! There's a transvestite in my toilet bowl!") The song "Don't Dream It. Be It" is now a call to participate in Frank's pleasure, no longer a command to be dominated by it. The masks disappear into the water while the now authenticated initiands lovingly touch Frank and one another, paralleling God conferring consciousness on Adam on the bottom of the pool. Their ritual change of status is celebrated by all five participants, who are now on equal footing, in a chorus-line song and dance, "Wild and Untamed Thing" (which is, musically, the continuation of the floor show confessions, "Rose Tint My World").

Spontaneous communitas, however, cannot be maintained indefinitely; it cannot survive the consensually agreed-upon demands of social life and must eventually settle into normative individual and collective attitudes and behaviors. Liminality is a phase, not a status. It is a bridge for crossing over to a new (or at least newly recognized) social space, but no human society intends for its members to take up residence on it: "Cognitively, nothing underlines regularity so well as absurdity or paradox. Emotionally, nothing satisfies as much as extravagant or temporarily permitted illicit behavior. Rituals of status reversal accommodate both aspects. By making the low high and the high low, they reaffirm the hierarchical principle. By making the low mimic (often to the point of caricature) the behavior of the high, and by restraining the initiatives of the proud, they underline the reasonableness of everyday culturally predictable behavior between the various estates of society" (Turner 176). Riff Raff and Magenta step in to "restrain the initiatives of the proud" and to restore "predictable behavior between the various estates of society." Riff Raff, dressed in gold lamé space gear, tells Frank, "It's all over. Your mission is a failure. Your lifestyle's too extreme." After Frank sings his Judy Garland swan song, Riff Raff tells him he's been "presumptuous" in assuming that he will accompany Magenta and himself back to Transsexual. (The title of the original stage production of Mary Shelley's book in 1823 was *Presumption, or the Fate of Frankenstein*.) As the simpering Dr. Scott tells Brad, "Society must be protected." It's time to reincorporate into society's normative structures or else reject them entirely—an alternative that seems unlikely for the affianced Brad and Janet.

Of course, even dead-below-the-waist Dr. Scott has been influenced by Frank's gift: His paralysis disappears, and his own fish-netted legs appear from beneath his invalid's wheelchair blanket. However, Scott is ultimately an establishment toady—a structure freak who will forgive anything and accept anything as long as he is promised a return to the status quo, even when the authority he submits to is as paranoid and duplicitous as Riff Raff's, "insolent in his lack of power, cruel when he holds it" (Henkin 61). "Absolute pleasure" is not a maxim that any structured society can tolerate for long, and the audience knows it. They will respond as warmly to Riff Raff and Magenta at the next showing as they did at the last one because they know that Frank will be back—he will traipse off that elevator into their lives and fill them with delightfully subversive pleasure again next week. If there is no crucifixion, there can be no resurrection, but in the meantime, order is reestablished, and the liminal is displaced by familiar hierarchical principles in order that it may reemerge another day.

John Kilgore points to van Gennep's final phase of initiation rituals—the necessary reintegration of initiands into formal society—when he defends the value of the *Rocky Horror* experience against those who would interpret it as merely profane adolescent indulgence: "The film moves from a raucous celebration of sexuality, through a lament for its dangers and confusions, to a final, sporting admission of the need to control it. Far from prompting rebellious sensuality, its ultimate balance and reconciliation of opposites leads in just the opposite direction—toward psychic detachment and an amiable acceptance of the need for compromise" (159). The liminal phase is always a leaving-from in order to arrive-at the normative roles a society's members are expected to perform for its own ongoing structural maintenance. Absolute pleasure has no meaning in the absence of normative restraint, any more than does compromise in the face of complete agreement. It is from our divergences with normative social realities that we return to discover who we are.

Community and Communitas

Turner quotes Martin Buber in describing what he means by communitas. He tells us, "Community is where community happens" (127). The audiences of *Rocky Horror* agree. A crowd of strangers comes together in an urban theater at midnight, ready to participate in a communal ritual of expressing their collective outsider status. It makes them feel better. In fact, it makes them feel great. "What makes it so infectious is the feeling of family and community within the theaters" (Piro, "Introduction" i). Many, but not all of them, are young. Many feel constrained by what Turner calls "structure," always experienced as more painful and overbearing by a society's marginalized persons—in our own, especially insecure teenagers, intellectual or overweight women, skinny or nearsighted men, and so on. As with some other forms of ritualistic expression, it's not for everybody, but some hardcore fans call it "going to church." According to Oppenheim,

> Like religious services, the midnight *Rocky* showings communally demarcate the end of a given week. There may, moreover, be an ingrained need or longing for some such gathering together: a voluntary event that reliably occurs like a pulse against time. . . . [There is] something comforting and stabilizing about ritualized repetition. But while ritual can provide a sense of containment in lives that are chaotic, it can also or even simultaneously provide a place for scheduled chaos in lives that are otherwise constrained. The latter, for example, occurred in the mad dancing of the Shakers, or in the ecstatic movement of dervishes. In *Rocky* too, the wildness and play-acting may happen because the film offers itself and the structure of its showings offer a ritual-like reassurance of a beginning and an end. (29)

A return to normative communitas does not just happen at the end of the film with the death of Frank, the departure of the aliens, and the freeing of Brad, Janet, and Dr. Scott to resume their lives in Denton, "The Home of Happiness." It also happens for participants in the exuberant *Rocky Horror* performance experience. Turner's insights into the ritual forms of liminality enacted in traditional societies transfer easily into the context of *Rocky Horror* as a cultural interperformance of initiation into social identity. The way he tells it, even "in complex industrialized societies, we still find traces in the liturgies of churches and other religious organizations of institutionalized attempts to prepare for the coming of spontaneous communitas. This modality of relationship, however, appears to flourish best in spontaneously liminal situations—phases betwixt and between states where social-structural role-playing is dominant, and especially between status equals" (138). The way Sal Piro tells it, Louis Farese, a kindergarten teacher from Staten Island, suddenly started talking back to the screen at Manhattan's Waverly Theater on Labor Day weekend in 1976. The costuming started on Halloween that year. The floor shows began a few regulars lip-synched to the record as it played before show time (Piro *Creatures of the Night*, 1–2). The audience loved it. They picked it up, and the interperformance rituals of *Rocky Horror* began.

Over thirty years later, there's another generation of people talking back to the screen. Still predominantly white and middle-class, they are male, female, trans- and intersexed, het, homo, transgendered, cross-dressing, queer, bi, and fluid. With luck and desire they ritualize with one another. In so doing, they find a collectively experienced sense of liminality, a "betwixt and between" wherein they can be unassailably vulnerable and safely dangerous for a few hours before reluctantly returning to their mundane, socially approved roles.

Works Cited

Bauman, Richard. *Verbal Art as Performance*. Prospect Heights, IL: Waveland, 1977.

Bryant, M. Darrol. "Cinema, Religion and Popular Culture." *Religion and Film*. Ed. John R. May and Michael Bird. Knoxville: U of Tennessee P, 1982. 101–14.

Chute, David. "Outlaw Cinema: Its Rise and Fall." *Film Comment* 19 (1983): 9–14.

Corliss, Richard. "Across the Land: The Voice of Rocky Horror." *Time Magazine* 126 (Dec. 9, 1985): 22–23.

Cosmo's Factory. 29 Sep. 2004. http://www.cosmosfactory.org/.

Day, Richard R. "Rocky Horror Picture Show: A Speech Event in Three Acts." *Sociolinguistics and Language Acquisition*. Ed. Nessa Wolfson and Elliot Judd. Rowley, MA: Newbury House Publishers, 1983. 214–21.

Dundes, Alan. "Metafolklore and Oral Literary Criticism." *The Monist* 50 (1966): 505–16.

Duranti, Alessandro. "The audience as co-author." *Text* 6.3 (1986): 239–47.

Eco, Umberto. "*Casablanca*: Cult Movies and Intertextual Collage." [1984]. *Travels in Hyperreality: Essays*. Trans. William Weaver. New York: Harcourt Brace Jovanovich, 1986. 197–211.

Eichler, Rolf. "In the Romantic Tradition: *Frankenstein* and *The Rocky Horror Picture Show*." *Beyond the Suburbs of the Mind: Exploring English Romanticism*. Ed. Michael Gassenmeir and Norbert Platz. Essen: Verlag Die Blaue Eule, 1987. 95–114.

Flynn, Rochelle O'Gorman. "Video News." *Tower Video Collector* (Dec. 1990). Tower Records: Sacramento, CA.

Gennep, Arnold van. *The Rites of Passage*. Trans. Gabrielle L. Caffee. Chicago: U of Chicago P, 1960.

Haring, Lee. "Interperformance." *Fabula: Journal of Folktale Studies* 29 (1988): 365–72.

Henkin, Bill. *The Rocky Horror Picture Show Book*. New York: Plume/Penguin Books, 1979.

Hoberman, J., and Jonathan Rosenbaum. "Curse of the Cult People." *Film Comment* 27.1 (1991): 18–22.

Hymes, Dell. "Folklore's Nature and the Sun's Myth." *Journal of American Folklore* 88 (1975): 345–69.

"Interview with Richard O'Brien." *The Rocky Horror Picture Show: 15th Anniversary Edition*. [VHS]. Twentieth Century-Fox Film Corporation, 1992.

Khan, Naseem. "Rocky On." *New Statesman* 110 (Dec. 20–27, 1985): 77.

Kilgore, John. "Sexuality and Identity in *The Rocky Horror Picture Show*." *Eros in the Mind's Eye: Sexuality and the Fantastic in Art and Film*. Ed. Donald Palumbo. New York: Greenwood, 1983. 151–59.

Oppenheim, Irene. "Rocky Redux." *The Threepenny Review* 44 (1991): 27–29.

Piro, Sal. *Creatures of the Night: The Rocky Horror Picture Show Experience*. Redford, MI: Stabur, 1990.

———. "Introduction." *The Rocky Horror Picture Show Movie Novel*. Ed. and adapted by Richard J. Anobile. New York: A&W Visual Library, 1980.

Piro, Sal, and Michael Hess. *Official Rocky Horror Show Audience Par-Tic-I-Pation Guide*. Livonia, MI: Stabur, 1991.

Rosenbaum, Ron. "Gooseflesh." *Harper's Magazine* v. 259 (Sept. 1979): 87.

Ruble, Raymond. "Dr. Freud Meets Dr. Frank N. Furter." *Eros in the Mind's Eye*. Ed. Donald Palumbo. New York: Greenwood, 1986. 163–68.

Schechner, Richard. "Collective Reflexivity: Restoration of Behavior." *A Crack in the Mirror: Reflexive Perspectives in Anthropology*. Ed. Jay Ruby. Philadelphia: U of Pennsylvania P, 1982. 36–81.

Siegel, Mark. "*The Rocky Horror Picture Show*: More Than a Lip Service." *Science-Fiction Studies* 7 (1980): 305–12.

Singer, Milton. *When a Great Tradition Modernizes*. New York: Praeger Publishers, 1972.

Sharman, Jim, and Richard O'Brien. *The Rocky Horror Picture Show*. Video [1975]. Dir. Jim Sharman. New York: CBS/Fox Video, 1990.

Stewart, Susan. *Nonsense: Aspects of Intertextuality in Folklore and Literature*. Baltimore: Johns Hopkins UP, 1979.

Studlar, Gaylyn. "Midnight S/excess: Cult Configurations of 'Femininity' and the Perverse." *Journal of Popular Film and Television* 1.2 (1989): 2–14.

Turner, Victor. *The Ritual Process: Structure and Anti- Structure*. Ithaca, NY: Cornell UP, 1969.

9

The Cult and Its Virgin Sacrifice

Rites of Defloration in and at
The Rocky Horror Picture Show

Kristina Watkins-Mormino

Rocky Horror is like sex, you can only have one first time so make the most of it.

—*James Norman, "What Every 'Virgin' Should Know"*

The loss of virginity is arguably the most important rite of passage in American society today. In the first place, it is a nearly universal experience cutting across ethnic, class, racial, religious, and gender lines. The event of "the first time" may occur in homosexual or heterosexual encounters and within committed or casual relationships. In short, sooner or later, in one way or another, the vast majority of Americans lose their virginity. Second, defloration is a critical rite of passage because it typically is experienced by young people yet always carries the possibility of serious adult consequences. For this reason, much of the political discourse about teen sexuality is motivated and fueled by statistics concerning sexually transmitted diseases, sexual assaults, and unwanted pregnancies. Third, the loss of virginity matters a great deal in a society in which sexual activity constitutes normative adult behavior. Although cotillion balls are fading away and weddings are occurring increasingly later in adulthood (if at all), the moment of defloration remains an important initiation into mature social interactions.

So, regardless as to whether the experience feels momentous or disappointingly meaningless to the individual, the loss of virginity is a significant event marking a critical change in status. Nonetheless, it normally takes place in secret. Whereas families, communities, and the state play a vital role in such rites of passage as proms, commencement ceremonies, the procurement of a first driver's license or house, weddings, and so forth, they exert limited influence on the circumstances of defloration and often do not know that a covert initiation has even taken place. Moreover, because virginity itself is hidden and difficult (if not impossible) to verify, and because the virgin lacks experiential knowledge of sex, one or both parties to a defloration may even be unaware or unsure of what has occurred. The surrender or loss of an individual's virginity is generally cloaked in secrecy and mystery.

Nonetheless, the event of the first time is collectively celebrated and ritualized through popular culture. In *Performing Virginity and Testing Chastity in the Middle Ages*, Kathleen Coyne Kelly discusses numerous relatively recent examples from television and film in which a character's virginity is called into question or teenagers agonize over whether and how to lose their virginity, including *Clueless*, *The Real World*, *Beverly Hills 90210*, *The X-Files*, and *Scream* (120–40). I might add to these *American Pie*, *Four Rooms*, *Cruel Intentions*, *American Beauty*, *Pleasantville*, and so on, but the list could go on indefinitely and would not even begin to address the ubiquity of the defloration theme in music, fiction, and news sources. (For example, the highly publicized preservation and subsequent loss of pop princess Brittany Spears' virginity made abstinence, teen sexuality, and defloration trendy topics in popular media.) Kelly notes that one result of this bombardment of cultural messages about virginity and its loss is that autobiographical defloration narratives tend to be rather formulaic: "It seems that one of the most intimate experiences of one's life, presumably and potentially the most pleasurable, resists language, falls into triteness and cliché, suggesting the degree to which the experience of virginity is culturally scripted and commodified" (126). Prepackaged defloration scenarios are disseminated in a uniform and far-reaching manner, so that young initiates into adult sexuality prove obliging consumers of sexual messages. Thus, although many families and communities may oppose teen sexuality, societal ritualization of the initial sex act proceeds through pop culture.

Of course, all rites of passage in Western societies have been more or less commercially regulated, but defloration is unique in its lack of actual ceremony and direct community involvement. Groups communally commemorate births, deaths, marriages, comings-out, graduations, and so forth, but only rarely in the United States does anyone celebrate that virginity has been lost. Old World customs such as the *chivaree* (raucous merrymaking and cat-calling at a newly wedded couple's door) and the public inspection of the bridal sheets for hymeneal blood have never been mainstream events in this country. In general, the wedding, which once heralded the deflowering of at least the bride, has largely lost its significance in this respect, and no one is surprised to see even divorcées and mothers of children walk down the aisle in white. As society has moved toward new normative positions on sexuality, there have been significant shifts in the way our culture deals with both matrimony and defloration—two rites of passage that were once intrinsically linked, at least for women. In spite of escalating divorce rates, marriage is celebrated with a luxury and pomp that borders on the absurd. Defloration, however, has ceased to be marked by any particular festivity.

There is one exception, and again it is to be found in popular culture. Perhaps the only widespread communal observance of the loss of virginity in America takes place every weekend at midnight screenings of *The Rocky Horror Picture Show*. This film, known for its celebration of outrageous libidinous exploits, also has a great deal to say about virginity and its loss. Three of its major characters begin as wide-eyed, inexperienced innocents but soon become sexually active—and even sexually transgressive. Similarly, each weekend cinematic showings draw newcomers to the film—mostly teenagers and very young adults, at least some of whom are as wide-eyed and inexperienced as the on-screen virgins—who participate in an event in which illicit dress, language, and behavior is publicly flaunted. At *Rocky Horror*, they enter into a communal encounter centered on the film, augmented with the lip-synching and performance of a live cast, and involving the participation of the general audience members, who sing along with the characters, direct crude or funny ripostes and interjections to the screen, and toss about prescribed props such as rice, rolls of toilet paper, or slices of toast. Drag, licentiousness, political incorrectness, and profanity are the order of the day. With reenactments and verbal suggestions of sex acts permeating both the film and the audience participation, it is not surprising that the first-time *Rocky Horror* viewer would come to be labeled as a sexual neophyte, a "virgin."[1] Thus, one's initial *Rocky Horror* experience is celebrated as a defloration; yet, far from private, it is an initiation in which the entire community takes part. All the while, the participants receive strong on- and off-screen messages about the nature of virginity and the conditions of its loss.

In the early years of the *Rocky Horror* phenomenon, Tim Curry remarked with more than a hint of ridicule that American kids were beginning to regard going to *Rocky Horror* as a sort of rite of passage (Hoberman and

Rosenbaum 193). In this chapter, I focus on how *Rocky Horror* represents, elides, and stands in for a specific rite of passage: defloration. First, I examine the bridal practices and sexual initiations that take place in the film itself. Then I turn my attention to the "deflowering" of "virgins"—that is, the hazing of first-time attendees—that has become part and parcel of the *Rocky Horror* experience. Finally, I consider the implications of the commodification of rites of passage in American society.

Defloration Rites in the Home of Happiness
and at the Frankenstein Place

As Mark Siegel points out in his 1980 article "*The Rocky Horror Picture Show*: More Than A Lip Service," the film centers on the ritualistic sexual initiation of Brad Majors and Janet Weiss, an exaggeratedly repressed young couple from the small Midwestern town of Denton, the "Home of Happiness" (305). Having just witnessed the wedding of their friends Ralph and Betty, Brad proposes to Janet during a campy musical number in which the two march down the aisle of the chapel, kneel before the altar, and finally kiss. They are next seen driving off to inform their former science teacher and friend Dr. Scott of their engagement. En route, they find themselves stranded with a flat tire in the middle of a rainstorm and make their way to a nearby castle to make a phone call. Unbeknownst to them, the castle is really a spaceship, and its owner, Dr. Frank-N-Furter, the leader of a band of aliens from the planet Transsexual in the galaxy of Transylvania, is about to bring to life his creature, Rocky Horror, a blond boy-toy with tanned skin and a sculpted physique (see Figure 9.1).

Frank-N-Furter, who can scarcely wait to bed his creation, soon escorts Rocky to their sumptuous chamber to the tune of Mendelssohn's wedding march. Later that night, Frank disguises himself as Brad to seduce Janet. When she discovers the ruse, she at first protests, "I was saving myself!" but then gleefully surrenders herself to his enticements. Next, Frank seduces Brad disguised as Janet, a ploy that perhaps works because Brad has no idea what a woman—or at least his fiancée—feels like. Realizing that he is in bed with Frank, he whines, "I thought it was the real thing," before himself succumbing to pleasure. What we have, then, are three marriages (the wedding of Ralph and Betty, the down-the-aisle dance of Brad and Janet, and the mock nuptials of Frank and Rocky) followed by three rapid-fire deflorations (Rocky's, Janet's, and Brad's).

The film is thus punctuated by two important rites of passage: the wedding and the loss of virginity. According to the values of the parodically old-fashioned, middle-American world in which we first see Brad and

Figure 9.1

Janet, the two rites are meant to coincide. The wedding graffiti on Ralph and Betty's car announces, "Wait 'til tonite! She got hers, now he'll get his!" This motto reinforces the traditional assignment of gender roles that the couple exemplifies. (She's "a wonderful little cook," and Ralph will be up for a promotion before long.) Betty has fulfilled the woman's dream of marriage. Janet gushes, "Oh, I can't believe it! An hour ago, she was plain old Betty Monroe, and now . . . now she's Mrs. Ralph Hapschatt!" Before the night is over, Ralph will fulfill the man's dream of heterosexual intercourse. Thus, the ceremony at the chapel is not only the couple's initiation into wedded life but is also their initiation into adult sexuality. Everything happens in the proper time, and Ralph hints that it is now Brad and Janet's turn to tie the knot.[2]

There are problems, however. Janet, as the woman, is supposed to want marriage above all, and it is true that she seems desperate to get a proposal out of Brad, greedily snatching up the engagement ring when it falls to the ground. Nonetheless, her initially unsuccessful attempts to kiss and embrace Brad reveal her already budding sexuality. Later, after her defloration, she will sing that she had never so much as engaged in heavy petting before. Nonetheless, at this early point in the film she is clearly eager to be initiated into both marriage and intimacy. Siegel sees the rites of passage of Brad and Janet as emblematic of the rites of intensification through which society was changing its sexual attitudes (307). It is noteworthy, then, that despite the girl-next-door camp with which the character is written and performed, Janet wants *both* sex and marriage. In addition, her catching the bride's bouquet is an omen of her readiness for passage into the next phase of life as wife and sexual partner.

Brad, in contrast, has a difficult time bringing himself to propose. When Janet catches the bouquet, Ralph assumes that Brad, her predetermined mate, will be the next to tie the knot, but he only responds with a non-committal "Who knows?" During his proposal, he resists Janet's advances, substituting romantic gestures for embraces. At one point, when she rushes into his arms, he swoops her up, places her in front of him, kneels and produces the ring, rather than hold her. At another, he puts distance between them by holding her literally at arms length and going into a dance. As Raymond Ruble notes in "Dr. Freud meets Dr. Frank N. Furter," both are virgins at the beginning of the film—Ruble regards them as equally innocent—and both "embark on an unwitting quest to discover their own sexuality," but Janet experiences a relatively healthy and liberating adjustment, whereas Brad remains repressed. Even in the film's climactic floor show, he struggles against sexual maturation, pleading, "Help me, Mommy . . . take this dream away!" until his sense of himself as a sexual being finally overwhelms him (Ruble 165). Before meeting Frank-N-Furter, however, he seems woefully underprepared for such a transformation (unlike his fiancée).

Already, the idea that through a wedding Janet would "get hers," and through defloration Brad would "get his," seems doubtful. Yet if their wedding had taken place, this notion would have been reinforced anyway, because of the impersonal nature of ritual. As initiates, the bride and groom are inducted into their new roles within and through the agency of a community. The writing on the car, it should be noted, is a traditional wedding prank, probably executed by Ralph's friends and relatives (including Brad). That is, it is a communal endorsement of the spousal and sexual union of the bridal couple. The opening scene of *Rocky Horror* is crowded with cheering friends and family members who participate in Betty and Ralph's initiation into normative adulthood. Likewise, when Frank, barely containing his anticipation, escorts Rocky to his bedchamber, it is amidst a crowd of approving Transylvanians. Echoing the cheering and tossing of rice of the Hapschatt-Munroe well-wishers, they chant, "Frank and Rocky, rah, rah, rah!" and toss confetti, a token of festivity (rather than fertility) better suited to celebrate Frank's pursuit of pleasure through production than traditional reproduction through pleasure.

Because Frank and Rocky's union is so evidently a union of the flesh, the attendance and approbation of the Transylvanians makes clear what might be overlooked at Ralph and Betty's wedding: that the community inaugurates the passage from virginity to sexual experience. Frank, of course, is no virgin, but then, even in the traditional marriage rites that he apes, the purity of the dominant (i.e., male) partner is generally irrelevant. Rather, the community certifies the inexperience of the bride and verifies his taking possession of her. On this the success of the entire marriage depends, for as Freud pronounces in "The Taboo of Virginity," the normal reaction of a bride after defloration is not only to embrace her groom with grateful satisfaction but also to embrace her lasting subjection to him (201). The properly deflowered bride accepts the sanctioned role of the good wife and enables her husband to assume the position of the father. As Kathleen Coyne Kelly states, the virgin is among other things, "the lynchpin in patrilinear cultures, a commodity to be exchanged between men, . . . the guarantee of as well as the reward for conforming to the heterosexual imperative" (Kelly 141). Thus, by overseeing the deflowering of the bride by the groom, the community plays a part in ensuring that each takes up his or her prescribed and gendered role both within the marriage and within heterosexist society as a whole.

This, at least, is how wedding traditions operate within the controlled confines of Denton, where, as Amittai F. Aviram puts it, "rather heavy-handed visual signs reinforce the conception of marriage not as a celebration of love but as the fulfillment of rigid social norms" (187). However, this program fails "over at the Frankenstein place." Even the nonvirgin party in the bridal couple is meant to be an initiate, but Frank holds fast to his role as initiator, controlling the community of Transylvanians as much as he does his string of sexual partners. *He* is not being inducted into a new status, and his lack of cooperation with the collective from Transsexual becomes clear at the film's climax, when his erstwhile servant Riff Raff assumes command of the mission and executes him, declaring, "your lifestyle's too extreme."

Moreover, although Frank and Rocky's Mendelssohn march to the site of consummation evokes the ritual of the wedding night, Frank dispenses with the necessary complement of actual matrimony, because he does not seek the homosexual analogue of a heterosexual institution. That is, he merely wishes to take possession of Rocky—the sole initiate in this rite—who has been created only for his enjoyment. Frank does not seek a meaningful partnership with him. In the Freudian model, Frank's deflowering of Rocky, Janet, and Brad should create in them a durable devotion to him, were it not for the obvious problem that Freud was describing an operation within the structure of heterosexual monogamy, a social system of which the mad doctor makes a mockery. Frank-N-Furter's actions are regulated not by a set of communal principles so much as by a narcissistic program of acting out all of his desires to live up to his motto: "Don't dream it. Be it." Because his driving principle is narcissistic, he does not submit himself to a larger communal regulation of desire, and therefore he cannot avail himself of whatever authority he might have derived through defloration within the heterosexist tradition he parodies. He cannot sustain the imposition on those around him of his desires as law, nor can he prevent others from mimicking his pursuit of personal pleasure.

Illustrative of this is Janet's seduction of Rocky. As previously mentioned, Frank easily persuades Janet to have sex with him, and the brief seduction scene ends as she playfully surrenders herself. The actual defloration takes place off camera. The next time we see Janet, Frank has already left her bedroom, and she is filled with remorse and a feeling of abandonment. As she boards the elevator to go find her fiancé, she cries "Brad, my darling, oh, how could I have done this to you?" "It was easy, but it would have been easier without the pantyhose!" retorts the *Rocky* audience, as Janet rises in the elevator and the camera shot takes in the length of her body down to her stockinged feet. Of course, this is but one of the many examples of editorial sloppiness in the film (the hose disappear in the following scene), but it does rather cast in doubt her actual defloration, which was never explicitly shown. Fundamentally, nothing has changed for Janet, whose remorse stems from a sense of having transgressed the laws to which she was subject—the directives that she marry Brad and surrender her virginity to him, as the bouquet catch predestined. She has not truly passed into a new stage of maturity, because she fervently wishes to undo what has been done. However, when she sees Brad on a television monitor enjoying a postcoital cigarette in bed with Frank, she begins to let go of the parameters that had formally set limits on her sexuality. Obviously, she, Brad, and Frank are not bound by the rules of heterosexual monogamy.

When Janet finds Rocky Horror hurt and hiding in the lab, she at once begins to loosen her repression of her desire for him. When initially asked her opinion of Frank's creature, Janet had cast a nervous glance at Brad, replied, "Well, I don't like men with too many muscles," and then looked back at Brad for approval. Later, when Frank was singing in rousing praise of the ideal masculine physique that Rocky embodies, Janet surprised everyone by piping in, "I'm a muscle fan!" Brad immediately quelled that burst of enthusiasm with a look of shock and disapproval. Now that Janet finds herself alone with her adored muscle man, however, Frank-N-Furter has destroyed the two things that might have constrained her from seducing the object of her desire: He has shattered her carefully preserved virginity, and he has placed Brad in flagrant violation of heterosexual monogamy, so that he can no longer represent the Law. As Janet tends Rocky's wounded hand, and he caresses hers, gazing at her with evident desire, she pauses for a moment in a state of indecision, even bewilderment, and then slowly smiles. This smile signals the completion of the process of defloration Frank began and unwittingly fostered but failed to control. Janet's true passage into sexual maturation occurs not when she surrenders her corporal virginity but when she recognizes and pursues her own fantasies, albeit fantasies prescribed within a male-dominated, heterosexist matrix. Janet quickly passes not from virgin to wife (as a conventional wedding with and defloration by Brad would have necessitated) but from virgin to whore (as her deflowering by Frank has made possible). She avidly strives to take up this new position, serenading Rocky with increasing brazenness:

> Touch-a, touch-a, touch-a, touch me!
> I wanna be dirty.
> Thrill me, chill me, fulfill me,
> Creature of the night!

As Aviram notes, "The disseminative Dionysian power to release, disrupt, seduce and sway is, unfortunately for Frank, not limited to the personality who locally represents it. Once Janet has been seduced, she cannot be stopped from seducing Frank's artificial man in turn, whom Frank had been reserving for his own pleasure as the perfect object of property" (189). Although she is no longer under Frank's direct control, the criminologist/narrator affirms that Janet is, in fact, slave to a "powerful and irrational master": emotion.

Emotion also replaces Frank as master over Rocky. Similar to Janet's and Brad's, Rocky's defloration has taken place off camera, and he next appears asleep, chained to the bed and lying on his stomach, suggesting that he had been the receptive partner in his interlude with Frank. During Janet's seduction, however, he eventually takes her underneath him, assuming for the first time the dominant position that Frank-N-Furter (who always seems to be on top) probably never intended him to take. His defloration is therefore also a process, rather than an event—one over which Frank loses sway.

Frank later tries to reassert his power over his "children" with his sonic transducer and medusa ray, which turns them into statues and ensures that they will reanimate in a state of debauchery centered on his pleasure. He stages their frozen bodies for a burlesque floor show and literally turns them on with the flip of a switch. Yet despite all these measures, Rocky warns, "Somebody should be told, / That my libido hasn't been controlled." Not surprisingly, the unchecked monster is destroyed along with his creator. As Riff Raff shoots at them again and again with his laser, Rocky, carrying Frank on his back, climbs a set piece representing the RKO radio tower. The fall of that phallic symbol signals the demise of them both.

Critics differ as to how Brad and Janet will proceed in their new sexual roles after their night at the Frankenstein place.[3] One reason for the range of opinions, most of them surprisingly optimistic, may be that the version of the film originally released in the United States omits parts of the song "Super Heroes," in which Brad and Janet writhe in the mire where the castle/spaceship once stood (it has blasted off to Transsexual), singing about their feelings of violation and suffering.[4] In any case, the lyrics from the reprise of "Science Fiction/Double Feature" that accompany the end credits in both versions reveal, "Darkness has conquered Brad and Janet." It is safe to say, then, that their experience has had a negative effect on their future lives. Nonetheless, it has served as a sort of rite of passage insofar as they emerge transformed and unable to return to their former status. Mark Siegel, following the work of Arnold van Gannep, identifies three stages in rites of intensification or passage: separation, transition, and incorporation. He observes that in *Rocky Horror*, the incorporation phase is aborted, leaving Janet and Brad's rites of passage incomplete (307). Into what group, after all, could they possibly be incorporated? Riff Raff cast them out of the castle before beaming it back to Transsexual, indicating that although they were inducted into sexuality by the renegade Frank-N-Furter, they were never initiated into Transylvanian society. Moreover, because their introduction into sexual maturity was removed from and in defiance of their own community, it is doubtful that their newfound status will allow them to assume their new roles harmoniously within Denton. Caught between Earth and outer space, the retro and the futuristic, and devoid of a context in which to understand their newfound identities, they are indeed, as the criminologist concludes, "Lost in time and lost in space and meaning."

Slaying Virgins

Despite its sober ending, most of *Rocky Horror* is an invitation to "swim the warm waters of sins of the flesh." Indeed, many of the regular audience members come to celebrate sexual transgression, and so they naturally relish the metaphorical defloration of "virgins." Nonetheless, it is curious that this term would come to be applied to *Rocky Horror* debutantes throughout North America, as the word "virgin" is never actually uttered in the film. When, for example, Janet tells Rocky that she only ever kissed before that night, Frank-N-Furter's minions Columbia and Magenta are spying on the two through a monitor. Stunned, Columbia asks, "You mean she . . . ?" to which Magenta, amused, answers "Uh-huh," much to her companion's disgust. It is as if "virgin" is a dirty word, better left unsaid. Perhaps it is only fitting, then, that Rocky fans scream the word at every midnight showing. What's more, each live action production company has developed and regularly practices rituals of defloration to which their "virgins" must submit. Yet, *virgin* is by no means a stable term, just as virginity is not an unambiguous concept.[5] To what, then, is the *Rocky Horror* "virgin" actually likened? What concepts of virginity and sexual experience are being drawn from through this analogy? What understandings of the transformation of defloration are performed by *Rocky Horror* "virgins" and by those who orchestrate their symbolic deflowering?

Let us begin with an exchange I witnessed on a recent Friday night, just after midnight at *Rocky Horror*. I was standing in line at the cinema ticket booth behind a small group of college-aged patrons, when a member of Lips Down on Dixie, the urban Atlanta *Rocky Horror* production company, approached, asking if any of them were coming to see *Rocky Horror* for the first time.[6] There was a tense pause for a few seconds, and then the *Rocky Horror* regular gleefully pointed at a tall, redheaded girl, identifying her as a "virgin"—a first-timer. The redhead unhesitatingly conceded: "You could see it in my eyes, huh?" "Yeah," replied the regular, "the virgin always twitches."

Several understandings of virginity were communicated through this exchange. First, the basis of the analogy between the *Rocky Horror* "virgin" and the literal virgin is a lack of experience. Virginity is conceived as lack, a "no" in response to the question "Have you ever . . . ?" The nonvirgin is distinguished through memory and history, both psychological and corporeal, and answers "yes" to the question "Have you ever . . . ?" From the moment the answer becomes "yes," it can never again be "no," meaning that virginity can only be had or lost once. However, it is precisely the problem of experience that has made it increasingly difficult in recent years to distinguish both the real virgin and the *Rocky Horror* "virgin."

The operative question in determining a person's virginity is "Have you ever . . . " *what*? The prevailing notion seems to be that a person who has had heterosexual intercourse involving vaginal penetration is definitively not a virgin. Anal, oral, and interfemoral sex and vaginal penetration with objects or body parts other than a penis, although clearly activities through which one can constitute oneself as a sexual being, are not necessarily considered as means of defloration. As Kelly points out, "There are other stories to be told about coming into sexual experience, stories that fall outside the paradigm of heterosexual description and metaphor, and as such, have been rendered as untellable and unreadable" (122).

The *Rocky Horror* communities I have known have provided privileged spaces wherein engagement in and initiation into nonnormative sexuality have been validated. However, *Rocky Horror* devotees have proven rather less flexible in defining the "virgin," as the understanding of what qualifies as experience of the film has become blurred. In 1990, CBS/Fox commemorated the fifteenth anniversary of *Rocky Horror* by releasing the film on video. For the first time, it was possible to view the movie independent of the audience culture that had made it so famous. Since then, it has also been regularly aired on television, and in 2002, Twentieth Century Fox Home Entertainment released it on DVD, with an added feature that allows the viewer to hear the audience participation while viewing the film. *Rocky Horror* regulars responded by making communal interaction at a public viewing of the film—rather than the actual viewing of the film itself—the sine qua non of the experience. The essay "What Every 'Virgin' Should Know" on the official *Rocky Horror* Web site bluntly states, "Seeing it on video doesn't count! Neither does seeing it on TV!" Its author, James Norman, recommends against watching it on video before seeing it in the theater, and he refers to the viewer who has only seen it at home as a "video virgin." The members of Lips Down on Dixie take a compromise approach that acknowledges degrees of inexperience: A person who has never seen *Rocky Horror* at all is a "virgin." A person who has seen it, but without the live theater experience, is labeled a "masturbator" and is treated as a slightly more experienced variation of the "virgin."

A second significant factor evoked in the exchange I witnessed at the ticket booth is the relationship between virginity and gender. If defloration has traditionally depended on vaginal penetration, it is largely because virginity is usually located in the female body. Yet, in *Rocky Horror*, there are two male virgins, each representing an archetypical understanding of what a virgin is: There is Brad, the repressed and awkward neophyte, and Rocky, the embodiment of pure sexual potential, pristine and untapped. The presence of male virgins fits well with the general gender blending of the film and with its openness to nonnormative sexualities and deflorations. Thus, when the *Rocky Horror* veteran asked the group of young men and women at the ticket counter whether any of them were attending for the first time, she considered them all potential "virgins."

The group's uncomfortable pause in response to her question points to a third important consideration in that encounter: the group dynamic. As I discussed in my reading of the film itself, defloration rites have traditionally involved a process of initiation into a new role within the larger community. At the cinema, the deflowering of the *Rocky Horror* "virgin" similarly takes the form of a ritualized induction. In the case of the ticket counter incident, the silence of the "experienced" theatergoers signaled their unwillingness to expose their friend, the redhead, who was a member of their own subgroup, but an outsider to the *Rocky Horror* community with which they were joined through common experience. All friends are not so generous. It is very common for enthusiastic attendees actively to participate in the initiation of their "virgin" friends or relatives, telling them about the fabulous experiences they have had, inviting them to come along, and then happily exposing their comrades' inexperience when asked to point out the "virgins." In their program book, Lips Down on Dixie welcomes this sort of operation: "Please tell your friends about Rocky Horror—Especially if they're Virgins! We live to embarrass! . . . We deflower the very best." Terrible as this may sound, it is important to keep in mind that the *Rocky Horror* experience is only possible through group effort. Lips Down on Dixie constantly recruits new regulars, and every "virgin" represents a potential member of the cast or crew. The defloration rituals enable them to build a sense of community, because once a newcomer has experienced *Rocky Horror*, he or she shares in a collective experience and is no longer a virgin. Furthermore, those "virgins" who are willing to have fun—even at their own expense—are the ones who are most likely to make a commitment to the communal experience, whether it be by coming again in costume, regularly and boisterously participating in the audience participation, or joining the production company.

The final and most obvious point that can be made about the outing of the redheaded "virgin" is the assumption that virginity may be visually perceived. In *Performing Virginity*, Kelly demonstrates that this has been an extraordinarily durable and universal belief that is to be found in both religious and secular conceptions of virginity. In fact, virginity continues to be read in demeanor. For example, one of the clearest signs of Brad and Janet's initial sexual inexperience is his uptight awkwardness and her frenetic giddiness after Ralph and Betty's wedding. The persistent belief in visible virginity is a guiding principle in the *Rocky Horror* defloration rituals as well. The redhead's virginity showed through her body (in her eyes) and her behavior (she twitched). When I asked several Lips Down on Dixie company members whether they could always tell a virgin on sight, the answer was a resounding "yes!" Even "hip virgins" who dress up for their first time give themselves away, I was told, because they are eager for the fullest possible experience. Nevertheless, despite the supposed visibility of "virginity," the first step in hazing first-time attendees is publicly to identify them. Regulars may "slay them and lei them"; that is, mark them with a visible sign and place artificial leis around their necks. Lips Down on Dixie designates their "virgins" by drawing the letter "v" on their foreheads in lipstick ("m" for "masturbators") and kissing them on the cheeks, leaving bright red lip prints. Of course, this practice places in doubt the idea that "virginity" is visibly evident. Why should "virgins" be marked if their inexperience is already visible? One reasonable reply to this question was that it makes them much easier to locate in the darkened theater after the movie has started. Even so, there remains the problem of why the cast member had to ask whether any of the students were "virgins."

Once the redhead was exposed, slayed, and leid, her symbolic defloration had only just begun. "Virgin" rites are numerous and vary among

Rocky Horror communities, ranging from the merely silly to the shockingly obscene. It is customary at viewings of *Rocky Horror* to have a preshow entertainment, and this is generally when the defloration rites take place, most of them reenactments of sex acts in the form of contests. The cast may request volunteer "virgins" for this, allowing only a few to stand in for all of the first-timers, or they may all be made to go to the front of the auditorium. For example, the virgins may compete to fake the best orgasm, play "Ring Around the Dildo," or see who can be the first to place a condom on a banana using only his or her mouth. In the "Twinkie Race," male contestants lay on their backs and place a Twinkie on their crotches, and their female partners, laying on top of them in the sixty-nine position, race to be the first to eat the Twinkie. In the "Suck-and-Blow Relay," the first team member holds a playing card to his or her mouth with suction and passes it to the next team member, who passes it to the next, and so on down the line. In "Make a Wish," far and away the most grotesque rite I have come across, two regulars lift a virgin with his or her legs spread, at which point a member of the cast jumps in front and mimes the sex act. Much less literal, Lips Down on Dixie cast members have "virgins" blow up red balloons during *Rocky Horror*'s dinner party scene. After leading the "virgins" in a choreographed dance to the song "Eddie's Teddy," they "pop their cherries."

The analogy of the "virgin's" first experience with *Rocky Horror* and the virgin's first experience of sex—oral, vaginal, heterosexual, or homosexual—is thus evoked often and without subtlety. The games seem to be only fictions of real sex, but because sex is a cultural construct as well as a bodily act, the possibility certainly exists that they can have real significance in the sexual development of the voluntary participants. For example, some "virgins" have had a great deal of actual sexual experience without their passage from virgin to nonvirgin having ever been recognized. The games provide them the opportunity obliquely to acknowledge this change in status by participating in the fun with zest or skill. Conversely, a "virgin" who is indeed sexually inexperienced can experiment, assuming the mock role of a sexually active person. A clandestine virgin may use the games to conceal actual virginity by performing sexual experience. *Rocky Horror* itself blurs the distinctions between sex (which occurs behind curtains and off camera) and the suggestion of sex (which is constant). So, too, audience participation activities such as mimicking the on-screen action, costuming oneself as a favorite character, and joining in "virgin" games provide a context through which *Rocky Horror* devotees can perform their fantasies and play with their identities, all the while eliding actual intercourse.

As previously mentioned, defloration rituals in the *Rocky Horror* cult vary widely, and I could not possibly list or discuss them all, but one merits special attention. It is the *Rocky Horror* "virgin" oath, sworn with the right hand raised and the left placed on the breast (for females) or crotch (for males): "I, virgin scum, do hereby admit in front of all these people that I am a *Rocky Horror* virgin, and I wish to lose all my morals and accept decadence into my heart. Yea, though I walk through the Valley of Heterosexuality, I shall fear no Republicans. Give us this day our daily head in the name of Frankie and Rocky and the holy Riff Raff. Klaatu barada nikto."

It is immediately apparent that what begins as an oath soon metamorphoses into a prayer. With its contempt for virginity and normative sexuality, its celebration of licentiousness, and its political commentary, all combined with a healthy dose of blasphemy, I imagine that a fan of the Marquis de Sade must have composed it. It is also Sadian insofar as it implies a sort of initiation into perversion. After all, the *Rocky Horror* defloration rituals are nothing if not an initiation into a cult. Members of the cult offer up "virgins" at midnight for "slaying." Up to and throughout the initiation, the "virgins" are in a state of nervous anticipation, not knowing what secret rites will be imposed on them. Through their participation in the prescribed ritual, they are instructed in the purpose and ethics of the cult ("to lose all my morals and accept decadence into my heart") and learn of its deities (Frank et al.). They chant, sing, and wildly dance (the "Time Warp"). In the end, their status has changed. No longer "virgins," they have been initiated into the cult that constitutes itself as communally other, as collectively alien. Klaatu barada nikto.

The concepts of virginity and defloration—which were never really stable ideas to begin with—have had to weather rapidly and radically changing attitudes about sex in recent years. Even in 1975, when *Rocky Horror* was released, the ideals and practices of the Hapschatts were becoming a thing of the past, and although today there remain in America subcultures in which brides and even grooms are expected to march down the aisle virginities intact, this is no longer the norm, nor do most people pretend that it is. This shift in societal standards has rendered the lack of ceremonial specific to defloration somewhat problematic. As I have demonstrated, public rituals allow communities to convey strong social messages to those passing from one status to another. For instance, the rites of the Hapschatt wedding herald that Betty will surrender her virginity to Ralph, that the two will assume prescribed gender roles, and that Janet and Brad will follow suit. Notably, the latter two are initiated into sexual maturity privately and in a manner that defies Denton's mandates. As a direct result, they find themselves "lost in time and lost in space and meaning"; they are unable to determine the significance of their sexual experiences and the future direction they should take vis-à-vis the community at large. "All I know," sings the violated Brad in "Super Heroes," "is down inside I'm bleeding." The sense of pain and meaninglessness of a modern neophyte may in fact be more acute, because unlike Brad and Janet, who at least know themselves to be in direct violation of clear communal signals, young people today lack ceremonial standards against which to evaluate their personal choices. There is no concerted performance to answer the questions of what virginity means, what conditions are normative for its loss, and what status the deflowered person assumes in relation to others. Of course, messages about virginity and sexuality are broadcast through popular media, but these tend to be contradictory and politically or commercially motivated.

Thus, young people possess the exhilarating and frightening freedom to assign or decline meaning in their first sex act, to adopt or reject those defloration narratives already in wide circulation. *Rocky Horror*, as so many other films, suggests multiple versions of the first time, ranging from the conservative to the transgressive. What is uniquely useful, however, is the way in which the cult experience allows the first-time participant to publicly perform his or her *own* virginity, defloration, and sexuality within a context that is ostensibly safe, because everything may be reduced to suggestion and metaphor, and because all actions are communally prescribed. Furthermore, however awkward or embarrassing the experience of "deflowering" may feel, the "virgin" knows that the "nonvirgins" present have gone through similar rites and are reliving their own defloration narratives. Thus, within this cult, all may avail themselves of an opportunity that no other community affords: to cast aside their status as innocents ceremonially and to claim for themselves publicly the pleasures of experience.

Works Cited

Aviram, Amittai F. "Postmodern Gay Dionysus: Dr. Frank N. Furter." *Journal of Popular Culture* 26.3 (1992): 185–92.

Freud, Sigmund. "The Taboo of Virginity." *The Standard Edition of the Complete Psychological Works of Sigmund Freud*, vol. 11. Ed. James Strachey. London: The Hogarth Press, 1957. 193–208.

Grant, Barry K. "Science Fiction Double Feature: Ideology in the Cult Film." *The Cult Film Experience: Beyond All Reason.* Ed. J. P. Telotte. Austin: U of Texas P, 1991. 122–37.

Hoberman, J., and Jonathan Rosenbaum. *Midnight Movies.* [1983]. New York: Da Capo, 1991.

Kelly, Kathleen Coyne. *Performing Virginity and Testing Chastity in the Middle Ages.* London: Routledge, 2000.

Norman, James. "What Every 'Virgin' Should Know." *The Official* Rocky Horror Picture Show *Web Site.* 1996–2002. 15 Dec. 2003 http://www.rockyhorror.com/virgknow.html.

Ruble, Raymond. "Dr. Freud Meets Dr. Frank N. Furter." *Eros in the Mind's Eye: Sexuality and the Fantastic in Art and Film.* Ed. Donald Palumbo. New York: Greenwood, 1986. 161–68.

Siegel, Mark. "*The Rocky Horror Picture Show*: More Than A Lip Service." *Science-Fiction Studies* 7.3 (1980): 305–12.

Notes

1. In this article, I refer to both actual virginity and the figurative virginity of the *Rocky Horror* novice. To distinguish between the two, I place the word "virgin" in quotes when referring to those attending the film for the first time.

2. It should be noted that Frank-N-Furter also presides over this initiation. Tim Curry plays the part of the minister at the wedding of the Hapschatts, and his minions Riff Raff, Magenta, and Columbia are present as church caretakers. In the next scene, the narrator, a criminologist, is shown viewing a slide of the wedding photo. A large handwritten red arrow points to the minister (Curry), and the sexton's face (O'Brien) is circled in red. A moment later, he peruses a casebook marked "The Denton Affair," containing more wedding pictures, typed notes, and head shots of Janet and Brad. These details suggest that the Transsexual Transylvanians have already infiltrated Denton, the traditionalist "Home of Happiness."

3. See Ruble 165; Hoberman and Rosenbaum 309; Aviram 190; Grant 21.

4. The song is included in the UK release, and this is the version currently being shown at my local cinema. The first two stanzas of "Super Heroes" are sung after the castle blasts off. The final lines of the criminologist actually constitute the third verse of the song.

5. For example, is Brad truly no longer a virgin after his interlude with Frank-N-Furter? Or, as virginity is usually defined in terms of heterosex, will he only be technically deflowered after vaginally penetrating a woman? Does it matter whether he penetrated Frank or was himself penetrated? And could it be that his awkward struggle against his newfound desires betokens that he is still a virgin after all? (In other words, and to borrow the phrase from Kathleen Coyne Kelly, does he perform his virginity?)

6. I am most grateful to the cast and crew of Lips Down on Dixie for the warm assistance they gave me in researching this article. The troupe is ranked number one in Georgia for offering the best experience to "virgins.")

Part III

Rocky Horror and Sexuality

10

In Search of the Authentic Queer Epiphany

Normativity and Representations of the Queer Disabled Body in *Rocky Horror*

Ben Hixon

The tendency toward normalcy and uniformity in popular culture often manifests itself in individual texts as subtle assumptions and underlying definitions of how a character should or should not act to be perceived as a person.[1] These implicit advocations of normalcy as "the way things are supposed to be" directly result in the marginalization and restriction of certain identities that are not acceptable from the normative point of view, and those who maintain and experience these "undesirable" identities are subject to disdain, disavowal, prejudice, victimization, or violence within a social system dominated by these norms. Attention to the marginalization of specific groups has focused historically on gender expectations, sexual preference, and ethnicity; however, recently a new category of marginality and victimization has come into critical focus: disability. The disabled body traditionally has been conceived of in mass culture as "broken," "inferior," or "bad"; as an identity situation in need of fixing; or if unfixable, then in need of segregation and seclusion—as something to be thought of with sadness or get well cards, but not with openness or equality. Recently, many political strategies have been developed to "break out" the disabled body into popular society; to highlight the arbitrary, socially constructed prejudice against the disabled; and to fight against their marginalization. One particular strategy used to undermine prejudice is the sexualization of the disabled body. Given that the disabled body frequently has been represented as asexual, this process of sexualization thereby may render the disabled body less "alien." In this consideration of the sexuality of the disabled, queerly sexual and queerly disabled identity categories can overlap, and their respective theorists can work together.[2] An alliance between queer and disability theory has produced an awareness of the body as both a source of fluctuating identity and as a site of lived experience of marginalization.

An analysis of the normative forces that produce marginalization of the queer and disabled identity within *The Rocky Horror Picture Show* can help to expose those forces within larger social contexts. This chapter first looks for such queer-disabled identity positions represented in *Rocky Horror* or, as in the case of Rocky himself, normate identity positions that indicate the queer by contrast, and then discusses whether the "overall" plot flow of the film supports either normative marginalization or queer disruption. Although on the surface *Rocky Horror* is certainly replete with alternative bodies and sexualities, I discuss several methods by which a text such as *Rocky Horror* can use these alternative representations to serve a further strengthening of normative hierarchies. Beginning with an identification of styles of character representation and then moving to a discussion of those textual mechanisms by which the inclusion of queer or disabled characters may still uphold normative regulations, I attempt to show that *Rocky Horror* does indeed subvert normative regulation, and I argue for the presence in the film of an authentically queer, antiableist, counter-normative subtext—one whose effect on the audience includes a breaking out of those normative stereotypes that render the disabled body as inhuman monstrosity. By first establishing character positions on which plot movement is built and then studying plot resolution and identifying narrative "epiphanies" that are resolutions imbued with strong power and incite potentially transformative reactions within the audience, I attempt to make the case that *Rocky Horror* exhibits a type of "authentic" queer disruption of the norm that does not allow for a nullification or pacification of the queer's potency.

The most obvious disabled characters in *Rocky Horror* are doctor Frank-N-Furter's humpbacked butler Riff Raff and the wheelchair-bound government scientist Dr. Everett Scott. Also a site of dis/ability identity tension is Rocky Horror himself—a beacon of masculine, ableist normativity. *Rocky Horror* highlights difference and marginalization via parody, calling unavoidable attention both to marginalized subject positions—queer and disabled bodies—and to excessively normative positions such as that of Rocky; in both cases, the result is a self-awareness of the social fluidity of identity. If a body's difference through disability is made unavoidably obtrusive to the viewer, then it can be a site of subversion of its normative position, especially when that difference is even further underscored by sexuality. Because sexuality is a peculiarly "social" experience, a disabled body that also experiences sex could be attributed with a social identity or individuality that disrupts some of its fixed essentialism, perhaps working to show that disability is a social category as well as, or instead of, a merely physical one.

The disabled body in *Rocky Horror* is both clearly underscored, calling attention to its differential status, and sexualized or "queered." For example, when Scott first arrives at the castle and appears in the "Zen room," Dr. Frank-N-Furter turns on the electromagnet and pulls Scott into the laboratory by his wheelchair. This clear highlighting of the wheelchair brings to the forefront the crippled, contrary status of Scott, drawing attention to his disability rather than attempting to cover it up or pretend it is normal, which would elide the individual disabled identity and remove it from the normative perspective by making it "pass" as normal and unobtrusive. Instead of supporting a normative stance in the film, the use of the electromagnet draws explicit attention to the disability. Scott's disabled body then becomes sexualized when, during the floor show and the performative dragging of Rocky, Brad, Janet, and Columbia, he reveals his dragged, stocking-clad leg from underneath his blanket (see Figure 10.1).[3]

The effect the exposure of Scott's leg has is the depiction of the disabled body as both a product of and an occurrence of drag, of a social performance in which physical appearance or mannerisms construct perceived and experienced identity. Judith Butler has famously analogized drag and performativity, pointing out how performing a dragged identity—"dressing up" as another identity while leaving the prior identity still in evidence—highlights identity's social construction in that the identity is shown to be defined by its appearance, gestures, and mannerisms. Moreover, Butler has proposed that drag offers an opportunity to disrupt defined and normative identities through their parody. The explicit representation of the disabled body coupled with its sexual dragging first calls attention to that body and then exacerbates its status as marginal by having the representation parody itself through sexualization.

The other explicitly represented disabled body, Riff Raff, occupies a notably different position than Scott. He is also sexualized in his liaisons with his

Figure 10.1

sister Magenta, who is not represented as disabled, but these sexualizations are—especially when compared to Frank-N-Furter's escapades—asexual and devoid of passion or emotion. Indeed, in "Postmodern Gay Dionysus," Amittai Aviram refers to Riff Raff and Magenta as representing the pure Apollonian couple, Apollo and Artemis (189–90), indicative of Nietzsche's formulation of the Apollonian drive as striving toward order and purity. Aviram contrasts Riff Raff/Magenta's asceticism with Frank-N-Furter's Dionysian lust and chaos. Later in this chapter, I discuss the film's finale and the "victory" of the Apollonian drive over the Dionysian, involving a transformation of Riff Raff from marginal, disabled body to normate body with the removal of his hump. However, as the quotes I placed around the word "victory" suggest, I also argue that although *Rocky Horror* appears to resolve with an ascendancy of the norm, the more powerful resolution is counter-normative, disableist, and queer, because of the overriding of normative binaries via the disruptive power of a nonmarginalizing sexuality.

Not only can the sexualization of a marginalized or abjected body call attention to its "undesirability" but sexing or queering an icon of normative *authority* may reduce that icon's normative-inducing power and circumvent its authority. This occurs in *Rocky Horror* with the sexualization of the medical or scientific gaze. The medical gaze is a major regulatory power acting on bodies to partition them into normate and disabled. By over-medicalizing the body, by viewing it as a specimen of disease rather than as the site of a human identity, and by unilaterally imposing on an abnormal body the qualities of sickness, ill health, and unnaturalness—qualities in need of being removed, thereby rendering the body-person as itself needing to be removed—the gaze of medicine reduces the disabled body to an inferior "wrongness" that cannot be a valid identity in its own right. In this way, the medical gaze and the system of truth-images and definitions from which it gazes work to reify the norm by abjecting and marginalizing the disabled other. However, this gaze draws its social power from the perceived authority of the medical purveyors—the doctors and scientists.

By again invoking a queer emphasis on sexuality as a major site of normative unrest, we can see that *Rocky Horror* undermines the authority of the medical gaze by dragging and introducing desire into the figure of the doctor, the originator of the medical gaze, and the symbol of authority to which society attributes the essentialist and naturalist power of medical definitions. Giving the doctor a subjective and queer identity position cuts away the authoritative objectivity of medicine. Recent theorizing of the medical gaze has elucidated this method of socializing medicine and of blurring together medicine and desire; of particular interest is the work revolving around the poet-physician Rafael Campo. In a 2003 issue of *GLQ*, Joanne Rendell appraises Campo's work on sexualizing the doctor image and attributing desire and personality to the doctor-patient relationship, relocating that relationship from a rigid binary to a more hybridized dynamic. For Rendell, Campo's works "enact critical, often transformative reimaginings of the medical setting and of biomedical thinking, where power and bodies, illness, relations, and identities are envisaged very differently" (206). Rendell focuses on Campo's blurring of the bodies of the patient and the doctor, the sick and the healthy, the normal and the abnormal—a blurring that Campo enacts primarily through introducing a sexual underpinning to the doctor's gaze. Clearly, a similar sexualization occurs in *Rocky Horror*, in which the body of the doctor, the patient, and the sexual lover combine.

Two characters in *Rocky Horror* can be thought to represent the doctor: Scott and Frank-N-Furter himself. As mentioned, Scott's position is one of clearly demonstrated disability, blurring the lines between doctor and sick object-specimen. The much more powerful blurring, however, occurs in the character of Frank-N-Furter. As a scientist, he evokes the doctor's figure of authority; but rather than the humanist figure of scientific power and supremacy, Frank is a Dionysian figure of sexual desire and lust. Though significant to Frank-N-Furter's character, the scientist-doctor is secondary to the lover. Frank's primary scientific act is the creation of a new lover in Rocky, and Frank spends the entire film attempting to promulgate his own sexual extravagance. Because of Frank-N-Furter's own dragging and sexualization, and because of the continued use and reference to Frank as "doctor," his character representation helps to disrupt univocal medical authority and identity assignation. Frank-N-Furter represents an interesting blend of hyperactive sexuality and scientific humanism—a hybrid of the creator and desire for the creation usually absent in scientist tropes.

The product of Frank's science is Rocky Horror, a blond-haired blue-eyed muscle-bound normate-bodied stereotype. Does Rocky's own seemingly normative presence and prominence in *Rocky Horror* present a problem for a disability activist-oriented reading of the text? Regulatory power often acts to construct norms invisibly, to wrap around the mind of the reader and seep perniciously into the unconscious. An extremely normative character such as Rocky could be interpreted as reifying normative regulations. However, obtrusively emphasizing the normative location of a character, as exemplified with the electromagnetic highlight of Scott's disability, potentially can subvert and circumvent that invisible normative construction. Because Rocky is such a stereotype, such an extreme parody, his character does not cultivate a normative marginalization of disabled bodies but instead ironically highlights the normate body. His character could be said to masquerade as a masculine, white, able-bodied normate, to exaggerate the normative or socially dominant characteristics to play that subject position's normative-given power against the normative itself.

This is a disability appropriation of Mary Ann Doane's own adoption of Joan Riviere's theory of the masquerade. For Doane, Riviere's theory of "excess" femininity as a way to mask individual difference and marginality is "to dismantle the question of essentialism before it can even be posed" (37). Masquerade distances the subject from its actions and social identity and creates incoherence between the representation of woman and the subject that behaves as woman. A "glitch in the system," masquerade is "a way of appropriating this necessary distance or gap, in the operation of semiotic systems, of deploying it for women, of reading femininity differently" (37). Masquerade introduces instability in the signifier: A feminine representation does not necessarily imply a feminine subject. Similarly, a normate representation such as Rocky does not necessarily imply a normate able-bodied subject but, indeed, ironically can parody the normate and thus call attention to its artificiality.

Not only can Rocky be thought of as a body exaggeratingly masquerading as normate but he is also obviously the Frankenstein's monster to Frank-N-Furter's doctor Frankenstein. The monster has historically been represented by a negatively connotated body, but Rocky is both that hideous monster and the beautiful idealized bride of Frankenstein in one. Because Rocky is masquerading as normate but is also created, the normate is presented as both a social identity and one rooted in materiality: He is a physical, material identity in flux.

Frank-N-Furter sets this idea of physical identity construction into song when he sings, "In just seven days / I can make you a man," alluding of course to the biblical story of the creation of the world.[4] Frank in this song contrasts the "natural" construction of a "man" to his "better" construction:

He'll eat nutritious high protein
And swallow raw eggs . . .
Try to build up his shoulders,
His chest, arms, and legs.
Such an effort—
If he only knew of my plan
In just seven days. . . .

Frank acknowledges the "usual" way one becomes a "man"—the parodic definition of "man" as possessing big muscles and little brain—but contrasts it to his artificial construction. Rocky represents the normate as fabrication, and Frank-N-Furter represents the extreme authority that does the fabricating, as well as a potential source of *re*-fabrication or disruption—a combination that exemplifies and parodies the construction of the normate identity in society and its lack of a basis in any fixed reality.

Rocky is both lover and science project, subject and object, specimen and person. This position is the cyborg as put forward by Donna Haraway: a marginalized subject position that, because of its blurring of boundaries, especially of social with scientific, has particular power and freedom in the construction of its own identity. We can connect the socially constructed Rocky cyborg to the Scott cyborg as explicitly delineated by Scott's metal wheelchair—a cyborgian technological enhancement. Disability theory and the concept of the cyborg have had a small number of crossings-over; for example, Allison Frailberg, in her 1991 essay "Of AIDS, Cyborgs, and Other Indiscretions: Resurfacing the Body in the Postmodern," makes the connection between the cyborg and increasing medical actions and reactions against AIDS, calling attention to the human-machine hybridity performed by, for example, intravenous drug use and the encouragement of condoms and clean needles. She makes the point that resistance to "cyborg-like integration ultimately leaves intact traditional sites of authority, sites with various investments in the 'general public': for example, bio-medical research, the position of the Surgeon General, governmental and legal policy decisions" (28). However, although the cyborg integration Frailberg refers to is specifically on the "patient" side, Scott, as a representation of both medical and governmental authority, further erodes that authority by blurring the rigid boundaries between creator and creation, between medical gaze and object of medical gaze, between scientist and specimen, and between doctor and patient. *Rocky Horror*'s blurring of disabled body (Scott), exaggerated normate body (Rocky), medical gaze (Scott), and cyborg (Scott and Rocky) is a powerful tool for complicating power structures that construct and restrict body-identities.

Thus far, we have discussed power structures by simply studying character positions and representations in *Rocky Horror* from a disability studies perspective informed by queer theory's awareness of power, marginality, and normativity. Although static character representations are important in that they establish a basic viewpoint of the text, at least equally as important are the narrative and plot mechanisms—the changes in the story and character positions that move the text and pull the reader along. There are multiple methods by which a seemingly queer narrative such as *Rocky Horror* can resolve into one that is "favorable" to the norm. An important development in disability theory is the idea that the disabled character is frequently used by the norm to shore up an authoritative edifice by forwarding or cohering the narrative resolution. Terming this textual device "narrative prosthesis," David Mitchell and Sharon Snyder argue that the representation of disability in texts frequently occurs at the expense of marginalizing disabled bodies, that disability "is deployed in literary narrative as a master metaphor for social ills . . . [providing] a means through which literature performs its social critique while simultaneously sedimenting stigmatizing beliefs about people with disabilities" (Mitchell 24). Representations of disability, which could potentially disrupt the narrative flow by introducing an unruly subject position undefinable within the narrative's established definitions, are actually used in reverse, as prostheses that can "plug up the holes" in the norm's representational reach to empower the norm rather than destabilize it; the disabled body is assimilated and used "as a crutch on which literary narratives lean for their representational power" (17) and thereby robbed of its queer subversiveness. Similarly, Robert McRuer identifies ableist, heteronormative epiphanies—means by which the norm slightly tolerates the queer disabled subject to invite it into the narrative, to offer it "a sense of subjective wholeness, however illusory" (82). Describing an example of epiphany as a filmic device, McRuer defines the "epiphanic moment" as one "in which an individual is said to lose himself or herself briefly, [that] tends to be a moment of unparalleled subjectivity. As the music swells and the light shifts, the moment marks for the character a temporary consolidation of past, present, and future, and the clarity that describes that consolidation allows the protagonist to carry, to the close of the narrative, a sense of subjective wholeness that he or she lacked previously" (85). By giving the marginal identity a definite subject position, a narrative resolution can latch down the queer individual, offering it a carrot to take away its disruptive power. In this way, texts featuring queer characters often reinforce the norm.

A third method by which normative narratives can include queer representations while still shoring up the norm is abjection. The abject within a text is that which is not identifiable by the viewer—that which is made intentionally and narratively queer and unusual. By featuring an abject representation, a text can promote the expulsion of the queer from its reader by providing an opportunity to "get it out of the system"; the text can then close with a normative resolution that distills any lingering thoughts that the depravity is acceptable in "real" life. This concept of abjection, originally formulated by Julia Kristeva to understand works of literature such as those of Céline and Bataille, is applied by Barbara Creed to horror film. Although Creed does restrict her study of the abject to the idea of the female as monster and, in my opinion, overessentializes by locating archetypes or general classes of the abject, her insight on the abject as a realm of othered monstrosity can be applied to the disabled and the queer as well as to the female. According to Creed, and adopted directly from Kristeva, the abject is that which is unthinkable or unallowable to the life of the subject and so must be excluded from the subject, "propelled away from the body and deposited on the other side of an imaginary border which separates the self from that which threatens the self" (9). However, abjection is a necessary function of the dominant social order; it is a mechanism of regulating the norm, of accounting for the experience of the unallowable. Thus, "the activity of exclusion is necessary to guarantee that the subject take up his/her proper place in relation to the symbolic" (9).

The methods by which normative narratives circumscribe the queer and nullify its disruptive power are multifarious and pernicious, and the remainder of this chapter attempts to determine whether *Rocky Horror* falls prey to them. I argue that although by its resolution *Rocky Horror* does indeed implement the methods of abjection, narrative prosthesis, and normative epiphany to assimilate the marginal into the norm, this assimilation is at least ironically highlighted if not nearly completely subverted by a more powerful "queer" resolution.

Rocky Horror is ostensibly a normative text: Its ultimate resolution, the death scene of Frank-N-Furter, Rocky, and Columbia, represents a radical subjugation of the queer by the newly assimilated normative agents Riff Raff and Magenta. Because this normative resolution appears temporally later in the text, it is the "stronger" and the more dominant resolution internalized by the reader and structuring the reader's interpretation of the text. Riff Raff and his sister Magenta revert to their alien doubles and destroy Frank-N-Furter, Rocky, and Columbia, apparently tired of their queer lifestyle. "Frank-N-Furter, it's all over / Your mission is a failure /

Your lifestyle's too extreme," sings Riff Raff on his entrance, immediately following and contrasting with the Dionysian "Don't Dream It. Be It." sequence in which Frank and his company demonstrate their extreme and apparently offensive queerness.

Emissaries of normative backlash against queer instability, Riff Raff and Magenta transform from hybrid Apollonian-Dionysian characters still implicated in Frank's queer frenzy into full, asexual Apollonians. Riff Raff's hump is removed, rendering him normate, firmly associating the hump-back body with queer wrongness and the upright body with authoritative, victorious, and righteous restoration of order and linking the disabled or abnormal body with that in need of "fixing." Riff Raff and Magenta's "elbow sex" ritual is still performed subsequent to Frank's death, but unlike previous instances during which the siblings were still members of Frank's household, this elbow sex performance does not include passionate kissing, demonstrating a further removal from the sexuality that demarcates the queer subject.[5]

Frank-N-Furter's death at the hands of these icons of normativity is a depiction of normative "victory" and dominance and a defeat of queer depravity. It could function to cement the distancing and abjection of the queer and cause *Rocky Horror* to be a film-length purging of sexuality and abnormality. In Raymond Ruble's reductionist psychoanalytic account, for example, the normative doppelgängers of Riff Raff and Magenta represent the unambiguous triumph of the Superego over the Id, the latter of which is of course embodied by Frank. Ruble claims that the audience identifies with Frank, so that when Frank dies, the Id and sexual energy of the audience die with him: "Libido flowers, like Frank N. Furter, only to die" (164). John Kilgore, in another psychoanalytic analysis of the film, also feels that the death scene of Frank, Columbia, and Rocky is the triumph of normative authority: "It is clear all along that Frank's Reign of Pleasure must eventually give way to traditional authority.... [C]ommunity standards and 'American Decency' prove to be Frank's undoing" (157). Kilgore, instead of Ruble's straightforward equation of Riff Raff and Magenta to the power of the superego, at least recognizes ambiguity in Riff Raff's "nimble switch from fellow 'creature of the night' to the Party of Decency" (157–58) but persists in a reading of the "final" normative resolution as the more triumphant.

What Ruble and Kilgore do not take into account is the possibility that a temporally penultimate and secondary resolution, the orgy, may have more power than its temporally ultimate but symbolically parodic shadow, the death scene. If a secondary resolution is stronger and more "satisfying" than the final normative narrative resolution, and if this normative resolution parodies normative "happy endings" and the normative in general, then the mechanisms for normative assimilation previously discussed are rendered ineffective. Such is the case in *Rocky Horror*: Frank's death scene, the final end of the film's narrative, is pale and unsatisfactory compared with the Dionysian swimming pool orgy and the "Don't Dream It" anthem because Frank's death prohibits his assimilation into the norm required in the mechanisms previously discussed, and the result is a final normative resolution that does not resolve the narrative for the viewer and so fails to expunge the queer.

The normative resolution lacks puissance, a lack seemingly felt by many fans, because, rather than assimilating the queer to use as a crutch or narrative prosthesis, the normative force—Magenta and Riff Raff—instead kills its potential queer crutch.[6] The audience identifies with the marginalized subjects, preventing the abjection and expulsion described by Creed. Instead, the normative space itself becomes alienated and ejected; the parodies of normative order and propriety, space aliens Magenta and Riff Raff, kill the characters identified with by the audience, and so "kill" the audience, proving very unsatisfying and laughable. Rather than serving as an edifying epiphany, this normative resolution bows to its more powerful predecessor, the queer resolution, which culminates in the pool orgy scene and the anthem "Don't Dream It." The normative must surrender the laurel wreath of textual epiphany, and *Rocky Horror*'s edifying epiphany is queer.

The resolution builds from a drag performance in which Brad, Janet, Columbia, and Rocky sing of their emotions and conflicting desires toward Frank, followed by Frank beginning the "Don't Dream It" sequence by entering a glittering swimming pool, where he is soon joined by the others. Frank sings "Give yourself over to absolute pleasure / Swim the warm waters of sins of the flesh," an acclamation of pleasure inseparable from the idea of the body as flesh rather than some socially defined, idealized subject position; this is followed by "Don't Dream It. Be It," a Nietzschean-style avowal of personal power—a Will to Power touted by queer-theory godfather Michel Foucault as a way to resist social hegemonies. As Brad, Janet, Columbia, and Rocky enter the pool with Frank, their bodies entwine amorously, rejecting any cookie-cutter distinctions of singular identity or subjective wholeness. Scott, although not actually in the swimming pool— further calling attention to his disability rather than hiding it—embraces the bacchanalia by exposing his dragged leg and exclaiming a life lived "for the thrill."

Frank's own authority and dominance is, before the pool orgy, nearly total and could, as Betty Robbins and Roger Myrick argue in "The Function of the Fetish," represent a phallic/normative subjugation of the marginal or feminine individual (274). However, in this scene this phallic authority is negated by the representation of Frank's previously authoritative body as simply one of a mass of bodies pleasuring each other, lacking any central authority; the revision of normative, subjugating authority such as Frank's by an antiauthoritarian "utopia" is the aim of much of queer praxis and political/cultural activism.[7]

The queer apotheosis of this scene, the mass of flesh eradicating any notion of ability or disability and destroying subjective hierarchy, represents a queer "utopia" that is only enhanced and given increased poignancy by its subsequent destruction at the hands of Riff Raff and Magenta's normative doppelgängers. McRuer's notion of the normative epiphany, discussed earlier, can be contrasted to the queer epiphany evinced here, in the penultimate resolution to *Rocky Horror*: Rather than a flood of narrative power and feeling that will entice the reader into accepting the subservient role of the queer to the norm, the queer epiphany is one that rides a wave of subversive power and feeling and, through the mechanisms discussed here—parody, masquerade, and the overthrow of abjection and prosthesis—shakes down the normative and prevents its assimilation of the queer or disabled, resulting instead in a promotion of the queer as a site of audience empathy and power.

Rocky Horror is a parody on multiple levels, and just as Rocky himself parodies the masculine normate, the "victory" of the norm is here a parody of normative subjugation, a parody of abjection and its associated exclusion of the queer, and a parody of texts that pacify queerness. Frank-N-Furter and his queer company are not abjected and excluded, thrown out as unfit and nonnormative, or made to bow down to normative goodness; rather, it is that act of abjection that is itself abjected and expunged. The destruction of Frank and Rocky, and the normative victory it implies, is overpowered by the preceding queer epiphany. Susan Purdie offers an engaging critique of Kilgore and Ruble's psychoanalytic descriptions, previously described, as part of her discussion of ritual in Rocky Horror. She notes that although Kilgore is convincing, at least more so than Ruble, he fails in that he "ignores the destabilizing effect of the penultimate, forest-crawling song (Brad and Janet are not unambiguously returned to 'order')" (181).[8] She decides that Kilgore's "pattern of energetic excess finally leading to restored calm" (182)—the nullification of the queer by the subsequent normative resolution—is insufficient to describe the uniqueness of the *Rocky Horror* audience reaction among film followings. Purdie also powerfully points to the self-awareness and self-parody of the audience: "Their mood is consistently humorous, with all the self-awareness and distancing that this involves. These participants are not in any way 'enthralled' with the film" (176). A normative epiphany relies on an engaged and satisfied audience—on subjects enthralled to its message—but the death of Frank and Rocky is for many fans anything but epiphanically satisfying.

Rocky Horror is unique in that it offers "authentic" queerness: Unlike far too many instances of queer representation in popular texts, the queer in *Rocky Horror* is not made to serve the normal, the right, the proper, or the way things are supposed to be. *Rocky Horror* has no happy, normative, "fairy tale" ending, whereby the queer is offered a place in the norm and is allowed to live happily ever after. The authentic queer does not live happily ever after; it is murdered by the normative society in which it lives. The authentic queer epiphany brings that oppression home to the viewer or reader on a wave of narrative force and acts as a barricade or firewall against the pernicious, omnipresent assimilation techniques employed by the norm to disempower the queer. *Rocky Horror's* queer epiphany makes it unique among the homogenous mass of popular cultural texts that provide so many avenues for the normative to infiltrate the individual and, if taken as a grain of salt amid the mass consumption necessitated by life within popular society, a dose of *Rocky Horror* may work toward allowing the queer to remain queer and free from inculcation by the pernicious tendrils of the happily normal ever after.

Works Cited

Aviram, Amittai. "Postmodern Gay Dionysus: Dr. Frank N. Furter." *Journal of Popular Culture* 26.3 (1992): 183–92.

Creed, Barbara. *The Monstrous-Feminine: Film, Feminism, Psychoanalysis*. London: Routledge, 1993.

Doane, Mary Ann. *Femmes Fatales: Feminism, Film Theory, Psychoanalysis*. London: Routledge, 1991.

Frailberg, Allison. "Of AIDS, Cyborgs, and Other Indiscretions: Resurfacing the Body in the Postmodern." *Postmodern Culture*. 1991. Project Muse. 7 January 2004 http://muse.jhu.edu/journals/postmodern_culture/v001/1.3fraiberg.html.

Kilgore, John. "Sexuality and Identity in *The Rocky Horror Picture Show*." *Eros in the Mind's Eye*. Ed. Donald Palumbo. New York: Greenwood, 1986. 151–59.

McRuer, Robert. "As Good As It Gets: Queer Theory and Critical Disability." *GLQ* 9.1–2 (2003): 79–105.

Mitchell, David. "Narrative Prosthesis and the Materiality of Metaphor." *Disability Studies: Enabling the Humanities*. Ed. Sharon Snyder, Brenda Jo Brueggemann, and Rosemarie Garland-Thomson. New York: The Modern Language Association of America, 2002. 15–30.

Purdie, Susan. "Secular Definitions of 'Ritual'; the *Rocky Horror* Phenomenon." *Theatre and Holy Script*. Ed. Simon Levy. Brighton: Sussex Academic Press, 1999. 171–90.

Rendell, Joanne. "A Very Troublesome Doctor: Biomedical Binaries, Worldmaking, and the Poetry of Rafael Campo." *GLQ* 9.1–2 (2003): 205–31.

Robbins, Betty, and Roger Myrick. "The Function of the Fetish in *The Rocky Horror Picture Show* and *Priscilla, Queen of the Desert*." *Journal of Gender Studies* 9.3 (2000): 269–80.

Ruble, Raymond. "Dr. Freud Meets Dr. Frank N. Furter." *Eros in the Mind's Eye.* Ed. Donald Palumbo. New York: Greenwood, 1986. 161–68.

Notes

1. The use of the terms "norm," "counter-norm," "normative," "normativity," and so on is meant to signify the prevailing points of view in a society—points of view that tend to be unable to tolerate opposition and thus try to marginalize/ erase proponents or symbols of opposing minority viewpoints. Furthermore, the term "normate" as introduced by Rosemarie Garland Thomson refers specifically to an ableist "normal" body, a fictional "standard" or "average" body whose representation as that average is disseminated throughout popular culture.

2. I follow the suggestion of Teresa de Lauretis, given when she coined the term "queer theory" in a 1991 issue of *differences*, that the "queer" is not simply a sexual identity category but can be any that is unpleasing to the norm.

3. As argued by Robbins and Myrick, the stockinged leg is also a fetishistic image, and its placement upon Scott links it with government authority, exposing the patriarchal source of the fetish (274); additionally, however, Scott's assumption of the fetishistic image subverts the power of that fetish by imposing it on what is seen by the phallic normative gaze as an "old male crippled" body, creating a disconcerting hybrid.

4. The biblical allusion casts Frank as the typical "God-scientist" trope—the scientist who considers himself a divine all-powerful authority—this trope may serve to undermine scientific authority/"divinity" by calling attention to the extravagance and unilateralism of that authority, the self-avowed divinity of scientific proclamation that becomes holy writ for normative society, as in the case of biological essentialism and disabled bodies discussed earlier.

5. The phrase elbow sex is commonly used in audience participation scripts to refer to the ritual in which Riff Raff and Magenta perform apparent sibling-Transylvanian bonding by bringing their arms together, most notably at the elbows.

6. Abundant on the scores of Internet fan sites dedicated to *Rocky Horror* are castigations of the "bad ending" of the film, along with fan-proffered revisions of the ending. This distaste of fans for the ending may also be part of the reason for the phenomenon of audience participation, by which audience members can rewrite the text as they see fit.

7. See, for example, Michael Warner's classic edited collection *Fear of a Queer Planet*, in which the "Queer Planet" is the disauthoritative dis/utopia, feared by the norm.
8. The scene to which Purdie refers is the scene that did not originally appear in the American version of the film in which Brad and Janet crawl around in the forest and sing "Super Heroes," a short song about how the 'beast is still feeding."

11

The Queer Pedagogy of Dr. Frank-N-Furter

Zachary Lamm

In her essay "Revisiting Bodies and Pleasures," Judith Butler reflects on what she experienced as a "heady moment" at the end of Foucault's first volume of *The History of Sexuality* in which he "held out the possibility that we might cease to think of sexuality as a specific attribute of sexed persons, that it could not be reducible to the question of his or her 'desire', and that overcoming the epistemic constraint that mandated thinking of sexuality as emanating from sexed persons in the form of desire might constitute an emancipation, as it were, beyond emancipation" (11).[1] For Butler, "The effort to separate the study of sexuality from the study of gender has been an important move to make"—one that she believes has only been made in the Foucauldian milieu of gender and sexuality studies that has pervaded certain sectors of the academy since the late 1980s and that continues to resonate in contemporary discussions of queerness and intimacy (11).[2]

The idea that one might separate sexuality from the prejudicial influence of gender and instead explore pleasures that one might experience as emanating from one's own body as well as the bodies of others—regardless of gender, or apart from the influence of gender—seems not just license to pursue yearnings that may not easily align themselves with the contemporary sex-gender system of sanctioned desires but license to do so without the obscuring effects that such socially coerced systems might have on the naked body—a body that might be more canvas, for oneself and others, than predetermined object of meaning.[3] By not yoking meaning to biology, the sexuality produced within this new realm of possibility would, in theory, leave us without the socially malignant forces of sexism and homophobia and instead create a world in which "queer" need not serve as an indexical category. Those behaviors that now seem "queer" could become part of the everyday.[4] Distancing gender and sex from the necessary components for sexuality's conception creates a space of liberty in which the freedom to pursue sexuality uninhibited by such—to use Foucault's term—"regulatory ideas" is offered to every individual.

However, before Foucault's valorization of bodies and pleasures (in 1978), there was *Rocky Horror* (1975). Within O'Brien's world, gender and sex become so ostentatiously stylized that their association with sexuality is detached, such that what looks likes gender must be recognized as a game played for one's own enjoyment and the joy that one might receive from giving pleasure to others. This breakdown of regulatory systems is the result of a pedagogy initiated by Dr. Frank-N-Furter, the headmaster of the queer facility in which the majority of the film takes place. He creates an institution in which knowledge of identities—commonly taken as foundational—is recognized as constructed and, therefore, mutable. Frank challenges the epistemological foundations of the conventional and constrained sexualities of his newest pupils: Brad and Janet.

For Michael Warner, queerness is not an "orientation" but, rather, a way of being politically, socially, and sexually an outsider in a normative culture that would shame those individuals who dare deviate from preset moral (and usually religious) doctrine; he calls this usage of "queer" "deliberately capacious" (38). The ultimate goal of a truly democratic society for Warner is sexual autonomy, which, as he explains, "requires more than freedom of choice, toleration, and the liberalization of sex laws. It requires access to pleasures and possibilities, since people commonly do not know their desires until they find them. . . . If the goal is sexual autonomy, consistent with everyone else's sexual autonomy, then it will be impossible to say in advance what form that will take" (7).[5] Because the majority of the population is presumed to be, and presumes itself to be, conventionally heterosexual, society's conception of "normal" is rooted in an ethics that deems monogamy and reproduction to be central concerns of a cultural sexual politics.[6] Heterosexuality occupies the privileged position of "normative" within American culture, privileged not just by religious and political institutions (and heterosexuals themselves) but even by those homosexuals who allot heterosexuality a special consideration when contemplating moral systems.

Introducing queerness into such a system not as an alternative model, but as an appeal to all individuals' desire for sexual liberty, generates the idea that autonomy may have been stunted for everyone somewhere within the process of enculturation and thereby subversively challenges the status quo by teaching that limitless possibilities for sexual expression exist and that a yearning for such expressions may already be present in even those individuals who most seem to conform—especially when one considers the possibility that *hyper*-conformity might function as a disavowal of queerness that has the potential to make the door of "the closet" all the more visible.[7]

Sometime over the course of my many viewings of *Rocky Horror*, it occurred to me that pedagogy is an overriding concern in the film. The film occurs as an intervention between a ceremony of traditional American "family values"—a wedding—and a return visit to the teacher who first introduced the newly engaged Brad and Janet to each other. The events of the early portions of the film represent two forms of education for the couple, first leading them through the circumscribed narrative of sexual morality derived from American normative culture and then introducing them into a "queer culture" highlighting intimacy's innumerable possible manifestations.[8] That the film posits a connection between learning the protocols of normalized everyday life and the formal educational system is apparent in (at least) two ways from the very beginning of the film: Brad and Janet fell in love while at school in such a way that civil marriage, which functions as a way of regulating sexual behavior through the state (so as to prevent deviation from preconceived notions of normalcy), seems the natural outcome of what the couple imagines to be the love narrative of proper citizens—of which Brad and Janet clearly are representative (they are, after all, members of the Junior Chamber of Commerce).[9] In addition, a return visit to Dr. Everett Scott, the former teacher who introduced Brad and Janet (he is "the man who began it"), seems to them the natural action after becoming engaged—a sort of prewedding honeymoon for the newly engaged couple.[10] In other words, Brad and Janet's engagement, which ostensibly takes place in the private world outside of academic space, is seemingly surrounded on both sides by educational institutions: a transition from an educational institution to the institution of marriage (via engagement) and back again. Of course, they wind up getting off track: physically, socially, and epistemologically.

The world of institutional, academic knowledge that the film associates with conventional morality is embodied in the person of Dr. Scott, Brad and Janet's "ex-tutor" and now "friend"; this world is rivaled by the alien counter-knowledge of Dr. Frank-N-Furter, whose queer views on sex, gender, and science have allowed him access to unexplored possibilities for sexual expression, as well as the secret to the "spark" of life for which Scott and his colleagues at the CIA (where he is now employed) have long been searching. Scott introduced Brad and Janet to conventional scientific knowledge and normative heterosexual coupling; Frank introduces them

to queer science and queer forms of sexual intimacy. The sexual productivity of the queer population (the "unconventional conventioners"), of
which Frank is leader, is exemplified in the pleasure we observe in the final
floor show and its orgiastic climax, whereas the parallel productivity of
queer science is verified in Frank's ability to achieve scientific feats still
not realized by the mainstream scientific community. Because queerness
succeeds as an epistemological endeavor both scientifically and sexually,
it can be assumed that queerness has the capacity to become a viable way
of living. Of course, this can only be the case if queerness is taken not as a
regulatory ideal but as a foundational principle for ideology—an unstable
and contingent foundation, to be sure, but one that can serve to educate
mainstream culture about not only the pleasures of queerness but its transformative potential as well.

The destabilizing effects of queerness can be observed throughout the
film, but perhaps no instance is more demonstrative of these effects than
Scott's revelation of the hose and high-heel shoes he is wearing underneath
the blanket that covers his legs when seated in his wheelchair; their exposure forces us to ask the question: Did Frank and his minions adorn him,
or was he wearing them when he arrived (and before he arrived as well)?
His seeming embrace of this transgendered performance, observable by
his groping of his own leg and kicking it up over his head during the floor
show, points to Scott's adoption of a queer persona. There are, to my mind,
two potential readings of this mise-en-scène: We are to understand either
that queerness is desirable for "conventional folk" when opportunity for
its presentation (and re-presentation) without stigma is made available, or
that queerness is close to the heart of conventionality, veiled by the regulatory functions of socially prescribed normalcy. It makes sense then that
Scott's revelations take place during the show's torch song, "Don't Dream
It. Be It."

This song represents perhaps the film's most explicitly pedagogical
moment, as the addressee of the song's lyrics is more the viewing audience
than the film's characters, the latter of which seem to have already picked
up on the lesson. Addressing them in this manner at this moment in the
film would literally be preaching to the choir, as the majority of the cast
sings the refrain behind Frank's lead vocals. The plea for us to dream, as the
cast has apparently already done, or—as the presence of the phantasmatic
audience seems to indicate—is doing, is a call for us to engage with fantasy,
the liminal psychical realm existing between reality and representation
that one must access to heed Frank's call. Judith Butler theorizes fantasy as
"what is not *yet* real, what is possible or futural, what belongs to a different
version of the real" ("The Force of Fantasy" 105).[11] *Rocky Horror* serves to
show the pleasures that enactment of sexual fantasy can bring, especially

when identity no longer serves as an obstacle to object-desire; as the orgy begins in the pool, with the music still in the background, one can observe same-sex eroticism (Brad and Rocky), opposite-sex eroticism (Brad and Columbia), and whatever sort of eroticism occurs between human beings and "transvestite transsexuals" from outer space. The sexual frenzy that erupts, in which no object is "proper," seems the culmination of queer thinkers' fantasies of queer world-making from Foucault onward, and the audience's elation and demand for repeat viewing mirrors this critical effect. Thus, the not-yet-real-world fantasy of the scene is manifested in a way that does no harm to the real world but brings pleasure to both on-screen participants and viewers (via the orgiastic performance of the cast members), especially when the mantra that inspired the action ("Don't dream it, be it!") is picked up during audience participation.

How then, one might ask, does this pedagogical process begin that produces the sexually liberated subjects we observe at the film's end? Leaving their native Denton—"The Home of Happiness"—Brad and Janet are forced (by car trouble and inclement weather) to inquire as to whether or not the castle they recently passed has a phone with which they can call for assistance. The film's first large dance number follows shortly, as the couple is introduced to the "Time Warp," which Brad presumes to be the "folk dancing" of "foreigners with ways different than our own"; he, of course, has no idea how right he is. It is important to note, however, that the "Time Warp" itself is a pedagogical anthem, teaching listeners both the steps of the dance and some of the fantastical effects that the dance might have on those who perform it. Even the stuffy criminologist who narrates the film gets in on the action, both performing the dance while standing on top of his desk and providing the instructional lines during a round of the chorus. Although Brad and Janet remain too intimidated by the environment into which they have been introduced to dance themselves, we can clearly see their perception of the queerness of the dancers, and we also see at several points Brad's attempt to disrupt the queerness with interjections of the bland normativity of their outside lives; for instance, after the conclusion of the dance, at Janet's urging, "Say something!" Brad can only think to ask, "Do any of you guys know how to Madison?" The crowd's unenthusiastic reaction illustrates the lameness of the question.

Although at this point Brad and Janet remain largely unmoved from their heteronormativity, Frank's first appearance sets the stage for their conversion into the sexual rebels they become by the final scene. On first viewing Frank through the bars of the elevator, Janet exhibits what we might assume to be the most typical reaction to difference: fear. She screams and begins to flee from Frank but is prevented from escaping. She and Brad are then witness to what has become the show's signature performance,

Tim Curry's rendition of "Sweet Transvestite." Frank's boasting, "I'm not much of a man / By the light of day / But by night I'm one hell of lover" rhetorically constructs ideas that are key to our understanding the events that unfold as the film progresses: By acknowledging the fact that his seeming physical manhood is obscured under the female-gendered clothing and makeup that he wears, Frank problematizes gender assumptions based on visual appearance, as he is commenting on his appearance "by the light of day." At night, however, when visibility is decreased, thereby making gender less perceptible through visual cues, Frank is able to act as a virile lover, one whose gender is irrelevant to the pleasure he (apparently) can provide to partners, regardless of their sex. Syntactically, then, Frank's declaration not only disassociates him from manhood but degenders the term "lover" such that, for him, "lover" seems to replace traditional gender categories as significant components of identity.[12]

What is doubly troubling about this song in terms of gender is its indecipherable concept of the "transvestite transsexual." Although it is true that Transsexual refers to a place on the alien home world of Transylvania, transsexuality also becomes part of the queer world that this song posits. The logic of such a construction of gender is indeed deconstructive by nature, and the systems of sex and gender thus seem inscrutable and, it would seem, undesirable. Logically, if we assume that Frank is biologically male, then his transvestism would cause him to dress as a woman, but his transsexuality would actually make him a woman, thus producing a "female woman," which he seems not to be; if he is female, then following the same logic, he would become a "male man." Neither seems to be the case. Essentially, Frank's original sex would reverse when entangled with gender, and it seems that what is going on here is much more complicated than any sort of simple reversal. Frank's body, regardless of its anatomical properties, becomes a canvas for play with genders while simultaneously refusing to be naturalized by them. This transcendence of gender makes Frank an appealing sexual partner for a plethora of individuals, even when his partners insist (for a while, anyway) on maintaining their own gender identities. He will eventually have sex with both Brad and Janet, but we can see in their initial encounter a resistance to Frank's gender insubordination (to use another of Butler's terms), particularly when Brad refuses to sing and merely speaks his lines in "Sweet Transvestite."

Thus, as we observe Frank's body serving as the embodiment of queered gender, we are tempted to consider Frank's sexuality, for, as both Foucault and Butler observe, Western cultures have tended to render sexuality unthinkable without the application of the filter of gender to the body. Because we cannot consider Frank's body in gendered terms without gender's contingency making our assumptions uneasy, classifying his sexuality—and the sexuality of those who have sex with him—is problematic, as our taxonomic systems have no place for those outside of the naturalized sex-gender system.[13] The temptation might be to call Frank bisexual, but his inability to fit into a dyadic gender system makes the notion that the most omnivorous form of sexuality possible is simply "bi-" unthinkable, and as we cannot exactly put our finger on Frank's sexuality, it is impossible for him to fit into a hetero/homosexual paradigm, as both require knowledge of the desiring individual's sex-gender classification. As a desiring agent, Frank illustrates just how homogenous heterosexuality truly is and challenges us, along with Brad and Janet, to consider what a sexuality that is truly heterogeneous might look like.

Indeed, Frank plays with gender anxieties in his sex scenes with Brad and Janet to rouse questions of imitation and the naturalization of identity. Although it is true that Brad and Janet both remain autonomous subjects throughout, Frank's ability to impersonate them both makes problematic the notion that the only proper object of desire is "the real thing"; if his play on gender teaches us nothing else, it is that "real thing"-ness is simply a quality that we perceive as "natural." It is also clear that Frank intends to be discovered in his disguise, as his costume is easily removed with the simple ruffling of hair and clothes. This intentional revelation functions pedagogically as a means of seducing the two naive youngsters into crossing the sexual boundaries set by regulatory sociosexual systems, and the temptation to indulge is too much for either of them.

Frank's promise that their transgression will be kept secret is undermined by the surveillance cameras he has installed in each of the rooms. From one of the monitors connected to this system, Janet observes Frank and Brad enjoying a postcoital smoke, and for a moment, her world seems to fall apart. It is clear, though, that both Brad and Janet have enjoyed their first foray into fornication—particularly Brad, who allows Frank to continue fellating him even after Riff Raff announces over the communication system that the situation with Rocky has become dangerous. What happens in the revelation of Frank's identity is not recognition of him as an insufficient or inappropriate sex partner—in fact, he seems to become something more than just a singular being: As he seems a hybrid of genders and sexualities, so too does his inauthenticity allow him to become a hybrid partner, such that Brad and Janet might indulge in his sexual knowledge all the while making love to a fantasy partner, or for the first time acknowledging the desirability of a queer lover.

As for the as-yet-unaddressed issue of the presence of Rocky, the most ostentatiously gendered character in the film, I would like to read him, as I believe Frank does, as a mold of Frank's sexual fantasies, which he has cast and brought to life through his recent scientific endeavors. Rather than claiming that Frank finds Rocky's "masculine" identity (if he could have such a thing) desirable, I would claim that Frank finds the appearance of "masculinity" desirable, and that the manly package that we associate with "masculinity" is not necessarily attractive to Frank wholesale as a way of being in the world. In the "Charles Atlas" song, Frank composes a list of the anatomical parts for which he lusts ("deltoid," "bicep," "hot groin," "tricep"), all of which Rocky has in abundance; it is this spectacular stylization of Rocky's body that makes him an object of lust. This is not an elusive masculinity that might be claimed by a variety of individuals, and as the contrast between Frank and Rocky makes clear, "masculinity" might not always signify the same thing—though we are taught by our culture to think it does. Indeed, the gay male obsession with musculature might serve as a destabilizing example in which masculinity seems to be outwardly observable but is undercut by the allegedly effeminizing effects of homosexuality.[14] Rocky's seemingly masculine attributes are inborn but not by any means natural, as he is fully a product of Frank's sexual fantasy and scientific genius. When, toward the end of "Sweet Transvestite," Frank announces that he has "been making a man / With blond hair and a tan," he sounds as if this amalgamate being he has produced is akin to something he might have ordered out of a catalogue; his reason: "he's good for relieving my tension." Therefore, Rocky seems fully a product of Frank's autonomous imagination. Frank lacked the object he desired (after tiring of his former lovers, Eddie and Columbia, who subsequently become lovers of each other), so he made what he wanted; he could have made him differently but chose not to.

Though Janet is initially resistant to the muscular appeal of Rocky ("I don't like men with too many muscles"), she is compelled to indulge in the figure who was literally made as a canvas for sexual desire, though someone else's desire to be sure. She does not, however, address him in gendered—or for that matter, even human—terms, referring to him instead as "creature of the night." Rocky began life as the receptacle of Frank's queer desires; he then succumbs to Janet's, as she makes him over in her mind for her own purposes. Her self-indulgent language ("I've got an itch to scratch / I need assistance"; "Touch-a touch-a touch touch-a touch me / I wanna be dirty / Thrill me, chill me, / Fulfill me") illustrates that Rocky serves only as a vessel for Janet's pleasure—though, as with Frank's objectification, he seems to enjoy it. The answer to Frank's question to Janet, "When we made it / Did ya hear a bell ring?" seems to be an affirmative; that is, having sex with Frank seems to have set Janet down a course that would ultimately lead to her seeking out new means of fulfilling her desires—desires that, until meeting Frank, she never seemed to know she had, or, if she did know of them, never dreamed of expressing. Frank occupies the role of tutor that

Scott once filled, imparting knowledge of sexual liberty instead of science, though Frank's approach is clearly more "hands-on."

When Rocky and Janet have sex, however, we might note an interesting circumstance in that both have been trained by Frank in the performance of sexual desires. We cannot entirely be sure whether Frank taught either of the two to be top, bottom, or both—they all seem to be viable options where Frank is concerned—and it is unclear from the filming of their sex scene which position they assume during the exchange. Of course, their apparent gender—that which we presume by looking at them—is no clue to how they actually identify or what role they would prefer during sex. This ostensibly heterosexual scene is queered not only by the lack of interpretive narratological precedence but also because the pedagogical function of their earlier flings with Frank allows for this triangulated scenario in which his two sexual pupils have sex to be read as Frank virtually having sex with himself, as it is from him that each of them has gained his or her knowledge of sexual performance. The spectrum of lovers that Janet envisions hovering over her body (including Rocky and Frank as well as Riff Raff, Magenta, Columbia, and Brad—with whom she has not yet had sex) shows that Janet has indeed "wised up" to her sexual potential, imagining the erotic potential of heterosexual and lesbian, as well as transgendered, sex. Disrupting the cinematic real with an intervention of fantasy short circuits the normative cultural narrative of sexuality and puts on display for the viewer the numerous possibilities for erotic rendezvous available for Janet within even her seemingly limited immediate circumstance. Audiences are thus edified as to the prospective erotic scenarios possible when bodies and pleasures are prioritized over the fetishized versions of gender Western culture has naturalized.

One problem that remains unresolved in this discussion is the issue of dominance, for surely Frank does his best to blur the lines between pedagogue and dominator/dominatrix. To be sure, Frank's household is not a democracy, which raises the question of whether or not what looks like the enacting of others' desires within the film is truly an expression of the individuals' fantasies or a regulated system by which Frank manipulates others for his own pleasure. To my mind, the ecstatic floor show acts as hedonistic counterevidence to the claim that the sex we see is only the product of domination. If domination does occur, it seems to be a scenario in which the dominated or objectified partner participates willingly and receives pleasure equal to or exceeding that of the dominant. Frank may hijack his cast for the floor show using the medusa ray, but once on stage, the whole lot not only indulges in pleasures formerly taboo but expresses the debt they owe to Frank for liberating them from cultural constraints. Although Rocky and Columbia still register a certain amount of "trouble and pain,"

Brad and Janet both profess the libratory effects that their interment at Frank's castle has had upon them: Brad's exploratory query, "What's this? Let's see," demonstrates the erotic lure of the unfamiliar, or queer, and his declaration, "I feel sexy!" reassures us that the effects of queerness have been positive. In turn, Janet's newfound pleasure registers in her gratitude toward Frank:

> Oh I—I feel released
> Bad times deceased
> My confidence has increased
> Reality is here.
> The game has been disbanded
> My mind has been expanded
> It's a gas that Frankie's landed
> His lust is so sincere.

For Janet, her prior heteronormative life has been a "game" that she has ceased to play now that her "mind has been expanded." What is significant about her proclamation is its positing that queerness—signified here by Frank's lust—is more real than the sexuality enacted in the "real" world; his queer lust is genuine such that it can serve as a typifying example even as it creates new venues for "release" for his disciples. Even if he dominates, he nevertheless asserts the sort of "bodies-and-pleasures" ideology for which queer theorists since Foucault have yearned.

The sexual education of Brad and Janet, which necessarily involves their casting off of prior heteronormative ideals, enacts for the audience positive effects that exposing individuals—even ones seemingly content with heteronormative ideology—to queerness can produce. Although Frank's queer counter-knowledge does not guarantee happiness or even produce a happy ending, it does provide a space of freedom within which scenarios can be played out and lives can indeed be lived without the oppressive shame that societies thrust upon their citizens.[15] Frank's death thus becomes a tragedy, which Brad and Janet mourn at the film's close; the fact that they, along with Scott, choose to lie in the vacant lot left after the castle's launch into space indicates unwillingness to return to conventionality—or even their car. Their notions of appropriateness and desirability have been changed in ways that leave their futures wide open: Marriage no longer seems the natural next episode in the couple's relationship, and the film refuses to participate in the normative cinematic narrative tradition that would end the film either with a wedding or with a wedding in the imminent future.[16]

By putting on display those pleasures that might have been forbidden to audiences not only within their lives but within cinematic history, *Rocky*

Horror demonstrates the positive potential that escape from civilization's regulatory ideology can have on subjects who, within such systems, are necessarily repressed (or so the film's, and Foucault's, logic goes). The audience is witness to Brad and Janet's education in queerness, which thereby makes available that same education to the masses. It makes sense then that those individuals most in need of "release" would seek out and enjoy the film, as its pedagogy of sexual subversiveness is virtually unparalleled within the tradition of major studio films. Finally, its long-lasting appeal and insatiable fan base attest to the film's relevance in today's culture, more than thirty years after its initial release.

Works Cited

Aviram, Amittai F. "Postmodern Gay Dionysus: Dr. Frank N. Furter." *Journal of Popular Culture* 26.1 (1992): 183–92.

Berlant, Lauren, ed. *Intimacy*. Chicago: U of Chicago P, 2000.

Berlant, Lauren, and Michael Warner. "Sex in Public." *Intimacy*. Ed. Lauren Berlant. Chicago: U of Chicago P, 2000. 311–30.

Butler, Judith. *Bodies that Matter: On the Discursive Limits of "Sex."* New York: Routledge, 1993.

———. "The Force of Fantasy: Feminism, Mapplethorpe, and Discursive Excess." *Differences* 2.2 (1990): 105–25.

———. "Revisiting Bodies and Pleasures." *Theory, Culture, and Society*. 16.2 (1999): 11–20.

Clarke, Eric O. *Virtuous Vice: Homoeroticism and the Public Sphere*. Durham, NC: Duke UP, 2000.

Duggan, Lisa. *The Twilight of Equality?: Neoliberalism, Cultural Politics, and the Attack on Democracy*. Boston: Beacon, 2003.

Foucault, Michel. *The History of Sexuality, Vol. I: An Introduction*. Trans. Robert Hurley. [1978]. New York: Vintage, 1990.

Freeman, Elizabeth. *The Wedding Complex: Forms of Belonging in Modern American Culture*. Durham, NC: Duke UP, 2002.

Nealon, Christopher. *Foundlings: Lesbian and Gay Historical Emotion Before Stonewall*. Durham, NC: Duke UP, 2001.

Robbins, Betty, and Roger Myrick. "The Function of the Fetish in *The Rocky Horror Picture Show* and *Priscilla, Queen of the Desert*." *Journal of Gender Studies* 9.3 (2000): 269–80.

Studlar, Gaylyn. "Midnight S/Excess: Cult Configuration of 'Femininity' and the Perverse." *The Cult Film Experience: Beyond All Reason*. Austin: U of Texas P, 1991. 138–55.

Warner, Michael. *The Trouble with Normal: Sex, Politics, and the Ethics of Queer Life*. Cambridge, MA: Harvard UP, 1999.

Notes

1. The line to which Butler refers is the following: "The rallying point for the counterattack against the deployment of sexuality ought not to be sex-desire, but bodies and pleasures" (Foucault 157).

2. See in particular the Foucauldian tinge of the Lauren Berlant–edited volume *Intimacy*. In her introduction, Berlant notes, "Foucault's work on recognizing the multiplicity of relations engendered at every moment by sexuality has been central to this project" (4).

3. According to Butler, "Sexual difference . . . is never simply a function of material differences which are not in some way both marked and formed by discursive practices. . . . The category of 'sex' is, from the start, normative; it's what *Foucault* has called a 'regulatory idea.' In this sense, then, 'sex' not only functions as a norm but is part of a regulatory practice that produces the bodies it governs, that is, whose regulatory force is made clear as a kind of productive power, the power to produce—demarcate, circulate, differentiate—the bodies it controls" (*Bodies that Matter* 1; emphasis added). In other words, we see bodies and unconsciously (in most cases) associate those bodies with a sex category—usually because of visible anatomical features—because that is what we have been trained to do: We see "men" and "women" because we are told that they exist and what they look like.

4. On the interpellation of queer behavior into mainstream culture, see Eric O. Clarke, *Virtuous Vice: Homoeroticism and the Public Sphere*.

5. Warner also argues for the validity of sexualities that are not inherited: "Sex does not have to be primordial in order to be legitimate. Civilization doesn't just repress our original sexuality: it makes new kinds of sexuality. And new sexualities, including learned ones, might have as much validity as ancient ones, if not more" (11).

6. Lisa Duggan describes these neoliberal homosexual thinkers as "homonormative," implying that they desire the normalization of homosexuality—that is, that rather than working toward a revolutionary movement that would remove heteronormativity as a core value of society, these individuals believe homosexuals should strive to more closely imitate the normative model of heterosexuality. Warner and Duggan cite conservative gay commentator Andrew Sullivan as the most outspoken proponent of this opinion.

7. Consider, for example, the increasing rapidity in recent years with which those conservative cultural and political leaders who most virulently oppose homosexuality—and indeed often seek to persecute homosexuals—have been "outed" as homosexuals.

8. Lauren Berlant and Michael Warner describe queer culture as "a world-making project, where 'world,' like 'public,' differs from community or group because it necessarily includes more people than can be identified, more spaces than can be mapped beyond few reference points, more spaces than can be mapped beyond a few reference points, modes of feeling that can be learned rather than experienced as a birthright." Further, "the queer world is a space

of entrances, exits, unsystemized lines of acquaintance, projected horizons, typifying examples, alternate routes, blockages, incommensurate geographies" ("Sex in Public" 322). Although the queer culture of the film exists within the contained space of Frank's castle, the partner switching, orgies, and unpredictable manifestations of sexuality embody most of the proper elements for Berlant and Warner's characterization.

9. Michael Warner argues, "A marriage license is the opposite of sexual license. Sexual license is everything that the state does not license, and therefore everything the state allows itself to punish or regulate" (*Trouble* 97). In other words, the (hetero)sex that occurs between married couples is the only clearly permissible form of sexual behavior within a state that regulates and legitimizes the romantic lives and sexuality of its citizens at the expense of those individuals whose romantic and sexual desires do not conform to the state's model of normalcy and morality. Warner claims, "As long as people marry, the state will continue to regulate the sexual lives of those who do not marry. It will continue to refuse to recognize our intimate relations—including cohabitating partners—as having the same rights or validity as a married couple. It will continue to criminalize our consensual sex" (96). The state, of course, also regulates the sex of married individuals when they wish to engage with sexual partners outside of the marriage bond, and until recently, some sodomy laws made nonreproductive forms of sex illegal even for married couples.

10. Elizabeth Freeman describes the honeymoon as a "supplement [to] the wedding: the honeymoon . . . physically separates the couple from peers and natal family, isolates them with one another and puts them into contact with a new place, and moves them along a narrative trajectory toward adulthood and (or as) dyadic heterosexual marriage" (146). Perhaps, as Brad and Janet are not married, or perhaps because they wind up in an alternate, improper venue for their preemptive honeymoon, they deviate from the "narrative trajectory" Freeman describes.

11. Butler offers her interpretation of fantasy as an alternative to those feminists associated with the antipornography movement who, in their portrayal of fantasy and its repercussions, "rel[y] upon a representational realism that conflates the signified fantasy with its (impossible) referent and construes 'depiction' as an injurious act and, in legal terms, a discriminatory action or 'real'-effect" (*Force of Fantasy* 105–06). In other words, antipornography feminists have assumed that the fantasy that pornography both enacts and inspires is capable of doing real harm to women through a tendency to conflate the degraded portrayal of women in pornography with the real sexual degradation of women in life. Although certainly not claiming that women do not suffer degradation, Butler sees that the ontological move that feminists want to make between representation and reality misses the intervention of the psyche that occurs as an intermediary between the representative and the real.

12. Betty Robbins and Roger Myrick read Frank's play on gender differently. In their discussion of *Rocky Horror* and *Priscilla, Queen of the Desert*, they make the following claim: "The extent to which either film critiques or subverts

gender norms is emphatically limited to the sole domain of masculinity, offering new registers of that gendered position . . . but ultimately maintaining a sexual indifference" (269). Their argument is based on a psychoanalytic reading of the film that associates power in the films with a fetishized phallus (in *Rocky Horror*, Frank has the phallus and leads its worship), and thus power is associated with masculinity. This argument hinges then on an automatic association of power—especially sexual power—with masculinity. We might also compare Robbins and Myrick's view to that of Gaylyn Studlar, who asserts that *Rocky Horror* "construct[s] a deeply ambivalent discourse that depends upon 'femininity' as a vector point uniting revulsion and fascination, excess and lack, pleasure and the perverse" (139). He claims that Frank only flirts with femininity in an effort to explore perversity, but that he "would never be caught dead on the bottom" (155); sexual power here is, for Studlar, unproblematically associated with not only masculinity but sexual positioning—as if there was no way for a "bottom" to be in control (and I believe we are unclear on Frank's positional preference, for while he tops Janet, he is clearly orally receptive with Brad and positioned to receive Rocky after their wedding march). To my mind, Frank and his followers do so much work to subvert gender norms and notions of gendered power that it seems likely critics' insistence on masculinizing Frank may arise more from the theory they bring to the film than from the film itself, especially because the primary evidence of Frank's masculinity, apart from what we can garner of his (alien) physiological composition, is his dominance, which might be the case for any number of reasons.

13. This situation is exemplary of the problem that has arisen in mainstream culture when attempting to classify the sexuality of transgendered individuals. Although "transgendered" clearly does not qualify as a sexual orientation, the individuals who are considered part of that group have not been easily assimilated into either hetero- or homosexual cultures.

14. See Christopher Nealon's essay on 1950s physique magazine culture, "The Secret Public of Physique Culture" (*Foundlings* 99–139). Rocky is clearly modeled on the aesthetic ideals these magazines promote, as Frank's references to Charles Atlas and Steve Reeves indicate. Nealon describes this culture as a manifestation of "foundling," a transitional state of the gay population in which homosexuality was at a liminal stage in the cultural consciousness between an "inversion model," in which homosexuals were assumed to posses the qualities identified with the opposite sex, and the "ethnic notion," in which "homosexual" serves as a viable category of identification, like a gender category.

15. Warner calls this system "the politics of shame."

16. Amittati F. Aviram reads the film as "an allegory of freedom," with numerous classical references as well as a resistance to heteronormative culture that he sees as formative within what he calls the "gay community" (191). The ambivalence and uncertainty within the film is, he believes, representative of the numerous and destabilized sexual identities he believes are available within the gay community, and thus symbolic of the potential for freedom that community offers.

12

"Be Just and Fear Not"

Warring Visions of Righteous Decadence and Pragmatic Justice in *Rocky Horror*

Thomas G. Endres

When I was an undergraduate in the early 1980s, I wrote a paper for my rhetorical criticism class titled, "Terrible Thrills: Hedonistic Pleasure in *The Rocky Horror Picture Show*." The thesis of the paper was that *Rocky Horror* advocated hedonism, or the desire to achieve pleasure and avoid pain. It traced, in particular, Janet's journey throughout the film and the pervasive "pleasure-seeking attitude, primarily sexual pleasure, that eventually coerces young Janet to give herself over to 'sins of the flesh'" (Endres 1). Looking through my twenty-something eyes, and integrating philosophies from John Stuart Mills, Jeremy Bentham, and even hedonism's founding father Epicurus, I concluded that *Rocky Horror* "embodies the search for, and delivery of, feelings of pleasure" (5).

Now, more than two decades later, I still see and am entertained by the pleasure-seeking principle of the film. However, I now recognize that there is an obvious undercurrent in the film that has a surprisingly conservative message. My forty-something perspective recognizes two parallel and competing tracks in *Rocky Horror*: the decadent hedonism for which the film is so popular and the subtle, yet eventually victorious, message that serves as a warning against such a flamboyant lifestyle. Ruble describes this battle as the "age-old human conflict between reason and desire" (161).

That message of reason, however, is often lost in traditional analyses of the film that focus heavily on the outrageous antics of participating audiences. Austin argues that a film is defined more by its audience than by its content or the filmmaker's intent and that cult films such as *Rocky Horror* "are not *made* (as for example, one sets out to make a musical, western, etc.) as much as they *happen* or *become*" (44). Although there is truth to these observations, the critic must also look specifically at the messages and meanings inherent within the actual artifact. Not only should we analyze *Rocky Horror* for what it becomes but we should also examine what it literally says and does. This chapter provides a textual analysis of the competing messages within the film itself, and Bormann's Symbolic Convergence Theory (SCT), a humanistic tool for interpreting dramatic imagery, provides the methodological tool for the analysis. Following a brief description of the method, descriptions are provided for both the decadent and conservative visions within the film, and the chapter concludes with comments regarding the usefulness of the method and the effect of the communicative medium.

Symbolic Convergence Theory

Developed in 1972 by Ernest G. Bormann, SCT is a method used to identify and interpret the "dramatizations which catch on and chain out" in group, public, or mass-mediated contexts ("Fantasy and Rhetorical Vision" 37). A primary assumption of SCT is that human interaction is characterized by the sharing of stories and dramatic imagery; we make sense of our world by combining our internal symbols and meanings with others to create a shared symbolic reality. The specific tool that a scholar uses to interpret a community's symbolic convergence is called Fantasy Theme Analysis (FTA), which provides the drama-based terminology for the critique.

The primary unit of analysis is the fantasy theme, which Bormann defines as a dramatizing message such as "a pun or other wordplay, a double entendre, a figure of speech, an analogy, an anecdote, allegory, fable, or narrative" ("The Force of Fantasy" 4). Obviously, *Rocky Horror* is replete with dramatic messages, both within the film itself and between the members of the audience. Cragan and Sheilds summarize all of FTA's technical terms, though this essay will focus only on those most pertinent to this analysis ("Corporate Strategic Planning" 200–203). Fantasy theme messages may reference a specific plot line (action) or scene (location) within a drama. Dramatic images frequently refer to the *dramatis personae* (characters) within a story, which helps the audience differentiate between protagonists, antagonists, and supporting players. Once the original fantasy theme has been shared, it can be elicited via a symbolic cue such as a "code word, phrase, slogan, or even a nonverbal sign or gesture" that makes a cryptic reference to the larger dramatic reality (200). For example, the catch phrase "publish or perish" has specific meaning to a college professor within the larger scenario of professional engagement and annual evaluation. Themes and cues also give insight into the sanctioning agent (legitimizing force) that condones and explains the reason and motivation for the story line. Examples of such forces given by Cragan and Shields include "a higher power—like God, the Supreme Court, or Democracy—or a well accepted code of conduct like the West Point honor code" (202).

Most important to this analysis are the terms rhetorical vision and master analogue. All the dramatic elements previously described coalesce and create for the adherents a rhetorical vision; that is, a composite drama that forms the basis for a common symbolic reality. Bormann, Cragan, and Shields call it a "unified putting-together" of the various themes that "gives the participants a broader view of things" (Bormann, "In Defense Of" 281). In other words, an audience that adheres to a common set of heroes and villains, that gets the humor of the same inside jokes, and that believes in the authority and rationale that justifies the plot line constitutes a community with a shared rhetorical vision.

Cragan and Shields observe that, in theory, there could be as many different rhetorical visions as there are people, but their research concludes that individuals adhere to one of three major deep structure dramas (*Applied Communication* 40). They call these the master analogues. The three types of underlying metaphors to which people adhere are righteous, social, or pragmatic in nature: "A rhetorical vision based on a righteous master analogue emphasizes the correct way of doing things with its concerns about right and wrong, proper and improper, superior and inferior, moral and immoral, and just and unjust. A rhetorical vision with a social master analogue reflects primary human relationships as it keys on friendship, trust, caring, comradeship, compatibility, family ties, brotherhood, sisterhood, and humaneness. A vision with a pragmatic master analogue stresses expediency, utility, efficiency, parsimony, simplicity, cost effectiveness, and minimal emotional involvement" ("Corporate" 202).

Rhetorical visions are viewed as warring with one another in their attempt to muster adherence within a community. When one vision loses its novelty and explanatory power, it tends to be replaced with a more compelling competing vision framed within a different master analogue. For example, our presidential elections often serve as opportunities to elect candidates who offer platforms in direct opposition to those of the incumbents. One vision diminishes; another takes its place. In my own work, I have made the case that, in addition to opposing camps, a single artifact may have multiple rhetorical visions with coexisting master analogues (Endres, "Co-Existing" 306). This seems to be the case with *Rocky Horror*, in which decadence and justice run side by side. The battle takes place within the artifact itself, and as the following analysis demonstrates, a subtle and surprisingly conservative vision emerges victorious. In the end, it does boil down to audience action and reaction, as "people act on the meanings, emotions, motives, and values of the rhetorical visions in which they participate" (Bormann, Cragan, and Shields, "Imaginary" 368). Before examining audience response, however, we must first interpret the dramatic imagery to which they are responding.

The Vision of Righteous Decadence

The back cover of *The Official Rocky Horror Picture Show Movie Novel*, edited and adapted by Richard J. Anobile, provides the following synopsis of the film: "Meet Brad (Barry Bostwick) and Janet (Susan Sarandon), two strait-laced [*sic*], middle-American kids confronted by the defiantly decadent morality of the '70s as represented in the person of Dr. Frank N. Furter [*sic*] (Tim Curry), a 'sweet transvestite' from the planet of Transexual [*sic*] in the galaxy of Transylvania." The phrase "decadent morality" provides an apt symbolic cue for this rhetorical vision. Although one would not normally define decadence as a form of morality, this paradoxical spin on the traditional definition is exactly what occurs in *Rocky Horror*. Recall that a righteous master analogue is one that advocates a superior, proper, and correct path for its adherents. In the case of *Rocky Horror*, decadent behavior is the righteous way. As Kilgore notes, the movie is a "manifesto for sex-and-whatever else feels good" (153).

At the center of this vision is protagonist Dr. Frank-N-Furter, the charismatic cross-dressing scientist who dominates not only the screen but also all the characters within it. His sanctioning agent is pleasure, evidenced in the main plot line of his creating a muscle-bound man as his personal plaything, as well as multiple subplots involving the on-screen sexual conquest of both Brad and Janet and the prescreen sexual conquest of Columbia and Eddie. Frank's entire persona—his looks, his words, his actions—is the driving force behind the decadent morality of the vision.

Bormann notes that fantasies that "clearly divide the sympathetic, good people (we) from the unsympathetic or evil people (they)" are crucial to the successful emergence of a rhetorical vision ("The Force of Fantasy" 12). If Frank is the hero of this vision, then the "they" must be all those whose lifestyle contradicts his code of sexual pleasure. Most vilified, of course, are the nerdish Brad and the prudish Janet. Following closely behind is the wheelchair-bound Dr. Scott, who stands in opposition to Frank as both a rival scientist and as the late Eddie's kin. Finally, the no-necked Criminologist who narrates the film poses a threat to Frank. They are the representations of moderation, status quo, and traditional morality—which Frank so strongly opposes.

They sympathetic "we" of the vision includes Frank's servants—the elbow-rubbing siblings Riff Raff and Magenta, and the partygoers (Frank's "unconventional conventionists"), who dance the "Time Warp" and witness Rocky's creation. Of course, there is also Rocky himself, who marches arm-in-arm with Frank to the bridal suite while the wedding march blares in the background. Granted, as the vision shifts, so do the allegiances, but the initial scorecard of "us" versus "them" is clearly the Transylvanians and crew against the Earthly establishment types.

Subtle symbolic cues solidify Frank's role as the central protagonist of the vision. Not only do his corset and fishnet stockings set the pace for the eventual stages of characters' undress throughout the film but the tattoo on his upper arm clearly proclaims him to be the "BOSS." In addition, both Riff Raff and Magenta refer to him as "Master," and Riff Raff elaborates by explaining, "We are simply his servants." In one telling scene, as Frank describes to onlookers the accidental discovery that allowed him to create Rocky, the camera zooms in to a close up of his face as he proclaims, "I hold the secret to life itself." In the vision of righteous decadence, Frank is the godlike persona of the creator and master of his universe.

A rhetorical vision is most effective when it not only differentiates the "us" from the "them" but also converts the "them" to "us" status. Bormann recognizes that convergence can occur when "one creative person fantasizes a powerful personal consciousness and does so with such skill that his or her consciousness is shared by converts" ("Force of Fantasy" 10). In Twitchell's evaluation of Frank's persona, which he describes as "'Frederick's of Hollywood' at Fire Island," he concludes that, "what makes it so startling is that it is so alluring" (74). As the movie progresses, Frank casts his spell over his competition and gets them to cross over enemy lines.

This conversion is most obvious with Janet. It begins early in the film, when she coyly grins at Frank's inquiry about whether or not she has any tattoos. Following Rocky's creation, Janet placates Brad by announcing that she doesn't like a man with too many muscles. However, as Frank sings of his ability to create a man in just seven days, right after he proclaims, "I don't want no dissension," Janet demurely discloses, "I'm a muscle fan."

From there, the conversion escalates. Frank visits the bedrooms of both Janet and Brad and, following a sexual encounter with each, gets them to admit that they enjoyed it and promises not to tell the other of their infidelity. Fidelity, then, becomes immoral under righteous decadence. Over the surveillance monitors, Janet inadvertently discovers Brad's tryst. Her reaction is less about indignation and more about sexual liberation. The next scene finds her in the lab with Rocky, explaining that "I've tasted blood and I want more." While Magenta and Columbia look on via the monitors, Janet places Rocky's hands on her breasts. The entire song "Touch-A, Touch-A, Touch Me" is an anthem to Janet's rebirth as a sexual being who needs "action." With that rebirth comes devotion to a new master. As the Criminologist somberly explains, Janet has fallen prey to a "powerful and irrational" emotion, and "there seemed little doubt that Janet was indeed its slave." Of course, giving oneself over to emotion and desire is simply part of the Frank-N-Furter mantra.

With the intrusion of Scott and the disturbing dinner party where conversation takes place about, and over, Eddie the delivery boy, Frank's influence starts to unravel. Janet runs screaming from the room, and Frank follows. As he tells her to wise up, he reminds her, "I've laid the seed / It should be all you need." Unfortunately, it's not enough. By the time all parties gather in the laboratory, Frank is at odds with many in his congregation. Still, the practice of moral decadence prevails, with the help of a sonic transducer and the medusa ray, which immobilizes and eventually transforms Brad, Janet, Scott, Rocky, and Columbia into statues. Frank offers commentary on the burden of being in charge of hedonistic fulfillment as he laments, "It's not easy having a good time."

At this point, the Criminologist cuts in to explain that "Brad and Janet had both tasted forbidden fruit. This in itself was proof that their host was a man of little morals—and some persuasion." This line is a perfect example of a fantasy theme that acknowledges the rhetorical vision founded in the influence of immorality. When the quartet of statues is unfrozen, each finds himself or herself to be a participant in a floor show of unparalleled decadence. Each is garbed in Frank-N-Furterish corsets and fishnets, coupled with white makeup and feather boas. Each sings, to varying degree, the hymns of the church of Frank. Columbia's is the least praise-filled, though she acknowledges she was a "regular Frankie fan." Rocky follows with his recognition that "the only thing I've come to trust is an orgasmic rush of lust." Brad is next, initially anguishing, "It's beyond me! Help me, Mommy!" He converts in the next verse, however, as he observes, "What's this, let's see. I feel sexy. What's come over me? Whoa! Here it comes again." Even Scott, still in the laboratory, reveals a stockinged and high-heeled leg and reports that the decadence potentially has the power to sap his will.

As implied throughout the film, Janet has the most complete conversion to the vision. When she is unfrozen, her lyrics most clearly contain the dramatic imagery of righteous decadence:

I feel released
Bad times deceased
My confidence has increased
Reality is here. The game has been disbanded
My mind has been expanded
It's a gas that Frankie has landed
His lust is so sincere.

At this point, Janet offers an exaggerated kiss to the audience. That kiss is the prelude to Frank's entrance on the stage, and his song, "Don't Dream It. Be It," is the movie's most overt portrayal of his pleasure-seeking philosophy. Frank croons,

Give yourself over to absolute pleasure
Swim the warm waters of sins of the flesh
Erotic nightmares beyond any measure
And sensual daydreams to treasure forever.

The choir of converts joins in as Frank sings, "Don't dream it. Be it." They leap into a swimming pool on the stage and bob and weave together in a tangle of arms, legs, and lips. As Janet surfaces, she smiles and sings, "God bless Lilly St. Cyr," referring to the famous burlesque legend and pinup girl from the 1940s and '50s. Following the pool scene, Frank and his decadent dramatists take to the stage again to proclaim that they are wild and untamed things.

As any *Rocky Horror* viewer knows, the plot line turns at this point. In FTA terms, the competing rhetorical vision—which to this point had been muted—surfaces and supplants the vision of decadence. Before moving forward, we must acknowledge that the decadence of the vision just described is precisely why *Rocky Horror* is so popular. The movie's status as a cult film is based in its over-the-top sensuality. Sal Piro, former president of the national *Rocky Horror* fan club, writes the following in the introduction to Anobile's movie novel: "A feeling of love pervades this cult as they give themselves over to pleasure and exhort the philosophy of becoming all the things they have dreamed" (par. 3). Although this chapter agrees with Piro's observation, it argues that the pervasive feeling is sublimated and defeated by the following warring vision.

The Vision of Pragmatic Justice

Although the obvious shift in the vision occurs near the end of the film, the warring perspective is evident throughout. Early in the film, outside the Denton Episcopal Church where Ralph and Betty have just exchanged vows, an ominous warning is given. Whereas most viewers focus on the large billboard in the scene proclaiming Denton "The Home of Happiness," attention should be turned to a small sign on the church property that reads "Be Just and Fear Not." This sign is a symbolic cue for the subtle yet eventually victorious vision of Pragmatic Justice. Though the sanctioning of justice may seem to fall under the master analogue of righteousness, it is presented in a more expedient and parsimonious fashion. Unlike the righteousness of the decadence vision, which is loudly proclaimed throughout the film, the vision of justice is understated. Its message is simple: Do the right thing or suffer the consequences. Kilgore argued this as early as 1986, when he wrote, "The film only seems to preach the gospel of absolute pleasure; in reality it acknowledges the existence of sensible limitations" (156). And what could be more pragmatic than a sensible limitation?

The vision actually begins in the very first words uttered in the movie. In the opening song, "Science Fiction/Double Feature" (sung by Richard O'Brien but lip-synced by Patricia Quinn), the first verse is, "Michael Rennie was ill the day the earth stood still / but he told us where we stand." The reference is to the 1951 science fiction classic, *The Day the Earth Stood Still*. Michael Rennie played a thinly disguised Christlike figure who comes from the heavens, takes the earthly name of Carpenter, is killed by the violent masses but is resurrected, and who warns the world that they must repent of their evil ways or be destroyed. He is speaking of the evils of atomic weapons, not sexual impropriety, but the pragmatic warning is just the same. Michael Rennie, similar to the little sign outside the Denton church, tells us where we stand: "Be Just and Fear Not."

Though a slight digression, it is important to note that all of *Rocky Horror*, not just the opening song, is an homage to Saturday afternoon science fiction and B-movie matinees. Richard O'Brien, the creator of *Rocky Horror*, explains that his intent was to write a musical that "any ten-year-old could enjoy" (Hoberman and Rosenbaum 4). Hoberman and Rosenbaum compare the audience participation with *Rocky Horror* to children clapping in stage productions of *Peter Pan* to save Tinkerbell: The intent is simple, not sensual.

This intent is further communicated in the opening credits. Characters are named, followed by a parenthetical description of who or what they are. Frank-N-Furter is simply labeled "A Scientist." Not a prophet, not a messiah, not a savior. Scott is simply labeled a "rival scientist," not an enemy or a traitor. Brad and Janet, in contrast, are announced as a "Hero" and "Heroine," respectively. Rather than painting them as establishment antagonists, as the righteous decadence vision would imply, they are actually heralded as protagonists. Even the Criminologist, who receives a great deal of abuse from pleasure-seeking audiences, is referred to as "An Expert." Though subtle, these simple titles establish a strong pragmatic foundation.

Following the wedding and the warning at the Denton church, Brad and Janet set out on a journey to meet with their former teacher, Scott. During a rainstorm, they get a flat tire not far from Frank-N-Furter's castle. In the theater, there is much ado about the rain and the newspaper that Janet uses to shield herself from the water. This activity often overshadows an important piece of the pragmatic vision. As Brad and Janet are driving, the radio is tuned to Richard Nixon delivering his resignation speech following the Watergate debacle. In this actual recording, Nixon declares, "I must put the interests of America first." There is no more powerful example during the decade of *Rocky Horror*'s production of someone who has violated standards and must therefore suffer the consequences of his acts.

Brad and Janet arrive at the castle and are eventually escorted to Frank's laboratory, where Rocky is brought to life. Rather than reveling in his birth, Rocky begins his life by singing the song, "The Sword of Damocles." The song is a classic form of fantasy theme, which refers to story lines outside the tensions of the here-and-now reality. As tradition tells it, King Dionysius was a wealthy but cruel tyrant. Many were envious of the king's riches and pleasures, particularly his friend Damocles, so the king offered to let Damocles spend a day imbibing all the pleasures of his office. At first, Damocles enjoyed having servants wait on him and providing him with vast banquets. On looking up, however, Damocles noticed a sword, suspended by a thin thread, hovering above his head. The king explained that he always has the sword above his head, and he never knows when it might fall. Damocles quickly changed places back with the king. The moral of the story is the myth of pleasure and the presence of imminent danger. Such is Rocky's fate: Pleasure is merely an illusion, and to partake of the illusion puts one at risk of death. Denounce the pleasure and you live. Be Just and Fear Not.

The next character we meet is Eddie, the delivery boy turned Frank's lover, who was partially lobotomized to provide half his brain to Rocky. In his song, "Hot Patootie—Bless My Soul," Eddie laments his loss of innocence and the simplicity of dressing up to go out on a Saturday night. The arrival of Frank and his pleasure-principle caused Eddie to believe that "cosmic light" came into his life. Eddie announces, "I thought I was divine," but the viewer realizes that he was adhering to an illusion. In a fit of rage, Frank grabs an ax, chases Eddie into the vault, and murders him. Twitchell provides a sobering interpretation of the scene, noting that "there is always the image of Eddie being axed to death for staying too long under the spell, for not pretending but believing" (75). He offers an extremely pragmatic conclusion to the struggle between the warring visions of decadence and justice: "we realize Eddie's fate could be ours if we ever took it seriously" (76).

As noted in the previous vision, there is a moment when Frank's righteous immorality has an upper hand, particularly with Janet's willingness to have sex with Rocky. Its dominance is short lived. After Scott arrives, the guests are invited to dinner. By the end of the meal, it becomes apparent that Eddie was the main course. Frank's outrageous behavior, which initially seemed focused primarily on sexual antics, has now crossed over into murder and cannibalism. The latter is such a taboo in our culture that, from this point forward, there is no way for the righteous decadence vision to succeed.

As the movie progresses to its climatic floor show, Frank must rely on science and technology to maintain control over the other characters. During the floor show, Janet seems the most willing to support the decadent vision, yet she was also the most active in retreating from Frank following the dinner scene. As noted earlier, Columbia, Rocky, and Brad (and, indirectly, Scott) all participate in the floor show. However, each character is obviously struggling with the transformation. Their guilt for their transgressions is obvious—the vision of Pragmatic Justice is calling.

Then the tides turn completely. Riff Raff and Magenta interrupt the floor show dressed in alien garb and no longer servants. Riff Raff then informs Frank that he is the new commander, giving as a reason, "Your mission is a failure. Your lifestyle's too extreme." That message is the consummate fantasy theme for the pragmatic vision. Frank overdid it—now he must pay. Using a weapon that shoots laser beams, Riff Raff kills both Frank and Rocky. They fall into the pool, where the ultimate fantasy theme is revealed. Painted on the bottom of the pool is the scene from Michelangelo's fresco *The Creation of Adam* that adorns the ceiling of the Vatican's Sistine Chapel. The message is clear and concise: The mock-creator has been punished for his sins. Justice has been served.

Though Kilgore is not looking at the movie using SCT, his conclusion about Frank epitomizes the ongoing, bipolar drama: "Hedonism has transformed him into an endearingly ridiculous freak, a sexual Charlie Chaplin more likely to attract sympathy than emulation. If giving oneself over to pleasure means becoming what Frank is, the price seems rather high" (156). In this vision, Frank is the antagonist. Ironically, Riff Raff becomes the emergent protagonist. As Kilgore observes, Riff Raff is not viewed as a traitor by the audience but as "an attractive realist and middleman" (158). This interpretation, which is almost formal and businesslike in its tone, affirms that the victorious vision is a pragmatic one (rather than righteous or social).

The denouement of the movie reifies the pragmatic perspective. Riff Raff and Magenta transport themselves and the castle back to Transylvania. The camera shows Brad, Janet, and Scott laying or crawling in the grass, and the scene starts to spin out of control. Kinkade and Katovich argue that the trio "escape" in this scene (199), though it seems less of an escape than an abandonment. In the closing scene, the Criminologist confirms their sentence as he says, "And crawling on the planet's face, some insects called the human race. Lost in time and lost in space . . . and meaning." This is not escape; this is not victory. The pragmatic drama has expanded to read, "Be Just, or be killed or be left behind to face a life with no meaning." Still, Kinkade and Katovich are correct in their conclusion that "traditional norms are validated; Frankenfurter is merely a distraction" (201).

Conclusions: The Methodology and the Communicative Medium

SCT provides a useful lens for understanding communicative artifacts. The language of FTA provides a terminology set for identification and measurement of the converged symbolic reality. Still, a full SCT/FTA analysis needs to look more closely at the members of the rhetorical community, who accept, reject, or are neutral to the artifact's messages. Because other chapters in this collection do so, this chapter does not focus heavily on the role of audience; however, their part in the process cannot be completely overlooked. In many respects, the audience is the real-life manifestation of the dialectical tension between the warring visions, and we must conclude that, as with the previous textual interpretation, the audience—although temporarily giving themselves over—also concludes that pragmatic justice prevails.

Twitchell refers specifically to the meaning audiences must draw from the message when he states, "What this movie says (if such a movie may be said to 'say' anything) is that it is okay to be sexually confused; it is okay for boys to run around in corsets and garters, to prance and flout and dance and sing; it is okay for girls to be naughty and dirty, to be sexual, bisexual, transsexual—you name it as long as you enjoy it. Or perhaps, to be more accurate, it is okay to *pretend* to be this way" (75). Eventually, the audience must go home. The makeup comes off, the costumes are put away for another late-night outing, and we return to our simple and practical lives. Evidence of this, ironically, can even be found with Frank-N-Furter himself. According to Hoberman and Rosenbaum, Tim Curry, wanting to see the audience participation phenomenon for himself, attended a midnight showing in Manhattan wearing a suit and tie. Theater workers would not believe it was him and made him wait in line with the rest of the crowd.

Finally, we must add to this analysis the fact that viewing modalities have changed. When I wrote my first *Rocky Horror* paper back in college, the only place to see the movie was at the theater. The audience participation went hand-in-hand with the viewing experience. For this two-decade-later revisit, I watched the movie on VHS. The experience was very different. Not only was it was the first time I heard the Nixon speech but I found myself continually struck by the messages of the pragmatic vision.

Aviram addresses the irony of attempting to experience *Rocky Horror* in the privacy of one's home. "The irony is that the Rocky Horror Cult ought to be celebrated in public spaces, late at night, in the dark, and not trivialized by suburban solitude and trips to the kitchen for beer" (183). Perhaps, though, this is *Rocky Horror*'s fate, or at least the most natural phase of its evolution. The '70s are behind us, and in this new era, we are simply drawn more quickly to the conservative ideology that was always there. Even the copy of the video I own begins with the following disclaimer: "Dream it in your living room. Be it in the theater!" Nowhere does it say, "Be it in your life." Although we may still occasionally transport ourselves in the live theater experience, the predominant venue will be muted to simply wishful thinking as we stare at our televisions.

And why not? *Rocky Horror* is, ultimately, a morality play that only can lead us to the conclusion that pure hedonism is an illusion and that those who attempt such a life will face retribution. It may not have been created for this specific purpose, unlike the 1936 propaganda film *Reefer Madness*, which eventually achieved cult status because of its inherent ridiculousness. I liken the message more to another cult classic, 1969's *Easy Rider*. On the surface, many see the movie as the celebration of freedom, drugs, and the hippie movement—similar to Frank's righteous decadence. In reality, Wyatt "Captain America" (Peter Fonda) concludes that, "We blew it." In the end, he and riding partner Billy are killed in a drive-by shooting. The final scene, where the camera pans back to reveal the burning motorcycles on the side of the road, seems a precursor to *Rocky Horror*'s spiraling final scene where Brad, Janet, and Scott—victims of their own indulgences—crawl about.

Rocky Horror is a temporary escape from normalcy and traditional definitions of morality. For one hundred minutes, audiences can join Frank and share in the vision of righteous decadence. However, whether it be on the big screen surrounded by costumed congregants or on the small screen surrounded by one's furniture, the outcome remains the same: Pragmatic Justice prevails.

Works Cited

Anobile, Richard J., ed. *The Official Rocky Horror Picture Show Movie Novel*. New York: A&W Visual Library, 1980.

Austin, Bruce A. "Portrait of a Cult Film Audience: *The Rocky Horror Picture Show*." *Journal of Communication* 31 (1981): 43–54.

Aviram, Amittai F. "Postmodern Gay Dionysus: Dr. Frank N. Furter." *Journal of Popular Culture* 26.3 (1992): 185–92.

Bormann, Ernest G. "Fantasy and Rhetorical Vision: The Rhetorical Criticism of Social Reality." *Quarterly Journal of Speech* 58.4 (1972): 396–407.

———. *The Force of Fantasy: Restoring the American Dream*. Carbondale: Southern Illinois UP, 1985.

Bormann, Ernest G., John F. Cragan, and Donald C. Shields. "Defending Symbolic Convergence Theory from an Imaginary Gunn." *Quarterly Journal of Speech* 89.4(2003): 366–72.

———. "In Defense of Symbolic Convergence Theory: A Look at the Theory and Its Criticisms After Two Decades." *Communication Theory* 4.4 (1994): 259–94.

Cragan, John F., and Donald C. Shields. *Applied Communication Research: A Dramatistic Approach*. Prospect Heights, IL: Waveland, 1981.

———. "The Use of Symbolic Convergence Theory in Corporate Strategic Planning: A Case Study." *Journal of Applied Communication Research* (May 1997): 199–218.

Endres, Thomas G. "Co-Existing Master Analogues in Symbolic Convergence Theory: The Knights of Columbus Quincentennial Campaign." *Communication Studies* 45.3–4 (1994): 294–308.

———. "Terrible Thrills: Hedonistic Pleasure in the Rocky Horror Picture Show." Unpublished manuscript, 1982.

Hoberman, J., and Jonathan Rosenbaum. *Midnight Movies*. New York: Da Capo, 1983.

Kilgore, John. "Sexuality and Identity in The Rocky Horror Picture Show." *Eros in the Mind's Eye: Sexuality and the Fantastic in Art and Film*. Ed. Donald Palumbo. New York: Greenwood, 1986. 151–59.

Kinkade, Patrick T., and Michael A. Katovich. "Toward a Sociology of Cult Films: Reading *Rocky Horror*." *Sociological Quarterly* 33.2 (1992): 191–209.

Ruble, Raymond. "Dr. Freud Meets Dr. Frank N. Furter." *Eros in the Mind's Eye: Sexuality and the Fantastic in Art and Film*. Ed. Donald Palumbo. New York: Greenwood, 1986. 161–68.

Twitchell, James B. "*Frankenstein* and the Anatomy of Horror." *Georgia Review* 37.1 (1983): 41–84.

13

"Your Lifestyle's Too Extreme"

Rocky Horror, Shock Treatment, and Late Capitalism

Kevin John Bozelka

It's around two o'clock in the morning at the nearest *Rocky Horror* venue. Somewhat imperceptibly, the tone of the film, if not the evening, has shifted. Instead of an orgiastic, Dionysian display, the scenes after the reprise of "I Can Make You A Man" feel progressively sleepier. This effect is only exacerbated if the theater's print contains "Super Heroes," the song cut out from the original American run of the film, and the mournful reprise of "Science Fiction/Double Feature." If one takes a break from the audience participation and really concentrates on these moments, it becomes clear that *The Rocky Horror Picture Show* has turned in on itself, that its wildest propositions have grown tragically untenable. Suddenly, the chants of "Don't Dream It. Be It" start to sound like a trap.

John D'Emilio's epochal "Capitalism and Gay Identity" refined Michel Foucault's history of sexuality by arguing that, along with other nineteenth-century discourses such as psychology, medicine, and criminology, capitalism was one of the chief components in the formation of a homosexual identity in the United States. As abstract money began funding an increasing number of industries, individuals were drawn away from the family (the primary haven for economic stability) into largely urban areas and a system of wage labor. As with Foucault, D'Emilio rejects the hypothesis that this system repressed sexuality. Quite the contrary, it helped create the spaces for a homosexual identity, if not identity in general, to thrive. And with this migration into cities, of course, comes the precondition for the formation of gay and lesbian communities as we know them today.

However, if homosexuality and capitalism are such tight bed partners, how do we account for the persistence of job discrimination, lack of insurance benefits for significant others, and other virulent strains of homophobia? D'Emilio himself wondered about this paradoxical incompatibility and, writing in 1979, came to the following conclusion: "On the one hand, capitalism continually weakens the material foundation of family life, making it possible for individuals to live outside the family, and for a lesbian and gay male identity to develop. On the other, it needs to push men and women into families, at least long enough to reproduce the next generation of workers. The elevation of the family to ideological preeminence guarantees that capitalist society will reproduce not just children, but heterosexism and homophobia. In the most profound sense, capitalism is the problem" (474).

In the first decade of the twenty-first century, capitalism is still the problem—albeit in a rather different way. Increasingly, capitalism is experiencing problems reproducing homophobia because of the need to constantly expand into new markets. As the success of a show like *Queer Eye for the Straight Guy* makes clear, there is now a legible homosexual subject that capitalism actively (if often ambiguously, especially in the case of a lesbian subject) addresses. Certainly, one can make the case that *Queer Eye* merely adds fuel to the ideological preeminence of the heterosexual family—after all, most episodes center around the maintenance of a well-oiled heterosexual courtship ritual—and although the Fab Five scrutinize this ritual at every turn, the show's format never allows for a strong expression of collectivity among them. In the end, they remain atomized in their flexibly specialized custodial roles.

Then again, this atomization is exactly what capitalism wants, or to be more precise, it is the ultimate goal of the more virulent strain of capitalism most commonly referred to as late capitalism. The exodus of individuals away from the family thus needs to be updated historically for this new era as more and more individuals go into business for themselves, not as multinational tycoons, of course, but as severely localized independent contractors. Angela McRobbie's unflinching portrait of the culture industries (where, it should be emphasized, many gay men become successful) offers a useful perspective on this development. As McRobbie notes, self-employment and freelance work transfer the onus of workplace politics from corporations (and social welfare institutions) onto the individual, thus increasing the profit margins of big business. Self-employed individuals, then, must adopt a modicum of reflexivity and essentially become their own institutional structures responsible for social welfare. The logistics of undertaking such an endeavor in this era of neoliberal individualization are obviously dumbfounding—however much time labor takes up, the remainder is usually reserved for maintaining the late capitalist system as a whole through consumption.

Going back to *Queer Eye*, then, what some gay men have won in their successful interpellation as capitalist subjects is impeccable shopping credentials. These credentials can then be transformed into capital as they are transferred to heterosexual lunkheads and other clueless consumers. There is something undeniably, gleefully subversive about this long overdue recognition of the enormous contributions gay men have made to the discourse on heterosexuality. "Like the Jewish studio moguls who propagated images of an overwhelmingly gentile United States," Kamal Al-Solaylee reminds us, "gay men and lesbians in Hollywood defined heterosexuality for Americans in the 20th century by influencing its outward trappings." However, the wide-open queer eye of the twenty-first century peers out from a distinctly middle-class—if not higher—vantage point. In praising an ever-increasing visibility, celebrants of this exciting new era of progress tend to forget that the eyes of other disenfranchised groups are peering right back at them. Richard Goldstein summarizes this state of affairs succinctly: "TV shows featuring well-heeled, happy homos feed the perception that gays are doing fine—so why should they qualify for 'special' rights?" Some of those disenfranchised groups are not only lower-class communities of various racial backgrounds but also other gays and lesbians (again, of various racial backgrounds) for whom trailer parks and welfare lines comprise a more accurate queer geography than the well-appointed apartments on *Queer Eye*. That these groups remain invisible to a portion of the well-heeled, happy, and usually white homos on television and in the television audience speaks to the more pernicious aspects of the homosexuality–capitalism matrix—namely, that it now allows some gays and lesbians to make their own significant, widely visible contribution to the unequal distribution of wealth. In short, they are now baldly implicated in the inequities of late capitalism and cannot afford (quite literally) to ignore the precise forms those inequities take.

In this chapter, I discuss *Rocky Horror* as a cautionary tale about the inequities that can result in the marriage between homosexuality and capitalism. Far too much of the commentary on *Rocky Horror* emphasizes the Dionysian aspects of the film—its hybridity in relation to genre and sexuality. For instance, in an analysis of *Shock Treatment*, the sequel to *Rocky Horror*, J. Hoberman and Jonathan Rosenbaum write "[*Shock Treatment*] was as quintessentially a work of the seventies as *Rocky Horror* was an expression (again slightly delayed) of the sixties" (210). I would counter that *Rocky Horror* contains a critique of the polymorphously perverse sexual politics of the counterculture—a critique very much informed by a distinctly 1970's brand of cynicism and disappointment. Particularly in the later sequences alluded to in my introduction, the film takes on the contours of such sour countercultural hangovers as *Last Tango in Paris* (1972) and *Some Call It Loving* (1973).

Of course, this is the most common complaint brought against *Rocky Horror* qua film. As Danny Peary notes, "the picture peters out (and, to a first-time viewer, becomes a bit confusing) and by the time Frank-N-Furter was killed, I wished the film had ended twenty minutes earlier. The hectic pace was too much to maintain" (305). One might surmise instead that *Rocky Horror* is about the petering out of the countercultural activity of the '60s and its inability to maintain its own hectic pace.

Furthermore, what *Rocky Horror* dramatizes is how amenable radical sexual politics are to late capitalism and how easily gays and lesbians can get sucked into perpetuating its inequities. Over the course of the next section, I draw out these implications in *Rocky Horror*. I also pay close attention to *Shock Treatment*—its much-reviled sequel—for the way in which it puts these implications into sharper (and, hence, more uncomfortable) relief. Ultimately, I want to demonstrate how the mantra of "Don't Dream It. Be It," *Rocky Horror*'s unchallenged motto, drowns out two of the film's equally significant mottos: "It's not easy having a good time" and, more tragically, "Your lifestyle's too extreme."

In his classic essay "Entertainment and Utopia," Richard Dyer has demonstrated that the classic Hollywood musical functions as an expression of utopia (2–13). Despite the successful fusion of conflicting impulses into one happy community by the film's end, however, musicals only show us what utopia might feel like, not how it can be organized. The climactic floor show in *Rocky Horror*, appropriately titled "Rose Tint My World," illustrates Dyer's notion perfectly. During the "Fanfare/Don't Dream It" portion of the floor show, Dr. Frank-N-Furter, the figure most revered by the *Rocky Horror* cult, sings about the tactile qualities of his utopia as a series of rather inactive second person commands and sleep-like states. He entreats us to give ourselves over to absolute pleasure and swim the warm waters of sins of the flesh. He tells of erotic nightmares beyond any measure and sensual daydreams to treasure forever. Eventually, he becomes so intoxicated by his own advertising slogans that he cannot continue and instead asks gushingly, "Can't you just see it?" But how exactly does one attain such utopian heights? We *can* just see it, Frank—but how do we get it?

Bearing out Dyer's analysis, the film never answers these questions. Or, more precisely, it offers the slightest suggestion of a fundamental capitalist answer—money. As the square representative of precounterculture middle

America, Brad Majors remarks early in the film that Frank's castle "is probably some kind of hunting lodge for rich weirdos." Giving oneself over to absolute pleasure implies the time and resources in which to do so. Brad's dismissive remark actually seals a connection between the queer liberation rhetoric of Frank's song and the money necessary to bring it into a radical sexual existence.

If Frank is the undisputed queen of these weirdos, however, in what way is he rich? For sure, the castle itself implies wealth, and the Zen Room, hazy with marijuana smoke and a pungent reminder of the countercultural 1960s, suggests a significant amount of leisure time, but beyond that, there are no overt economic markers in the film beyond dead-end conjecture about the system of exchange on Frank's home planet of Transsexual in the galaxy of Transylvania. And although his work as a scientist produces a gorgeous playmate, Rocky, as well as an audiovibratoryphysiomolecular transport device, Frank never hints at how he might transform his creations into some form of capital.

Of course, as queen of his castle, he need not worry too much about capital—his absolute pleasure derives from absolute power—but Frank's brand of rule betrays the taints of fascism rather than the divine rights of feudalist monarchy. In contrast to signs of economic privilege, there is no poverty of fascist markers throughout the film. First of all, there is the swastika-like lightning bolt insignia that the Transylvanians wear on their right arms. It also rides atop the castle on a flag, which some *Rocky Horror* audiences salute with a "Sieg Heil!" during "Over at the Frankenstein Place." Next, there is Magenta's comment that Rocky is a triumph of Frank's will—an allusion to *Triumph of the Will*, Leni Riefenstahl's 1936 Nazi propaganda epic. Finally, Rocky himself fulfills and even epitomizes the requirements for blonde, physically fit Aryan beauty (see Figure 13.1).

Other signposts suggest that Frank may have been a victim of fascism in addition to one of its purveyors. For one, his fishnets and garters garb link him to the prefascist Weimar Republic or, in Hollywood's version, to Liza Minnelli as Sally Bowles in *Cabaret*, released only a year before the first stage production of *The Rocky Horror Show*. The name of a popular German cologne, *4711*, is "tattooed like a concentration-camp identification on his leg" (Hoberman and Rosenbaum 187), and when Frank refers to his rival Dr. Scott as Dr. Von Scott, he is implying precisely that Scott has a Nazi past—a point made clear by audiences that again stand up at this point to salute "Sieg Heil!" Nevertheless, by the time we first see Frank in the film, he has come out on top to enjoy his radical sexual identity to its fullest potential. His character paradoxically imbues an image of Berlin decadence circa 1930 with fascist power. According to Gaylyn Studlar, fans respond to this aspect of Frank with the most fervor: "Frank's fans identify

Figure 13.1

with the Frank who, in juxtaposing the pearl necklace of a demure matron with a sequined lace-up corset, spiked heels, and gartered stockings, evokes Marlene Dietrich's erotic ambiguity in von Sternberg's *The Blue Angel*, while hinting at the tantalizingly taboo possibilities of sadomasochistic bondage. The joke is that Frank would never be caught dead at the bottom—and his fans know it" (Studlar 149).

The cyclical nature of fascism in this scenario gives pause, though, when one realizes how closely Frank resembles the self-employed creative laborers that McRobbie discusses. Similar to the freelance fashion designer or the rave promoter, Frank has "seemingly circumvented 'unhappy work' and [has] come upon a way of earning a living without the feeling of being robbed of identity" (McRobbie 521). Also like them, however, he necessarily becomes his own social support system, where "reflexivity marks the space of self responsibility, self blame . . . a de-politicizing, de-socializing mechanism" (McRobbie 522). So where creative laborers inevitably wonder "Where have I gone wrong?" as McRobbie surmises, Frank concludes that "It's not easy having a good time," wondering whether or not he made a mistake using half of Eddie's brain to create Rocky. In each instance, it is a larger structure that is the problem, revealing what Max Horkheimer and Theodor Adorno had already concluded in their 1944 Frankfurt School opus *Dialectic of Enlightenment*—that fascism and capitalism are two sides of the same coin.

It is only Frank who is rich in any significant way. What *Rocky Horror* demonstrates in the end, then, is the price of giving yourself over to absolute pleasure. "Don't Dream It. Be It" is an untenable proposition in any collective sense because someone has to mop the floor and dust the control panel as Magenta and Riff Raff do in one scene, fittingly after Frank has already slept with both Rocky and Janet (he gets to Brad by the very next scene). Frank never gains enough reflexivity to account for social welfare (not to mention janitorial services) in his radical sexual lifestyle. Instead, he opts to murder and even eat Eddie because such behavior makes another outrageous notch on his polymorphously perverse bedpost—a limits-bucking modus operandi adopted by infamous cultural laborer Michael Alig. Thus, in flexing his radical queerness, Frank perpetuates the inequities of the fascist/capitalist system. That Magenta and Riff Raff eventually turn on him should then come as no surprise, with the latter singing immediately after the floor show, "Your lifestyle's too extreme."

For the cyclical nature of Frank's fascist/capitalist individuality to function smoothly, however, it needs a cyclical process of production and consumption in place to move it along. It must ensure that there will always be someone in thrall to the demagoguery of fascism and to the seductive rationale of capitalism, as both attempt to seep into every facet of existence—and it certainly helps if these blissed-out monads remain blind to (or willfully ignorant of) the ways in which a lack of reflexivity comes back to haunt the atomized individuals in these systems. So where Riff Raff and Magenta are clearly fed up with how expansively Frank has (ir)rationalized his lifestyle, Columbia, as a groupie and "regular Frankie fan," is the *Rocky Horror* cult's surrogate in the film, and by the time of the floor show, Brad, Janet, and Rocky function in the same fashion as Columbia—clearly in thrall to Frank but avoiding the negative ramifications of their fanaticism as they sing "Rose tint my world, keep me safe from my trouble and pain."

As with most musicals, Frank's utopia has reenergized each character, to which they testify in song. Only Columbia expresses dismay over his tyrannical impulses—Rocky remains pure sexual desire, Brad feels sexy, and Janet's solo practically serves as an outline of Dyer's essay. The rejuvenated feelings she lists correspond to the musical's utopian solutions of abundance, energy, intensity, and transparency, and as Dyer adds, these are only responses to inadequacies that capitalism can address (Dyer 8). Crucially completing the cycle, Frank joins in on the "Rose Tint My World" chorus because he himself was in thrall once, to Fay Wray and her satin-draped frame. He himself was in a powerless position, moved to tears because he wanted to be dressed just like King Kong's favorite plaything, but he refused merely to dream about it. What movies taught him (and teach us every weekend at midnight) was that any dream, no matter how monstrous, can become viable—something to help stave off mortality and endear you to future generations until someone usurps your throne/zeitgeist (Hoberman and Rosenbaum 304)—but on and on the cycle goes. At this point in the film, we might truly ask ourselves whatever *did* happen to Fay Wray?—for her date with oblivion foreshadows Frank's.

Frank does indeed live out his dream and becomes Fay Wray to Rocky's King Kong. Unfortunately, as in all good melodramas, it comes too late. By the time Rocky hauls him up the RKO tower in homage to King Kong's trek up the Empire State Building with Fay Wray, Frank has already said "hello to oblivion," courtesy of Riff's pitchfork-pronged antimatter laser. Perhaps then what makes this dénouement so dreary to so many viewers is the horrible fates that await our surrogates up on the screen.

Columbia and Rocky are murdered, ostensibly for their expression of grief over Frank's death. Brad, Janet, and Scott stumble around in the aftermath of the castle's launch into outer space. They wail about superheroes who feed on them—a line that serves as a particularly stinging critique of how the cyclical drive of late capitalism imprisons them in cultish consumption—and for the very end, the narrator, a criminologist, bears witness to this ultimate crime against humanity, recalling Adorno in the oh-so-omniscient space in which he frequently positioned himself: "And crawling on the planet's face, some insects called the human race. Lost in time . . . lost in space . . . and meaning." When the audience asks "What's your favorite TV show?" before the narrator says "lost in space" here, our prison gates get padlocked shut for good. We are chained to capitalism's treadmill of the ever new, reveling in references and unable to step off toward an experience untainted by commerce. All that remains is the sad little reprise of "Science Fiction/Double Feature," a snippet plagued with loss, departure, and darkness conquering Brad and Janet—darkness because any system outside of Frank's now seems an unimaginable no place—the literal definition of utopia.

For Amittai F. Aviram, the ending holds subversive potential. "To be 'lost . . . in meaning' is to find oneself in the play of meanings and allusions, in a position that is both frightening and exhilaratingly free" (Aviram 190). But no matter how playful our sexual identities, someone, perhaps equally hybrid in his or her sexuality, is always standing at attention to market to us. We are exhilaratingly free to go shopping, free to maintain an unequal distribution of wealth—insects ripe to scurry through late capitalism's ant farm. In this regard, the much-ballyhooed generic hybridity of *Rocky Horror* gets sucked into this vortex as well. The film does indeed radically mix the musical with the horror film, the science fiction film, the rock and roll film, and perhaps even the melodrama. Yet again, however, this mélange only makes it a more ideal product because movie studios can spread it across different markets, and the speed on this cultural blender has been upped to "liquefy" in the decades after *Rocky Horror* debuted. Corey K. Creekmur goes as far as to suggest that the concept of genre itself is poised for gooey extinction in an era of multinational, thoroughly diversified Hollywood. There has been an implicit address to "everyone" in an increasing number of Hollywood films since 1975.[1] Horror film lovers can hold hands with musical lovers at the same screening. As with the CD box sets of the 1990s, these all/no genre films offer the illusion of a complete package, of complete satisfaction, but always there is something more to buy—the book based on the movie, the soundtrack album, the action figures, and so on.

There are few spaces to contest this hold because it seems to take up all space, so McRobbie's writes: "And after hours, in the dedicated club/networking space, with free vodka on tap all night thanks to the sponsorship of the big drink companies, who dares to ask 'uncool' questions about the minimal representation of women and non-white young people, about who the big clients are and what they do with the product, and about the downside of the 'talent-led' economy?" (McRobbie 523). Similarly, in the hail of toast and toilet paper, as you feel that kinky rush when you first connect your garter belt to your fishnet stocking, who dares to ask "uncool" questions about the lack of reflexivity in Frank's utopia? Who dares to suggest we take Scott more seriously, that living your life for the thrill is indeed a trap, and that society must be protected from Frank? Who dares to speculate on the economic situation of the theater, especially when, as in some cases, you are let in for free? And what of the sheer waste of toilet paper and toast, not to mention the Riff Raff and Magenta surrogates who have to clean it all up in the morning? Who dares to wonder about the entire mechanism that gets us to the theater every weekend and has us enlisting the services of record bounty hunters across the globe for a coveted copy of the New Zealand *Rocky Horror Show* cast album featuring Gary Glitter as Frank?

By the time of *Shock Treatment*, which was not a temporal sequel but can be more accurately described as a hangover from *Rocky Horror*, late capitalism's victory over everyday existence was now complete. The audience is built into the film as a panoply of slack-jawed cultists blissfully trapped inside Denton Television's studio. They even sleep at the studio—"the nerve center of operations" as Nation McKinley refers to it. Game show host Bert Schnick is so accustomed to the situation that he fails to understand the word "home." With the "everybody" market firmly in place within this hermetically sealed universe, they are perpetually sold that quintessential late capitalist product—mental hygiene—which is never fully attainable, as an endless assembly line of new products constantly reminds us.

In *Shock Treatment*, Janet takes over Frank's function in *Rocky Horror* and becomes the star to sell it to them. Only here, we see every angle of the star-making machine, as fast food magnate Farley Flavors and his minions work to transform her into "Miss Mental Health." Instead of offering a relentless deconstruction of the forces of commerce, however, the film renders them all the more mysterious and ultimately unknowable. Part of what makes *Shock Treatment* so confusing for so many viewers is that Janet's rise to superstardom seems to follow a predetermined logic known only to Farley Flavors and his minions—and sometimes not even them. Cosmo and Nation McKinley, for instance, are two neurospecialists who star in "DTV's most popular hospital series," *Dentonvale*, an eerie foreshadowing of such reality television shows as *Starting Over* and *The Swan*. Their backroom politics with Schnick suggest that they are implicated in the tangled game show machinations that win Brad, now an "emotional cripple," medical treatment on *Dentonvale*. To be sure, they all play an unquestionably integral role in prepping Janet for superstardom, but Schnick makes it clear from the beginning that Farley Flavors will be funding *Dentonvale*—a fact that throws Cosmo into a rage. In his monitor-cluttered office perched high above the studio, Flavors wields the power of a veritable Ideological State Apparatus unto himself. From this surveillance bank, he presides over all in what amounts to a manifestation of the utter omnipresence of capital. Eventually, it becomes clear to the viewer that no character in the film exists outside of the peculiar rationale of Farley Flavors and the Denton television matrix. Schnick sums up this total rationalization of life in his comment after Brad is wheeled off to the rest home/*Dentonvale*: "The subject is committed . . . as are we all."

In *Shock Treatment*'s arid world, disembodied announcer voices skip across the soundtrack. Sometimes we can connect them to characters, but more often, they belong to no one—not even a no-neck narrator. Television monitors clutter and sometimes take over the frame in constant transmission mode. During the *Marriage Maze* game show toward the beginning of the film, for instance, the camera turns away from Schnick to his image on a monitor. Eventually, a cut causes the edges of the monitor to disappear in a shot-reverse shot discussion with Ralph Hapschatt and Macy Struthers. The film thus becomes the television, which has filled up the entire frame. All throughout, monitors are as pervasive in the mise-en-scène as characters. Indeed, Brad and Janet sing to a monitor during "Bitchin' in the Kitchen." Where once they sang to and about Frank, now the superheroes are a fabulous array of appliances to which the couple turn for marital advice and aid. However, the shape of the song is not dictated by any form of self-expression—quite the contrary. Brad and Janet must respond to whatever pops up in the random flow of commercials. Thus, Janet wrinkles her face in bewilderment at the sight of toothpaste being squeezed on a toothbrush and proceeds to sing "Oh toothpaste—don't you put the squeeze on me!"[2] As for the products themselves, some of them traffic in the kind of pseudo-individualization Adorno uncovered as a representative tenet of capitalist illusion, whereby advertisers attempt superficially to differentiate an utterly standardized product (Adorno 307–9). For instance, the announcer refers to the alarm clock that rushes past Janet on the monitor as a "micro-digital awaker." Much like the *Rocky Horror* cult, characters eventually start to mimic the omnipresent television screens, as when Janet's parents grab for beverages exactly when the television announcer instructs them to do so. Furthermore, we hear the voices of Cosmo and Nation in this scene mimicking Janet's conversation with her parents from some unseen surveillance system (perhaps the television set itself).

This eerie absence of human interlocutors makes for a rather vexed musical. For sure, the musical numbers are firmly integrated into the narrative, but they fail to achieve the community that is the traditional end result of the musical. Only the title number manages to bring previously warring factions together, and there, the characters come under the collective spell of late capitalism in the figure of Farley Flavors. Elsewhere, characters sing into and dance with mirrors, or they sing to and about themselves. Janet begins one song "there's just the two of me alone at last together," while the chorus is nothing more than a rousing ode to "me, me, me!" And as with so many post–1960 musical numbers, the climactic duet between Brad and Farley takes place in their imaginations.[3]

In *Shock Treatment*, then, we have an entire town of atomized individuals, unable to distinguish between reality and television. In fact, most viewers of the film find themselves in the same predicament. After about twenty minutes, we are never quite sure when we are watching a television show within the film. Late capitalism's tentacles have wrapped so tightly around us that all concepts of inside and outside become irretrievably confused. With its claustrophobic setting and severely reduced visual palette, *Shock Treatment* offers a glimpse of what Fredric Jameson calls "a postmodern or technological sublime." Similar to *The Matrix* and other postmodern melodramas, it tries to represent the unrepresentable. We sit dumbfounded in the face of Denton TV's enormous, all-pervasive communicational network, which only duplicates our bewilderment at multinational capitalism. As Jameson might have said of the film, "it seems to offer some privileged representational shorthand for grasping a network of power and control even more difficult for our minds and imaginations to grasp: the whole new decentered global network of the third (late) stage of capital itself" (Jameson 37–38).

Yet the system does not go unchallenged. Similar to little Neos, Judge Oliver Wright and Betty Hapschatt—recently fired from the *Denton Dossier* talk show—embark on an investigation of the Flavors matrix. They break Brad out of *Dentonvale*, and eventually Janet comes to realize her status as nothing more than cog in the machine. However, when Flavors orders these newfound rivals out of the *Faith Factory* finale, one wonders where "out" might be. For the moment, the rebellious quartet winds up sequestered in an office on the soundstage. It would seem that they escaped the fate of the audience, who finally leave their auditorium seats only to find themselves happily singing the hometown song in straightjackets throughout the padded rooms and prison cells of the studio. Once the two couples manage to break out of the office holding cell, though, they merely take the audience's place in the auditorium seats, singing the last and perhaps oddest number in the film, "Anyhow, Anyhow." "We're gonna do it anyhow, anyhow," they chirp, but again, one wonders what exactly "it" is. As they drive off the set in a convertible at the end of the film, they pass a huge, neon Denton TV sign with an enormous Vegas-style arrow pointing back to the set, but rather than showing an escape from Denton TV and the cyclical pull of late capitalism, the end feels as if they will remain on its treadmill. As the song states, "we just gotta keep going."

The ability even to imagine utopia becomes severely limited in a space so thoroughly conquered by capital. Jameson has analyzed how architecture attempts to work out this problem: In a Santa Monica home built by Frank Gehry, he detects a tension between a predilection for cheap materials that underscores the economics of space and a kind of postmodern hyperspace that deliberately confuses inside and outside, thus effacing vectors of power. On the one hand, there is "the production of poverty and misery, people not only out of work but without a place to live, bag people, waste and industrial pollution, squalor, garbage, and obsolescent machinery"; on the other, "the postmodern United States of extraordinary technological and scientific achievement; the most 'advanced' country in the world, in all the science fictional senses and connotations of that figure, accompanied by an inconceivable financial system and a combination of abstract wealth and real power in which all of us believe, without many of us ever really knowing what that might be or look like" (128). According to Jameson, we must take up the challenge of working this tension out dialectically to begin ironing out the inequities of capital and to seize its material manifestations: "There must be a relationship between those two realms or dimensions of reality, or else we are altogether within science fiction without realizing it" (128).

What is missing from *Shock Treatment* is that first term—a visual register to counteract all the technological wonderment/bewilderment of late capitalism. The film leaves few material reminders of the havoc that capitalism wrecks on space and the environment, and no glimpse of the cheap materials alluding to poor communities. As such, *Shock Treatment* is pure science fiction, similar to *The Matrix*. Just as the movie comes to a conclusion, however, yet another disembodied voice provides us with the film's *de facto* moral: "The sun never sets on those who ride into it." I would like to take this aphorism as an opportunity briefly to wax more positive.

Despite the fact that *Shock Treatment* never attracted a cult of *Rocky Horror* proportions, the *Rocky Horror* cult audience is unquestionably built into it. The slack-jawed Denton TV viewers make this connection obvious, but one can also detect it in the constant allusions to *Rocky Horror* and in the broken cadences of the dialogue that seem to beg for audience participation. Perhaps, then, we could take the *Rocky Horror* cult audience as that missing first term.[4] In a crucial way, the *Rocky Horror* cult is an earlier, more primitive form of the culture industry jobs of late capitalism. What sets it apart, however, is its enormous morphability, and not just its ability to incorporate disparate disenfranchised individuals. I am thinking more of the ragtag nature of the casts, the constant movement in and out of membership, the temporary nature of their collectives, and the props and costumes that, no matter how much time and money is poured into them, can never measure up to their counterparts on the screen. I am also thinking about cast dues necessarily paid at infrequent rates and fluctuating sums, depending on the economic situation of various cast members. Deleuze and Guattari might call such ever-shifting conglomerations rhizomatic.[5] Despite these potential setbacks, the fan-practitioners of the *Rocky Horror* cult manage to perform a show every weekend at midnight.

Again, the vulgar mass watching endless hours of Denton TV programming represents this particular audience, but they have an even closer surrogate in a group of young people who step out from the crowd. Oscar Drill and The Bits are a punkish band "with a suburban garage sound" that plays before Farley's *Faith Factory* show. Fan-practitioners all, they are also Janet's unregenerate groupies. When Brad, Janet, Betty, and Oliver drive off at the end of the film, they bring Oscar Drill and The Bits along with them for their ride into the sun. The film provides no strong narrative reason for this particular dénouement, but conceptually, it narrows the distance—however temporarily—between star and fan, between the sleek, basic black of the upper class and the squeaky clean whites of the middle class.

I take this motley group of passengers as a model for collective behavior in the absence of larger social welfare structures and a sense of reflexivity. Perhaps what cultural laborers can do to ease the self-blame (and chip away at the monolith that indentures them) is to drag as many people as possible through their happy work world. These collective will necessarily be ragtag and temporary like the *Rocky Horror* cult itself, and certainly more connections to other groups of people will have to be made—the suburban garage is quite far from the squalor and misery of poverty. However, clearly what "the sun never sets on those who ride into it" means to say is that there is no way out of the clutches of late capitalism—only a disconnected series of attempts to burrow directly through it.

Works Cited

Adorno, Theodor. "On Popular Music." [1941]. *On Record: Rock, Pop and the Written Word.* Ed. Simon Frith and Andrew Goodwin. New York: Pantheon, 1990. 301–14.

Al-Solaylee, Kamal. "Queer Power: Makeover or takeover?" 31 Jan. 2006. http://www.evalu8.org/staticpage?page=review&siteid=3074.

Aviram, Amittai F. "Postmodern Gay Dionysus: Dr. Frank N. Furter." *Journal of Popular Culture* 26.3 (1992): 185–92.

Corrigan, Timothy. *A Cinema Without Walls—Movies and Culture After Vietnam.* New Brunswick, NJ: Rutgers UP, 1991.

Creekmur, Corey K. "Picturizing American Cinema: Hindi Film Songs and the Last Days of Genre." *Soundtrack Available.* Ed. Pamela Robertson-Wojick and Arthur Knight. Durham, NC: Duke UP, 2001. 375–406.

Deleuze, Gills, and Felix Guattari. *A Thousand Plateaus—Capitalism and Schizophrenia.* Trans. Brian Massumi. Minneapolis: U of Minnesota P, 1980.

Dyer, Richard. "Entertainment and utopia." *Movie* 24 (1977): 2–13.

Goldstein, Richard. "Get Back!: The Gathering Storm Over Gay Rights." *The Village Voice* 31 Jan. 2006. 14 Aug. 2003 http://www.villagevoice.com/issues/0332/goldstein.php.

Hoberman, J., and Jonathan Rosenbaum. *Midnight Movies.* [1983]. New York: Da Capo, 1991.

Horkheimer, Max, and Theodor Adorno. *Dialectic of Enlightenment.* New York: Continuum, 1972.

Jameson, Fredric. *Postmodernism, Or, The Logic of Late Capitalism.* Durham, NC: Duke UP, 1991.

McRobbie, Angela. "Clubs to Companies: Notes on the Decline of Political Culture in Speeded Up Creative Worlds." *Cultural Studies* 16:4 (2002): 516–31.

Peary, Danny. *Cult Movies: The Classics, the Sleepers, the Weird, and the Wonderful.* New York: Dell Publishing, 1981.

Studlar, Gaylyn. "Midnight S/excess: Cult Configurations of 'Femininity' and the Perverse." *The Cult Film Experience.* Ed. J. P. Telotte. Austin: U of Texas P, 1991. 138–55.

Notes

1. This is how Timothy Corrigan analyzes the notorious box-office failure of *Heaven's Gate* (1980) as a barometer for the shifts in post-Vietnam cinema: "[*Heaven's Gate*] seemingly appealed to no one because of its attempts to appeal to everyone (which is of course no one)" (13).

2. The "Bitchin' in the Kitchen" song contains remarkable echoes of X-Ray Spex's 1977 punk masterpiece "Oh Bondage! Up Yours!" Vocalist Poly Styrene shouts to bondage as if it were a person, laughing at its claims of radical rebellion and deconstruction. The message, of course, was that punk was so semiotically destructive that not even such taboos as whips and chains were effective in registering revolutionary commitment. Everything eventually becomes amenable to capitalism, rendering investment itself perpetually fraught. On their subsequent full-length album *Germfree Adolescents*, released just at the crack of dawn of postmodernism in Western popular music, Styrene romps through capitalism's fun house of commodities and joyously manages to make an affective investment in hygienic Weetabix and synthetic fibre see-through leaves. Janet, in contrast, remains confused.

3. One can see this operation in musical numbers ranging from the meeting at the dance in *West Side Story* (1961) to "I Can't Do It Alone" in *Chicago* (2002), as well as earlier in the "Blue Danube (Why Are We Here)" number from *It's Always Fair Weather* (1955).

4. Richard Pryor's turn as a pathetic wino serves this role in *Some Call It Loving*, where his scenes function as a cognitive clash with the elaborate erotic role playing that occurs at his friend's (Zalman King) mansion. One might indeed describe the latter as a hunting lodge for rich weirdos, populated by an upper class with the time and resources to indulge their most recondite sexual fantasies. Pryor's character, of course, does not enjoy the same privileges.

5. See Deleuze and Guattari, especially 7–13.

Contributors

Sarah Artt is lecturer in literature and culture at Napier University and lecturer in film and media at Queen Margaret University. She earned her doctorate in 2005 from Queen Margaret with a dissertation that dealt with contemporary film adaptations of the work of Edith Wharton and Henry James. Her research interests include adaptation and transnational cinema, and her article "Art of the Past: Adapting Henry James's *The Golden Bowl*" appeared in the inaugural issue of the *Journal of Adaptation in Film and Performance* in December 2007.

Kevin John Bozelka is a doctoral candidate in the radio television film department at the University of Texas at Austin. His film and popular music criticism has appeared in *Village Voice, Chicago Reader*, and *Popmatters*.

Michael Mark Chemers received a doctorate in theatre history and theory from the University of Washington and has an MFA in playwriting from Indiana University. He teaches in the School of Drama at Carnegie Mellon, where he founded and directs the school's dramaturgy program. His work has appeared in many journals including *Modern Drama, Journal of Theatre and Performance, Comparative Drama*, and *Disability Studies Quarterly*, and his book *Staging Cinema: A Critical Examination of the American Freak Show* is available from Palgrave Macmillan (2008).

Julian Cornell is an adjunct lecturer in media studies at Queens College, City University of New York. He is also a doctoral candidate in cinema studies at New York University and is working on a dissertation about recent apocalyptic American films entitled *The End at the End: Apocalyptic Cinema at the Close of the Millennium*. His publications include articles on H. G. Wells and zombies.

Thomas G. Endres is a professor of communication studies and director of the School of Communication at the University of Northern Colorado, Greeley. He has authored over two dozen book chapters and articles in predominantly communication-related publications, presented more than one hundred papers and keynote addresses worldwide, and is the author and photographer of *Sturgis Stories: Celebrating the People of the World's* awarded a grant that same year to present at the Society for Literature and Science's annual conference.

Zachary Lamm is a graduate student at Loyola University Chicago. He is currently completing a dissertation entitled "The Queer Work of Fantasy: The Romance in Antebellum America."

Heather Clampitt Levy is an Austin-based poet and lover of Frankenstein films. She taught English composition at the University of Texas at Arlington, and her areas of interest include psychoanalytic film theory, creative writing, and the ways in which technology and data growth inform capitalist culture.

Matthew A. Levy is an assistant professor of English at Pacific Lutheran University. Previously, he served as writing program administrator at the University of Texas at Arlington and as a Writing Center instructor at Texas Christian University. His research focuses primarily on cynicism as a political issue that affects college writing instruction.

Liz Locke holds a doctorate in folklore from Indiana University. Currently a lecturer in expository writing at Oklahoma University, she is coeditor (with Theresa A. Vaughan and Pauline Greenhill) of *The Encyclopedia of Women's Folklore and Folklife* (Greenwood Press, 2008). Her ongoing research interests include feminist classics; race, class, and gender theory; film semiotics; and the persistence of myth in American political and popular culture.

Sue Matheson teaches film and literature at University College of the North, Manitoba, Canada. A twentieth-century generalist, she earned her doctorate at the University of Manitoba. Her areas of interest include modern American literature and culture, women's literature, children's literature, and Western films. She has a book manuscript in progress on male initiation rites.

Kristina Watkins-Mormino is an assistant professor of French at Georgia Gwinnett College, the first four-year college to be founded in the United States in the twenty-first century, where she is building the French program. A medievalist, her research explores sacerdotal virginity in Old French hagiography, representations of Joan of Arc in French culture, and the characterization of love as a life-threatening wound in Old French romance.

Nicole Seymour is a doctoral candidate in English literature at Vanderbilt University, where she teaches undergraduate writing courses centered on queer theory, ecocriticism, and conceptions of authorship. Her dissertation project examines the relationship between narrative dynamics and the representation of queer bodily transformations in post–World War II literature and film.

Jeffrey Andrew Weinstock is associate professor of American literature and culture at Central Michigan University. He is the author of *The Rocky Horror Picture Show* (Wallflower Press, 2008) and *Scare Tactics: Supernatural Fiction by American Women* (Fordham UP 2008) and has edited academic collections on *South Park*, *The Blair Witch Project*, Edgar Allan Poe's prose and poetry, and "The Yellow Wallpaper." His work has appeared in journals including *American Literature*, *Studies in American Fiction*, *Arizona Quarterly*, and *Pedagogy*.

Index

CPI Antony Rowe
Chippenham, UK
2017-01-02 15:05